Praise for
Visual Studio Team Foundation Ser
Adopting Agile Software Practices

"Agile dominates projects increasingly from IT to product and business development, and Sam Guckenheimer and Neno Loje provide pragmatic context for users seeking clarity and specifics with this book. Their knowledge of past history and current practice, combined with acuity and details about Visual Studio's Agile capabilities, enable a precise path to execution. Yet their voice and advice remain non-dogmatic and wise. Their examples are clear and relevant, enabling a valuable perspective to those seeking a broad and deep historical background along with a definitive understanding of the way in which Visual Studio can incorporate Agile approaches."

—**Melinda Ballou**, Program Director, Application Lifecycle Management and Executive Strategies Service, International Data Corporation (IDC)

"Sam Guckenheimer and Neno Loje have forgotten more about software development processes than most development 'gurus' ever knew, and that's a good thing! In *Visual Studio Team Foundation Server 2012*, Sam and Neno distill the essence of years of hard-won experience and hundreds of pages of process theory into what really matters—the techniques that high-performance software teams use to get stuff done. By combining these critical techniques with examples of how they work in Visual Studio, they created a de-facto user guide that no Visual Studio developer should be without."

—**Jeffrey Hammond**, Principal Analyst, Forrester Research

"If you employ Microsoft's Team Foundation Server and are considering Agile projects, this text will give you a sound foundation of the principles behind its Agile template and the choices you will need to make. The insights from Microsoft's own experience in adopting Agile help illustrate challenges with scale and the issues beyond pure functionality that a team needs to deal with. This book pulls together into one location a wide set of knowledge and practices to create a solid foundation to guide the decisions and effective transition, and will be a valuable addition to any team manager's bookshelf."

—**Thomas Murphy**, Research Director, Gartner

"This book presents software practices you should want to implement on your team and the tools available to do so. It paints a picture of how first-class teams *can* work, and in my opinion, is a must-read for anyone involved in software development. It will be mandatory reading for all our consultants."

—**Claude Remillard**, President, InCycle

Visual Studio Team Foundation Server 2012: Adopting Agile Software Practices

Visual Studio Team Foundation Server 2012: Adopting Agile Software Practices

From Backlog to Continuous Feedback

■ Sam Guckenheimer
Neno Loje

✦✦Addison-Wesley

Upper Saddle River, NJ • Boston • Indianapolis • San Francisco
New York • Toronto • Montreal • London • Munich • Paris • Madrid
Capetown • Sydney • Tokyo • Singapore • Mexico City

The Library of Congress cataloging-in-publication data is on file.

ISBN-13: 978-0-321-86487-1
ISBN-10: 0-321-86487-5

Text printed in the United States on recycled paper at R.R. Donnelley in Crawfordsville, Indiana.

First printing September 2012

To Monica, Zoe, Grace, Eli, and Nick,
whose support made this book possible.
—Sam

Contents

Forewords		*xii*
Preface		*xvi*
Acknowledgments		*xxiii*
About the Authors		*xxiv*

1   The Agile Consensus   **1**

The Origins of Agile   2
Agile Emerged to Handle Complexity   2
Empirical Process Models   4
A New Consensus   5
Scrum   6
An Example   12
Self-Managing Teams   14
Summary   15
Endnotes   16

2   Scrum, Agile Practices, and Visual Studio   **19**

Visual Studio and Process Enactment   20
Process Templates   21
Process Cycles and TFS   24
Inspect and Adapt   37
Task Boards   37
Kanban   38
Fit the Process to the Project   39
Summary   42
Endnotes   43

3 Product Ownership   **45**
What Is Product Ownership?   46
Scrum Product Ownership   50
Release Planning   51
Qualities of Service   69
How Many Levels of Requirements   73
Summary   75
Endnotes   75

4 Running the Sprint   **77**
Empirical over Defined Process Control   78
Scrum Mastery   80
Use Descriptive Rather Than Prescriptive Metrics   86
Answering Everyday Questions with Dashboards   91
Choosing and Customizing Dashboards   98
Using Microsoft Outlook to Manage the Sprint   100
Summary   101
Endnotes   101

5 Architecture   **103**
Architecture in the Agile Consensus   104
Exploring Existing Architectures   107
Summary   124
Endnotes   126

6 Development   **129**
Development in the Agile Consensus   130
The Sprint Cycle   131
Keeping the Codebase Clean   132
Staying "in the Groove"   139
Detecting Programming Errors Early   143
Catching Side Effects   154
Preventing Version Skew   162
Making Work Transparent   170
Summary   171
Endnotes   173

7 Build and Lab   **175**
Cycle Time   176
Defining *Done*   177

Continuous Integration 179
Automating the Build 181
Automating Deployment to Test Lab 186
Elimination of Waste 199
Summary 203
Endnotes 204

8 Test 207
Testing in the Agile Consensus 208
Testing Product Backlog Items 211
Actionable Test Results and Bug Reports 215
Handling Bugs 223
Which Tests Should Be Automated? 223
Automating Scenario Tests 224
Load Tests, as Part of the Sprint 228
Production-Realistic Test Environments 234
Risk-Based Testing 236
Summary 238
Endnotes 239

9 Lessons Learned at Microsoft Developer Division 241
Scale 242
Business Background 243
Improvements after 2005 247
Results 256
Acting on the Agile Consensus 256
Lessons Learned 258
The Path to Visual Studio 2012 262
Endnotes 263

10 Continuous Feedback 265
Agile Consensus in Action 266
Continuous Feedback Allows Build/Measure/Learn 267
There's No Place Like Production 269
Summary 271
Endnotes 274

Index 275

Foreword to Third Edition

Sam and I met in 2003 over a storyboard. We were on this new team with a mission to take Visual Studio—the world's leading individual development environment—and turn it into the world's leading team development environment. He had just joined Microsoft and wanted to convince me that we would succeed not just by building the best tools, but by creating the best end-to-end integration, and he used a storyboard to show the ideas.[1] He convinced me and the rest of the team.

He also persuaded us that we should think of enabling Agile process flow from the beginning. A key idea was that we minimize time spent in transitions. We would build our tools to make all their data transparent and squeeze as much waste and overhead as possible out of the software process. That way, the team could focus on delivering a flow of value to its customers.

That vision, which we now call the Agile Consensus, informed the first versions of Team Foundation Server and Visual Studio Team System, as our product line was called in 2005. The first edition of this book was the explanation of the reasons we made the leap.

Neno was one of our first customers and consultants. He quickly became one of our strongest advocates and critics, seizing the vision and identifying the gaps that we would need to fill release after release. He is now one of the clear experts in the product line, knowing as much about how our customers use the Visual Studio product line as just about anyone.

Since we released v1, we've also been on our own journey of Agile transformation across Microsoft Developer Division. Our products have helped

---

[1] In VS 2012, we made storyboarding a part of the product too.

make that change possible. First, in the wave to VS 2008, we set out to apply Agile software engineering practices at scale. You'll recognize these in our product capabilities today like unit testing, gated check-in, parallel development, and test lab management. These helped us reduce waste and create trustworthy transparency. Once we achieved those goals, we could set out to really increase the flow of customer value, in the second wave leading to VS 2010. And most recently, with VS 2012, we have really addressed our cycle time. The clearest example of this is the hosted Team Foundation Service, which is now deploying to customers every three weeks. Chapter 9 tells this story well.

Together, Sam and Neno have written the *why* book for modern software practices and their embodiment in the Visual Studio product line. This book does not attempt to replace the product documentation by telling you which button to click. Rather, it covers your software life cycle holistically, from the backlog of requirements to deployment, and shows examples of how to apply modern best practices to develop the right thing.

If you are an executive whose business depends on software, then you'll want to read this book. If you're a team lead trying to improve your team's velocity or the fit of your software to your customers' needs, read this book. If you're a developer or tester, and you want to work better, with more time on task, and have more fun, read this book.

Brian Harry
Microsoft Technical Fellow
General Manager, Team Foundation Server

Foreword to Second Edition

It is my honor to write a foreword for Sam's book, *Agile Software Engineering with Visual Studio*. Sam is both a practitioner of software development and a scholar. I have worked with Sam for the past three years to merge Scrum with modern engineering practices and an excellent toolset, starting with Microsoft's VS 2010. We are both indebted to Aaron Bjork of Microsoft, who developed the Scrum template that instantiates Scrum in Visual Studio through the Scrum template.

I do not want Scrum to be prescriptive. I left many holes, such as what is the syntax and organization of the product backlog, the engineering practices that turned product backlog items into a potentially shippable increment, and the magic that would create self-organizing teams. In his book, Sam has superbly described one way of filling in these holes. He describes the techniques and tooling, as well as the rationale of the approach that he prescribes. He does this in detail, with scope and humor. As I have worked with Microsoft since 2004 and Sam since 2009 on these practices and tooling, I am delighted. Our first launch was a course, the Professional Scrum Developer .NET course, that taught developers how to use solid increments using modern engineering practices on VS (working in self-organizing, cross-functional teams). Sam's book is the bible to this course and more, laying it all out in detail and philosophy. If you are on a Scrum team building software with .NET technologies, this is the book for you. If you are using Java, this book is compelling enough to read anyway, and may be worth switching to .NET.

When we devised and signed the Agile Manifesto in 2001, our first value was "Individuals and interactions over processes and tools." Well, we have the processes and tools nailed for the Microsoft environment. In Sam's book, we have something developers, who are also people, can use to understand the approach and value of the processes and tools. Now for the really hard work, people. After 20 years of being treated as resources, becoming accountable, creative, responsible people is hard. Our first challenge will be the people who manage the developers. They could use the metrics from the VS tooling to micromanage the processes and developers, squeezing the last bit of creativity out and leaving agility flat. Or, they could use the metrics from the tools to understand the challenges facing the developers. They could then coach and lead them to a better, more creative, and more productive place. This is the challenge of any tool. It may be excellent, but how it is used will determine its success.

Thanks for the book, Sam and Neno.

Ken Schwaber
Co-Creator of Scrum

Preface

Seven years ago, we extended Microsoft Visual Studio to include Application Lifecycle Management (ALM). This change made life easier and more productive for hundreds of thousands of our users and tens of thousands of our Microsoft colleagues. In 2010, when we shipped Visual Studio 2010 Premium, Ultimate, Test Professional, and Team Foundation Server, we achieved our goal of being widely recognized as the industry leader.[1] In 2012, we complemented the Server with the public preview of the hosted Team Foundation Service and started delivering even more value more frequently to software teams.

We've learned a lot from our customers in the past seven years. Visual Studio enables a high-performance Agile software team to release higher-quality software more frequently. It is broadly recognized as the market-leading, innovative solution for software teams, regardless of technology choice. We set out to enable a broad set of scenarios for our customers. We systematically attacked major root causes of waste in the application life cycle, elevated transparency for the broadly engaged team, and focused on flow of value for the end customer. We have eliminated unnecessary silos among roles, to focus on empowering a multidisciplinary, self-managing team. Here are some examples:

No more no repro. One of the greatest sources of waste in software development is a developer's inability to reproduce a reported defect. Traditionally, this is called a "no repro" bug. A tester or user files a bug and later receives a response to the effect of "Cannot reproduce," or "It works on my machine," or "Please provide more information," or something of the sort. Usually this is the first volley in a long game of Bug Ping-Pong, in which no software gets improved but huge frustration gets vented. Bug Ping-Pong is especially difficult for a geographically distributed team. As detailed in Chapters 1, "The Agile Consensus," and 8, "Testing," VS 2012 shortens or eliminates this no-win game.

No more waiting for build setup. Many development teams have mastered the practice of continuous integration to produce regular builds of their software many times a day, even for highly distributed Web-based systems. Nonetheless, testers regularly wait for days to get a new build to test because of the complexity of getting the build deployed into a production-realistic lab. By virtualizing the test lab and automating the deployment as part of the build, VS 2012 enables testers to take fresh builds daily or intraday with no interruptions. Chapter 7, "Build and Lab," describes how to work with build and lab automation.

No more UI regressions. The most effective user interface (UI) testing is often exploratory, unscripted manual testing. However, when bugs are fixed, it is often hard to tell whether they have actually been fixed or if they simply haven't been found again. VS 2012 removes the ambiguity by capturing the action log of the tester's exploration and allowing it to be converted into an automated test. Now fixes can be retested reliably and automation can focus on the actually observed bugs, not the conjectured ones. Chapter 8 covers both exploratory and automated testing.

No more performance regressions. Most teams know the quickest way to lose a customer is with a slow application or Web site. Yet teams don't know how to quantify performance requirements and accordingly, don't test for load capacity until right before release, when it's too late to fix the bugs that are found. VS 2012 enables teams to begin load testing early. Performance does not need to be quantified in advance because the test can answer the simple question, "What has gotten slower?" And from the end-to-end result, VS profiles the hot paths in the code and points the developer directly to the trouble spots. Chapter 6, "Development," and Chapter 8 cover profiling and load testing.

No more missed changes. Software projects have many moving parts, and the more iterative they are, the more the parts move. It's easy for developers and testers to misunderstand requirements or overlook the impact of changes. To address this, Visual Studio Test Professional introduces test impact analysis. This capability compares the changes between any two builds and recommends which tests to run, both by looking at the work completed between the builds and by analyzing which tests cover the changed code based on prior coverage. Chapters 3, "Product Ownership," and 4, "Running the Sprint," describe the product backlog and change management, and Chapters 6 through 8 show test impact analysis and the corresponding safety nets from unit testing, build automation, and acceptance testing.

No more planning black box. In the past, teams have often had to guess at their historical velocity and future capacity. VS 2012 draws these directly from the Team Foundation Server database and builds an Excel worksheet that allows the team to see how heavily loaded every individual is in the sprint. The team can then transparently shift work as needed. Examples of Agile planning are discussed in Chapter 2, "Scrum, Agile Practices, and Visual Studio," and Chapter 4.

No more late surprises. Agile teams, working iteratively and incrementally, often use burndown charts to assess their progress. Not only does VS 2012 automate the burndowns, but project dashboards go beyond burndowns to provide a real-time view of quality and progress from many dimensions: requirements, tasks, tests, bugs, code churn, code coverage, build health, and impediments. Chapter 4 introduces the "happy path" of running a project and discusses how to troubleshoot project "smells."

No more legacy fear. Very few software projects are truly "greenfield," developing brand-new software on a new project. More frequently, teams extend or improve existing systems. Unfortunately, the people who worked on earlier versions are often no longer available to explain the assets they have left behind. VS 2012 makes it much easier to work with the existing code by introducing tools for architectural discovery. VS 2012 reveals the patterns in the software and enables you to automatically enforce rules that reduce or eliminate unwanted dependencies. These rules can become part of the check-in policies that ensure the team's definition of *done* to prevent inadvertent architectural drift. Architectural changes can also be tied to bugs or work, to maintain transparency. Chapter 5, "Architecture," covers the discovery of existing architecture, and Chapter 7 shows you how to automate the definition of *done*.

No more distributed development pain. Distributed development is a necessity for many reasons: geographic distribution, project complexity, release evolution. VS 2012 takes much of the pain out of distributed development processes both proactively and retrospectively. Gated check-in proactively forces a clean build with verification tests before accepting a check-in. Branch visualization retrospectively lets you see where changes have been applied. The changes are visible both as code and work item updates (for example, bug fixes) that describe the changes. You can visually spot where changes have been made and where they still need to be promoted. Chapters 6 and 7 show you how to work with source, branches, and backlogs across distributed teams.

No more technology silos. More and more software projects use multiple technologies. In the past, teams often have had to choose different tools based on their runtime targets. As a consequence, .NET and Java teams have not been able to share data across their silos. Visual Studio Team Foundation Server 2012 integrates the two by offering clients in both the Visual Studio and Eclipse IDEs, for .NET and Java, respectively. This changes the either-or choice into a both-and, so that everyone wins. Again, Chapters 6 and 7 include examples of working with your Java assets alongside .NET.

These scenarios are not an exhaustive list, but a sampling of the motivation for VS 2012. All of these illustrate our simple priorities: reduce waste, increase transparency, and accelerate the flow of value to the end customer. This book is written for software teams considering running a software project using VS 2012. This book is more about the *why* than the *how*.

This book is written for the team as a whole. It presents information in a style that will help all team members get a sense of each other's viewpoint. I've tried to keep the topics engaging to all team members. I'm fond of Einstein's dictum "As simple as possible, but no simpler," and I've tried to write that way. I hope you'll agree and recommend the book to your colleagues (and maybe your boss) when you've finished with it.

Enough about Visual Studio 2012 to Get You Started

When I write about Visual Studio (or VS) I'm referring to the full product line. As shown in Figure P.1, the VS 2012 family is made up of a server and a small selection of client-side tools, all available as VS Ultimate.

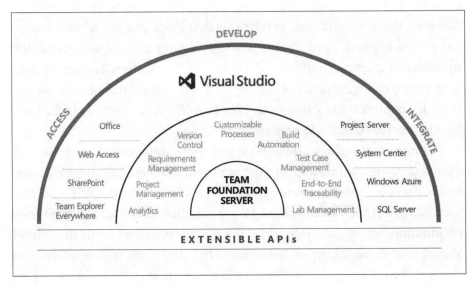

FIGURE P.1: Team Foundation Server forms the collaboration hub of VS 2012. The client components are available in VS Ultimate.

Team Foundation Server (TFS) is the ALM backbone, providing source control management, build automation, work item tracking, test case management, reporting, and dashboards. Part of TFS is Lab Management, which extends the build automation of TFS to integrate physical and virtual test labs into the development process.

If you just have TFS, you get a client called Team Explorer that launches either stand-alone or as a plug-in to the Visual Studio Professional IDE. Team Explorer Everywhere, a comparable client written in Java, launches as an Eclipse plug-in. You also get Team Web Access and plug-ins that let you connect from Microsoft Excel or Project. SharePoint hosts the dashboards.

Visual Studio Premium adds the scenarios that are described in Chapter 6 around working with the code. Visual Studio Test Professional, although it bears the VS name, is a separate application outside the IDE, designed with the tester in mind. You can see lots of Test Professional examples in Chapter 8. VS Ultimate, which includes Test Professional, adds architectural modeling and discovery, discussed in Chapter 5.

There is also a rich community of partner products that use the extensibility to provide additional client experiences on top of TFS. Figure P.2 shows examples of third-party extensions that enable MindManager, Microsoft Word, and Microsoft Outlook as clients of TFS. You can find a directory at www.visualstudiowidgets.com/.

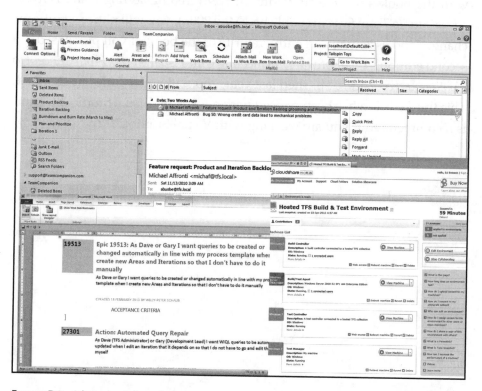

FIGURE P.2: A broad catalog of partner products extend TFS. Shown here are Ekobit Team-Companion, CloudShare hosted dev/test labs, and the open source TFS Word Add-in available on CodePlex.

Of course, all the clients read and feed data into TFS, and their trends surface on the dashboards, typically hosted on SharePoint. Using Excel Services or SQL Server Reporting Services, you can customize these dashboards. Dashboard examples are the focus of Chapter 4.

Of course, there's plenty more to learn about VS at the Developer Center of http://msdn. microsoft.com/vstudio/.

A Note to Readers about Editions of the Book

We are pleased to bring you the third edition of the book. If you have been with the book since the first edition, *Software Engineering with Microsoft Visual Studio Team System* (published May 2006), you will notice significant changes and essentially an entire rewrite of the book. If you purchased the second edition, *Agile Software Engineering with Visual Studio: From Concept to Continuous Feedback*, published last year, you will notice little has changed. This third edition has been revised with a focus on Visual Studio 2012 and is recommended if you are working with Visual Studio 2012.

Acknowledgments

Hundreds of colleagues and millions of customers have contributed to shaping Visual Studio. In particular, the roughly two hundred "ALM MVPs" who relentlessly critique our ideas have enormous influence. Regarding this book, there are a number of individuals who must be singled out for the direct impact they made. Ken Schwaber convinced me that this book was necessary. The inexhaustible Brian Harry and Cameron Skinner provided detail and inspiration. Jason Zander gave me space and encouragement to write. Tyler Gibson illustrated the Scrum cycles to unify the chapters. Natalie Wells, Martin Woodward, and Amit Chopra helped us with builds, virtual machines, and prerelease logistics to get the work done in time. Among our reviewers, David Starr, Claude Remillard, Aaron Bjork, David Chappell, and Adam Cogan stand out for their thorough and careful comments. And a special thanks goes to Joan Murray, our editor at Pearson, whose patience was limitless.

About the Authors

Sam Guckenheimer

When I wrote the predecessor of this book, I had been at Microsoft less than three years. I described my history like this:

I joined Microsoft in 2003 to work on Visual Studio Team System (VSTS), the new product line that was just released at the end of 2005. As the group product planner, I have played chief customer advocate, a role that I have loved. I have been in the IT industry for twenty-some years, spending most of my career as a tester, project manager, analyst, and developer.

As a tester, I've always understood the theoretical value of advanced developer practices, such as unit testing, code coverage, static analysis, and memory and performance profiling. At the same time, I never understood how anyone had the patience to learn the obscure tools that you needed to follow the right practices.

As a project manager, I was always troubled that the only decent data we could get was about bugs. Driving a project from bug data alone is like driving a car with your eyes closed and only turning the wheel when you hit something. You really want to see the right indicators that you are on course, not just feel the bumps when you stray off it. Here, too, I always understood the value of metrics, such as code coverage and project velocity, but I never understood how anyone could realistically collect all that stuff.

As an analyst, I fell in love with modeling. I think visually, and I found graphical models compelling ways to document and communicate. But the models always got out of date as soon as it came time to implement anything. And the models just didn't handle the key concerns of developers, testers, and operations.

In all these cases, I was frustrated by how hard it was to connect the dots for the whole team. I loved the idea in Scrum (one of the Agile processes) of a "single product backlog"—one place where you could see all the work—but the tools people could actually use would fragment the work every which way. What do these requirements have to do with those tasks, and the model elements here, and the tests over there? And where's the source code in that mix?

From a historical perspective, I think IT turned the corner when it stopped trying to automate manual processes and instead asked the question, "With automation, how can we reengineer our core business processes?" That's when IT started to deliver real business value.

They say the cobbler's children go shoeless. That's true for IT, too. While we've been busy automating other business processes, we've largely neglected our own. Nearly all tools targeted for IT professionals and teams seem to still be automating the old manual processes. Those processes required high overhead before automation, and with automation, they still have high overhead. How many times have you gone to a 1-hour project meeting where the first 90 minutes were an argument about whose numbers were right?

Now, with Visual Studio, we are seriously asking, "With automation, how can we reengineer our core IT processes? How can we remove the overhead from following good process? How can we make all these different roles individually more productive while integrating them as a high-performance team?"

Obviously, that's all still true.

Neno Loje

I started my career as a software developer—first as a hobby, later as profession. At the beginning of high school, I fell in love with writing software because it enabled me to create something useful by transforming an idea into something of actual value for someone else. Later, I learned that this was generating customer value.

However, the impact and value were limited by the fact that I was just a single developer working in a small company, so I decided to focus on helping and teaching other developers. I started by delivering pure technical training, but the topics soon expanded to include process and people, because I realized that just introducing a new tool or a technology by itself does not necessarily make teams more successful.

During the past six years as an independent ALM consultant and TFS specialist, I have helped many companies set up a team environment and software development process with VS. It has been fascinating to watch how removing unnecessary, manual activities makes developers and entire projects more productive. Every team is different and has its own problems. I've been surprised to see how many ways exist (both in process and tools) to achieve the same goal: Deliver customer value faster though great software.

When teams look back at how they worked before, without VS, they often ask themselves how they could have survived without the tools they use now. However, what had changed from the past were not only the tools, but also the way they work as a team.

Application Lifecycle Management and practices from the Agile Consensus help your team to focus on the important things. VS and TFS are a pragmatic approach to implement ALM (even for small, nondistributed teams). If you're still not convinced, I urge you to try it out and judge for yourself.

Endnotes

[1] See, for example: Thomas E. Murphy and Jim Duggan, "Magic Quadrant for Application Life Cycle Management," 5 June 2012 ID:G00218016, available at http://www.gartner.com/technology/reprints.do?id=1-1ASCXON&ct=120606&st=sb.

■ 1 ■

The Agile Consensus

A crisis is a terrible thing to waste.

—Paul Romer (attributed)

WARS AND RECESSIONS become focal points for economic and engineering trends that have developed gradually for many years before. The Great Recession of 2007 through 2010 is a case in point. In 2008, for example, Toyota—the youngest of the world's major automobile manufacturers—became the world market leader, as it predicted it would six years earlier.[1] Then in 2009, two of the three American manufacturers went through bankruptcy, while the third narrowly escaped. The emergence from this crisis underscored how much the Detroit manufacturers had failed to adapt to competitive practices that had been visible and documented for decades. In 1990, Jim Womack and colleagues coined the term *Lean* in their exquisitely researched book *The Machine That Changed the World* to describe a new way of working that Toyota had invented.[2] By 2010, Lean had become a requirement of doing business. As the *New York Times* headline read, "G.M. and Ford Channel Toyota to Beat Toyota."[3]

The Origins of Agile

Software companies, of course, experienced their own spate of bankrupt-cies in the years 2000–02 and 2008–10, while internal IT organizations were newly challenged to justify their business value. In this period, many industry leaders asked how Lean could have a similarly major impact on software engineering.

Lean was one of several approaches that became known as "Agile processes." On a weekend in 2001, 17 software luminaries convened to dis-cuss "lightweight methods," alternatives to the more heavyweight devel-opment processes in common use. At the end of the weekend, they launched the Agile Alliance, initially charged around the *Agile Manifesto*.[4] At the end of the decade, in a 2010 study of 4,770 developers in 91 countries, 90% of respondents worked in organizations that used Agile development practices to some degree (up from 84% the previous year).[5] Contrary to the early days of Agile, the most frequent champions for introducing Agile practices are now in management roles. By now, "agility" is mainstream. In the words of Forrester Research:

> Agile adoption is a reality. Organizations across all industries are increasingly adopting Agile principles, and software engineers and other project team members are picking up Agile techniques.[6]

It seems that every industry analyst advocates Agile, every business executive espouses it, and everyone tries to get more of it.

Agile Emerged to Handle Complexity

In prior decades, managers and engineers alike assumed that software engineering was much like engineering a bridge or designing a house. When you build a bridge, road, or house, for example, you can safely study hundreds of very similar examples. The starting conditions, requirements, technology, and desired outcome are all well understood. Indeed, most of the time, construction economics dictate that you build the current house or bridge according to a proven plan very much like a previous one. In this case, the requirements are known, the technology is known, and the risk is low.

These circumstances lend themselves to a *defined process model*, where you lay out the steps well in advance according to a previously exercised baseline, derived from the process you followed in building the previous similar examples. Most process models taught in business and engineering schools, such as the Project Management Body of Knowledge (PMBOK),[7] are defined process models that assume you can know the tasks needed to projected completion.

Software is rarely like that. With software, if someone has built a system just like you need, or close to what you need, chances are you can license it commercially (or even find it as freeware). No sane business is going to spend money building software that it can buy more economically. With thousands of software products available for commercial license, it is almost always cheaper to buy, if what you need already exists.

Accordingly, the software projects that are worth funding are the ones that haven't been done before. This has a significant implication for the process to follow. Ken Schwaber, inventor of Scrum, has adapted a graph from the book *Strategic Management and Organisational Dynamics*, by Ralph D. Stacey, to explain the management context. Stacey divided management situations into the four categories of simple, complicated, complex, and chaotic (as shown in Figure 1.1).[8]

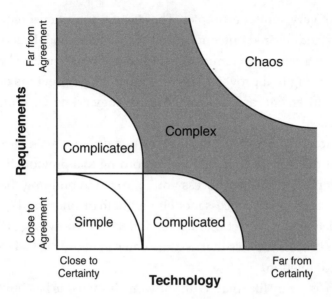

FIGURE 1.1: The Stacey Matrix distinguishes simple, complicated, complex, and chaotic management contexts and has been an inspiration for Scrum and other Agile practices.

Empirical Process Models

When requirements are agreed upon and technology is well understood, as in the house or bridge, the project falls in the simple or complicated regions. Theoretically, these simple and complicated regions would also include software projects that are easy and low risk, but as I discussed earlier, because they've been done before, those don't get funded.

When the requirements are not necessarily well agreed or the technology is not well known (at least to the current team), the project falls in the complex region. That is exactly where many software projects do get funded because that is where the greatest opportunity for competitive business differentiation lies.

The uncertainties put these projects in Stacey's complex category, often referred to as the "edge of chaos." The uncertainties also make the defined process model quite ill suited to these projects. In these cases, rather than laying out elaborate plans that you know will change, it is often better that you create more fluid options, try a little, inspect the results, and adapt the next steps based on the experience. Indeed, this is exactly what's known as

the *empirical process model,* based on what works well in product development and industries with continuous process control.[9]

An everyday example of an empirical process control is the thermostat.
We don't look up hourly weather forecasts and set our heaters and air con-
ditioners based on Gantt charts of expected temperatures. Rather, we rely
on a simple feedback mechanism to adjust the temperature a little bit at a
time when it is too hot or too cold. A sophisticated system might take into
account the latency of response—for example, to cool down an auditorium
in anticipation of a crowd or heat a room in anticipation of a cold spell—but
then the adjustment is made based on actual temperature. It's a simple control system based on "inspect and adapt."

A New Consensus

As software economics have favored complex projects, there has been a
growing movement to apply the empirical models to the software process.
Since 1992, Agile, Lean, Scrum,[10] Kanban,[11] Theory of Constraints,[12] System
Thinking,[13] Extreme Programming (XP),[14] and Flow-Based Product Development[15] have all been part of the trend. All of these overlap and are con-
verging into a new paradigm of software engineering. No single term has
captured the emerging paradigm, but for simplicity, I'll call this the *Agile
Consensus.*

The Agile Consensus stresses three fundamental principles that reinforce each other:

1. Flow of value, where *value* is defined by the customer who is paying
    for or using this project
2. Continual reduction of waste impeding the flow
3. Transparency, enabling team members to continually improve the
    above two

These three principles reinforce each other (as shown in Figure 1.2).
Flow of value enables transparency, in that you can measure what is important to the customer (namely, potentially shippable software). Transparency
enables discovery of waste. Reducing waste, in turn, accelerates flow and

enables greater transparency. These three aspects work together like three legs of a stool.

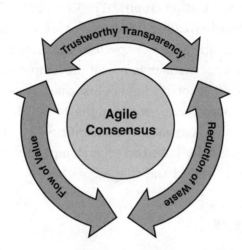

FIGURE 1.2: Flow of value, transparency, and reduction of waste form the basis of the Agile Consensus.

Microsoft's Visual Studio Team System 2005 and its successors were among the first commercial products to support software teams applying these practices. Visual Studio 2012 (VS 2012; Microsoft has dropped the words *Team System* from the name) has made another great leap forward to create transparency, improve flow, and reduce waste in software development. VS 2010 was one of the first products to tackle *end-to-end* Agile engineering and project management practices and, as you'll see in the following chapters, VS 2012 delivers a compelling workflow through them. A key set of these practices come from Scrum.

Scrum

As Forrester Research found recently, "When it comes to selecting an Agile methodology, Scrum is the overwhelming favorite."[16] Scrum leads over the nearest contender by a factor of three. Scrum has won acceptance because it simplifies putting the principles of flow of value, reduction of waste, and transparency into practice.

Scrum identifies three interlocking cadences: release or product planning, sprint (usually 2–4 weeks), and day; and for each cadence, it prescribes specific meetings and maximum lengths for the meetings to keep the overhead under 10% of the total time of the cycle. To ensure flow, every sprint produces a potentially shippable increment of software that delivers a subset of the *product backlog* in a working form. Figure 1.3 shows the cycles.[17]

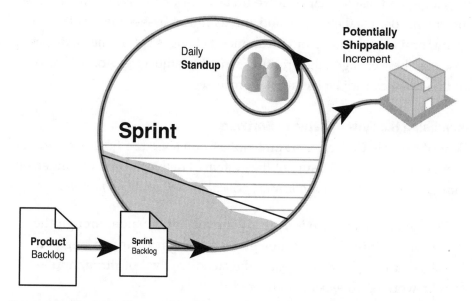

FIGURE 1.3: The central image of the Scrum methodology is a great illustration of flow in the management sense.

Core to Scrum is the concept of self-managing teams. Rather than rely on a conventional hierarchical structure with a conventional project manager, a self-managing team uses transparently available metrics to control its own work in process and improve its own velocity of flow. Team members are encouraged to make improvements whenever necessary to reduce waste. The sprint cadence formally ensures that a "retrospective" is used at least monthly to identify and prioritize actionable process improvements. Scrum characterizes this cycle as "inspect and adapt." Although more nuanced than a thermostat, the idea is similar. Observation of the actual process and its results drives the incremental changes to the process.

Potentially Shippable

Scrum also enables transparency by prescribing the delivery of "potentially shippable increments" of working software at the end of every sprint. For example, a team working on a consumer Web site might focus one sprint on catalog search. Without a working checkout process, the site would be incomplete and not actually shippable or publicly deployable. However, if the catalog search were usable and exercised the product database, business logic, and display pages, it would be a reasonable *potentially shippable* increment. Both stakeholders and the team can assess the results of the sprint, provide feedback, and recommend changes before the next sprint. Based on these changes, the product owner can adjust the product backlog, and the team can adjust its internal processes.

Increasing the Flow of Value in Software

Central to Agile Consensus is an emphasis on *flow*. The flow of customer value is the primary measure of the system of delivery. David J. Anderson summarizes this view in *Agile Management for Software Engineering:*

> Flow means that there is a steady movement of value through the system. Client-valued functionality is moving regularly through the stages of transformation—and the steady arrival of throughput— with working code being delivered.[18]

In this paradigm, you do not measure planned tasks completed as the primary indicator of progress; you count units of value delivered.

Scrum introduced the concept of the *product backlog*, "a prioritized list of everything that might be needed in the product."[19] This is a stack-ranked list of requirements maintained by the product owner on the basis of stakeholder needs. The product backlog contains the definition of the intended customer value. The product backlog is described in depth in Chapter 3, "Product Ownership."

The product backlog provides the yardstick against which flow of value can be measured. Consistent with Scrum, Visual Studio 2012 offers an always-visible product backlog to increase the communication about the flow of customer-valued deliverables. The product backlog is the current agreement between stakeholders and the development team regarding the next increments to build, and it is kept in terms understandable to the stakeholders. Usually, product backlog items are written as *user stories,* discussed more in Chapter 3. The report in Figure 1.4 shows product backlog and the test status against the product backlog. This bird's-eye view of progress in the sprint lets the team see where backlog items are flowing and where they are blocked. More detailed examples of a common dashboard, showing both progress and impediments, are discussed in Chapter 4, "Running the Sprint."

Stories Overview

Helps you track how far each user story has been implemented. Shows each story's actual number of hours of work remaining and completed, its acceptance test results, and the number of bugs that are linked to each story.

Related Reports
- Bug Status
- Status on All Iterations
- Stories Progress
- Test Case Readiness
- Test Plan Progress

Completed / Remaining

Passed / Failed / Not Run / Active / Resolved

Title	Work Progress		Test Status		
	% Hours Completed	Hours Remaining	Tests	Test Results	Bugs
⊞ As a new customer, I want to order a meal.	80 %	6634	3	33% 55 %	1 2
As a customer, I want to track my order history.	79 %	14053	0		6
Enable selection based on strength, intelligence, etc	19 %	144	2	48 % 52 %	1 2
As a returning customer, I want to order one of the meals that I've recently ordered.	78 %	17	2	48 % 52 %	
As a new customer, I want to choose a meal from a specific provider.	80 %	42	0		
⊞ As a customer, I want to save orders.	80 %	9432	0		
As an event planner, I want to let participants in my event choose meals from DinnerNow.	17 %	298	2	33 % 53 %	
As an event planner, I want to filter the menu to meet my constraints so that I can control the cost of the meals or so that I can offer only meals that are appropriate for the event.	40 %	126	0		
Gold member can search for villans	79 %	724	2	33 % 53 %	1
As a returning customer, I want to be able to override my default location so that I can order from DinnerNow when I'm on the road.	35 %	110	0		
As a delivery provider, I want orders to be submitted to my business at least 45 minutes before we pick the order up from the provider so that we can optimize the delivery.		28	0		
As a delivery provider, I want to provide a premium just-in-time service so that customers can decide at the last minute to order from DinnerNow.		0	0		
As a delivery provider, I want DinnerNow orders submitted to my dispatch system so that the cost of handling DinnerNow orders is minimized.		0	0		

FIGURE 1.4: The Stories Overview report shows each product backlog item on a row, with a task perspective under Work Progress, a Test Results perspective reflecting the tests run, and a Bugs perspective for the bugs actually found.

Reducing Waste in Software

The enemy of flow is waste. This opposition is so strong that reduction of waste is the most widely recognized aspect of Lean. Taiichi Ohno of Toyota, the father of Lean, developed the taxonomy of *muda* (Japanese for "waste"), *mura* ("inconsistency"), and *muri* ("unreasonableness"), such that these became common business terms.[20] Ohno categorized seven types of *muda* with an approach for reducing every one. Mary and Tom Poppendieck introduced the *muda* taxonomy to software in their first book.[21] Table 1.1 shows an updated version of this taxonomy, which provides a valuable perspective for thinking about impediments in the software development process, too.

TABLE 1.1: Taiichi Ohno's Taxonomy of Waste, Updated to Software Practices

Muda	In-Process Inventory	Partially implemented user stories, bug debt, and incomplete work carried forward. Requires multiple handling, creates overhead and stress.
	Overproduction	Teams create low-priority features and make them self-justifying. This work squeezes capacity from the high-priority work.
	Extra Processing	Bug debt, reactivations, triage, redundant testing, relearning of others' code, handling broken dependencies.
	Transportation	Handoffs across roles, teams, divisions, and so on.
	Motion	Managing tools, access rights, data transfer, lab setup, parallel release work.
	Waiting	Delays, blocking bugs, incomplete incoming components or dependencies.
	Correction	Scrap and rework of code.
Mura	Unevenness	Varying granularity of work, creating unpredictability in the flow.
	Inconsistency	Different definitions of done, process variations that make assessment of "potentially shippable" impossible.
Muri	Absurdity	Stress due to excessive scope.
	Unreasonableness	Expectations of heroic actions and commitments to perform heroic actions.
	Overburden	Stress due to excessive overhead.

Consistent with Ohno's taxonomy, *in-process inventory, transportation, motion,* and *waiting* often get overlooked in software development. Especially when many specialist roles are involved, waste appears in many subtle ways. As Kent Beck observed, "The greater the flow, the greater the need to support transitions between activities."[22] Some of the transitions take seconds or minutes, such as the time a developer spends in the cycle of coding and unit testing. Other transitions too often take days, weeks, or unfortunately, months. All the little delays add up.

Transparency

Scrum and all Agile processes emphasize self-managing teams. Successful self-management requires transparency. Transparency, in turn, requires measurement with minimal overhead. Burndown charts of work remaining in tasks became an early icon for transparency. VS takes this idea further, to provide dashboards that measure not just the tasks, but multidimensional indicators of quality.

VS enables and instruments the process, tying source code, testing, work items, and metrics together. Work items include all the work that needs to be tracked on a project, such as scenarios, development tasks, test tasks, bugs, and impediments. These can be viewed and edited in Team Explorer, Team Web Access, Visual Studio, Eclipse, Microsoft Excel, or Microsoft Project.

Technical Debt

In 2008, the plight of the financial sector plunged the world economy into the steepest recession of the past 70 years. Economists broadly agree that the problem was a shadow banking system with undisclosed and unmeasured financial debts hidden by murky derivatives. Fortunately, this crisis has led legislators to remember the words of U.S. Supreme Court Justice Louis Brandeis, "Sunlight is said to be the best of disinfectants; electric light the most efficient policeman."[23]

For software teams, the equivalent of these unknown liabilities is *technical debt.* Technical debt refers to work that needs to be done to achieve the *potentially shippable* threshold, such as fixing bugs, unit testing, integration testing, performance improvement, security hardening, or refactoring for sustainability. Technical debt is an unfortunately common form of waste. Unanticipated technical debt can crush a software project, leading to unpredictable delays, costs, and late cancellation. And similar to the contingent financial liabilities, technical debt is often not disclosed or measured until it is too late.

Among the problems with technical debt is the fact that it prevents the stakeholders from seeing what software is actually in a potentially shippable state. This obstacle is the reason that Scrum prescribes that every product backlog item must be delivered according to a definition of *done* agreed by the team. This is discussed more in Chapter 2, "Scrum, Agile Practices, and Visual Studio." Think of the transparency like Louis Brandeis's electric light: It makes the policeman less necessary. Together, the common definition of *done* and the transparent view of progress prevent the accumulation of technical debt, and thereby enable the team and its stakeholders to assess the team's true velocity.

An Example

Consider the effort spent in making a new build available for testing. Or think about the handling cost of a bug that is reported fixed and then has to get reactivated. Or consider writing specs for requirements that ultimately get cut. All of these wastes are common to software projects.

VS 2012 has focused on reducing the key sources of waste in the software development process. The build automation in VS Team Foundation Server allows continuous or regularly scheduled builds, and with "gated check-in" can force successful builds before accepting changed code. Lab Management can automatically deploy those builds directly into physical or virtualized test environments. These are discussed in Chapter 7, "Build and Lab."

An egregious example of waste is "Bug Ping-Pong." Every tester or product owner has countless stories of filing bugs with meticulous descriptions, only to receive a "Cannot reproduce" response from a programmer. There are many variants of this "No repro" response, such as "Need more information" or "Works on my machine." This usually leads to a repetitive cycle that involves every type of *muda* as the tester and programmer try to isolate the fault. And the cycle often leads to frustration, blame, and low morale.

Bug Ping-Pong happens not because testers and developers are incompetent or lazy, but because software bugs are often truly hard to isolate. Some bugs may demonstrate themselves only after thousands of asynchronous events occur, and the exact repro sequence cannot be re-created deterministically. Bugs like this are usually found by manual or exploratory testing, not by test automation.

When a tester files a bug, VS 2012 automatically invokes up to six mechanisms to eliminate the guesswork from fault isolation:

1. All the tester's interactions with the software under test are captured in an *action log,* grouped according to the prescribed test steps (if any).
2. A *full-motion video* captures what the tester sees, time-indexed to the test steps.
3. *Screenshots* highlight anything the tester needs to point out during the sequence.
4. *System configurations* are automatically captured for each machine involved in the test environment.
5. An *IntelliTrace log* records application events and the sequence of code executed on the server, to enable future debugging based on this actual execution history.
6. *Virtual machine snapshots* record the state of all the machines in the test environment in their actual state at the time of failure.

Eliminating Bug Ping-Pong is one of the clearest ways in which VS 2012 reduces work in process and allows quick turnaround and small batches in testing. Another is test impact analysis, which recommends the highest priority tests for each build, based both on completed work and historical code coverage. This is shown in more detail in Chapter 8, "Test."

Self-Managing Teams

A lot of ink has been used in the past 20 years on the concept of governance with regard to software development. Consider this quote from an IBM Redbook, for example:

Development governance addresses an organization-wide measurement program whose purpose *is to drive consistent progress assessment* across development programs, as well as the use of *consistent steering mechanisms.*[24] [Emphasis added.]

Most of the discussion conveys a bias that problems in software quality can be traced to a lack of central control over the development process. If only we measured developers' activities better, the reasoning goes, we could control them better. The Agile Consensus takes a very different attitude to command and control. Contrast the preceding quote with the following analysis:

Toyota has long believed that *first-line employees* can be more than cogs in a soulless manufacturing machine; they *can be problem solvers, innovators, and change agents.* While American companies relied on staff experts to come up with process improvements, Toyota gave every employee the skills, the tools, and the permission to solve problems as they arose and to head off new problems before they occurred. The result: Year after year, Toyota has been able to get more out of its people than its competitors have been able to get out of theirs. Such is the power of management orthodoxy that it was only after American carmakers had exhausted every other explanation for Toyota's success—an undervalued yen, a docile workforce, Japanese culture, superior automation—that they were finally able to admit that *Toyota's real advantage was its ability to harness the intellect of "ordinary" employees.*[25]

The difference in attitude couldn't be stronger. The "ordinary" employees—members of the software team—are the ones who can best judge how to do their jobs. They need tools, suitable processes, and a supportive environment, not command and control.

Lean turns governance on its head, by trusting teams to work toward a shared goal and using measurement *transparency* to allow teams to improve the flow of value and reduce waste themselves. In VS, this transparency is fundamental and available both to the software team and its stakeholders. The metrics and dashboards are instruments for the team to use to inspect its own process and adapt its own ways of working, rather than tools designed for steering from above.

Back to Basics

It's hard to disagree with Lean expert Jim Womack's words:

The critical starting point for lean thinking is value. Value can only be defined by the ultimate customer.[26]

Similarly for software, the Agile Consensus changes the way we work to focus on value to the customer; reduce the waste impeding the flow; and transparently communicate, measure, and improve the process. The auto industry took 50 years to absorb the lessons of Lean, until customer and investor patience wore out. In mid-2009, on the day General Motors emerged from bankruptcy, CEO Fritz Henderson held a news conference in Detroit and said the following:

"At the new GM, we're going to make the customer the center of everything. And we're going to be obsessed with this, because if we don't get this right, nothing else is going to work."[27]

Six months later, when GM had failed to show suitable obsession, Henderson was out of a job. It may be relatively easy to dismiss the woes of Detroit as self-inflicted, but we in the software industry have carried plenty of our own technical debt, too. That technical debt has cost many a CIO his job, as well.

Summary

For a long time, Scrum creator Ken Schwaber has said, "Scrum is all about common sense," but a lesson of the past decade is that we need supportive tooling, too.[28] To prevent the practice from diverging from common sense, the tools need to reinforce the flow of value, reduce the waste, and make the process transparent. These Agile principles have been consistently reflected in seven years of customer feedback that are reflected in VS 2012.

In practice, most software processes require a good deal of manual work, which makes collecting data and tracking progress expensive. Up front, such processes need documentation, training, and management, and they have high operating and maintenance costs. Most significantly, the process artifacts and effort do not contribute in any direct way to the delivery of customer value. Project managers in these situations can often spend 40 hours a week cutting and pasting to report status.

In contrast, the business forces driving software engineering today require a different paradigm. A team today needs to embrace customer value, change, variance, and situationally specific actions as a part of everyday practice. This is true whether projects are in-house or outsourced and whether they are local or geographically distributed. Managing such a process usually requires an Agile approach.

And the Agile Consensus requires supportive tooling. Collecting, maintaining, and reporting the data without overhead is simply not practical otherwise. In situations where regulatory compliance and auditing are required, the tooling is necessary to provide the change management and audit trails. Making the handoffs between different team members as efficient as possible becomes more important than ever because these handoffs happen so much more often in an iterative process. VS 2012 does that and makes Agile practices available to any motivated software team. The rest of this book describes the use of VS to support this paradigm.

In the next chapter, I look at the implementation of Scrum and other processes with VS. This chapter focuses on how VS represents the timeboxes and cycles. Chapter 3 pulls the camera lens a little further out and looks at product ownership broadly and the grooming of the product backlog, and Chapter 4 puts these topics together to discuss how to run the sprint using VS.

Endnotes

1   James P. Womack and Daniel T. Jones, *Lean Thinking: Banish Waste and Create Wealth in Your Corporation* (New York: Free Press, 2003), 150.

2   James P. Womack, Daniel T. Jones, and Daniel Roos, *The Machine That Changed the World: How Japan's Secret Weapon in the Global Auto*

Wars Will Revolutionize Western Industry (New York: Rawson Associates, 1990).

3   "G.M. and Ford Channel Toyota to Beat Toyota," *New York Times,* March 7, 2010, BU1.

4   www.agilemanifesto.org

5   "5th Annual State of Agile Survey" by Analysis.Net Research, available from http://agilescout.com/5th-annual-state-of-agile-survey-from-version-one/.

6   Dave West and Tom Grant, "Agile Development: Mainstream Adoption Has Changed Agility Trends in Real-World Adoption of Agile Methods," available from www.forrester.com/rb/Research/agile_development_mainstream_adoption_has_changed_agility/q/id/56100/t/2, 17.

7   Available from www.pmi.org/Resources/Pages/Library-of-PMI-Global-Standards-Projects.aspx.

8   Ken Schwaber, adapted from Ralph. D. Stacey, *Strategic Management and Organisational Dynamics, 2nd Edition* (Upper Saddle River, NJ: Prentice Hall, 2007).

9   Ken Schwaber and Mike Beedle, *Agile Software Development with Scrum* (Upper Saddle River, NJ: Prentice Hall, 2001).

10 Ken Schwaber and Jeff Sutherland, *Scrum: Developed and Sustained* (also known as the *Scrum Guide*), February 2010, www.scrum.org/scrumguides.

11 Henrik Kniberg and Mattias Skarin, "Kanban and Scrum—Making the Most of Both," InfoQ, 2009, www.infoq.com/minibooks/kanban-scrum-minibook.

12 Eliyahu M. Goldratt, *The Goal* (Great Barrington, MA: North River Press, 1986).

13 Gerald M. Weinberg, *Quality Software Management, Volume I: Systems Thinking* (New York: Dorset House, 1992).

14 Kent Beck and Cynthia Andres, *Extreme Programming Explained: Embrace Change* (Boston: Addison-Wesley, 2003).

15 Donald G. Reinertsen, *The Principles of Product Development Flow: Second Generation Lean Product Development* (Redondo Beach, CA: Celeritas Publishing, 2009).

16 West, *op. cit.*, 4.

17 This variation of the diagram is available from http://msdn.microsoft.com/.

18 David J. Anderson, *Agile Management for Software Engineering: Applying the Theory of Constraints for Business Results* (Upper Saddle River, NJ: Prentice Hall, 2004), 77.

19 Schwaber and Sutherland, *op. cit.*

20 Taiichi Ohno, *Toyota Production System: Beyond Large-Scale Production* (Cambridge, MA: Productivity Press, 1988).

21 Mary B. Poppendieck and Thomas D. Poppendieck, *Lean Software Development: An Agile Toolkit* (Boston: Addison-Wesley, 2003).

22 Kent Beck, "Tools for Agility," Three Rivers Institute, 6/27/2008, www.microsoft.com/downloads/details.aspx?FamilyId=AE7E07E8-0872-47C4-B1E7-2C1DE7FACF96&displaylang=en.

23 Louis Brandeis, "What Publicity Can Do," in *Harper's Weekly*, December 20, 1913, available from www.law.louisville.edu/library/collections/brandeis/node/196.

24 IBM IT Governance Approach: Business Performance through IT Execution, February 2008, www.redbooks.ibm.com/Redbooks.nsf/RedbookAbstracts/sg247517.html, 35.

25 Gary Hamel, "The Why, What, and How of Management Innovation," *Harvard Business Review* 84:2 (February 2006), 72–84.

26 Womack and Jones (2003), *op. cit.*, 16.

27 All Things Considered, National Public Radio, July 10, 2009, www.npr.org/templates/story/story.php?storyId=106459662.

28 Schwaber and Sutherland, *op. cit.*

2

Scrum, Agile Practices, and Visual Studio

One methodology cannot possibly be the "right" one, but…
there is an appropriate, different way of working for each project
and project team.[1]

—Alistair Cockburn

FIGURE 2.1: The rhythm of a crew rowing in unison is a perfect example of flow in both the human and management senses. Individuals experience the elation of performing optimally, and the coordinated teamwork enables the system as a whole (here, the boat) to achieve its optimum performance. It's the ideal feeling of a "sprint."

THE PRECEDING CHAPTER DISCUSSED the Agile Consensus of the past decade. That chapter distinguished between complicated projects, with well-controlled business or technical risk, and complex ones, where the technology and business risks are greater. Most new software projects are complex; otherwise, the software would not be worth building.

This chapter covers the next level of detail—the characteristics of software engineering and management practices, the "situationally specific" contexts to consider, and the examples that you can apply in Visual Studio (VS). In this chapter, you learn about the mechanisms that VS (primarily Team Foundation Server [TFS]) provides to support the team enacting the process. Whereas Chapter 1, "The Agile Consensus," gave an outside-in view of what a team needs, this chapter provides an inside-out overview of the tooling that makes the enactment possible.

Visual Studio and Process Enactment

Through three classes of mechanisms, VS helps the team follow a defined software process:

1. As illustrated in Chapter 1, TFS captures backlogs, workflow, status, and metrics. Together, these keep the work transparent and guide the users to the next appropriate actions. TFS also helps ensure the "doneness" of work so that the team cannot accrue technical debt without warning and visibility.

2. Each team project tracked by TFS starts off with a process template that defines the standard workflows, reports, roles, and artifacts for the process. These are often changed later during the course of the team project as the team learns and tunes its process, but their initial defaults are set according to the chosen process template.

3. On the IDE clients (VS or Eclipse), there are user experiences that interact with the server to ensure that the policies are followed and that any warnings from policy violations are obvious.

Process Templates

The process template supports the workflow of the team by setting the default work item types, reports, queries, roles (i.e., security groups), team portal, and artifacts. Work item types are the most visible of these because they determine the database schema that team members use to manage the backlog, select work, and record status as it is done. When a team member creates a team project, the Project Creation Wizard asks for a choice of process template, as shown in Figure 2.2.

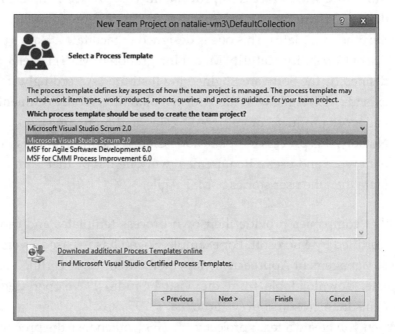

FIGURE 2.2: The Project Creation Wizard lets you create a team project based on any of the currently installed process templates.

Microsoft provides three process templates as standard:

1. **Microsoft Visual Studio Scrum:** This process template directly supports Scrum, and was developed in collaboration with Ken Schwaber based on the *Scrum Guide*.[2] The Scrum process template defines work item types for Product Backlog Item, Bug, Task,

Impediment, Test Case, Shared (Test) Steps, Code Review Request/ Response, and Feedback Request/Response. The reports are Backlog Overview, Release Burndown, Sprint Burndown, and Velocity.

2. **MSF for Agile Software Development:** MSF Agile is also built around an agile base but incorporates a broader set of artifacts than the Scrum process template. In MSF Agile, product backlog items (PBIs) are called *user stories* and impediments are called *issues.* The report shown in Figure 1.4 in Chapter 1 is taken from MSF Agile.

3. **MSF for CMMI Process Improvement:** This process template is also designed for iterative work practices, but with more formality than the other templates. This one is designed to facilitate a team's practice of Capability Maturity Model Integration (CMMI) Level 3 as defined by the Software Engineering Institute.[3] Accordingly, it extends MSF Agile with more formal planning, more documentation and work products, more sign-off gates, and more time tracking. Notably, this process template adds Change Request and Risk work item types and uses a Requirement work item type that is more elaborate than the user stories of MSF Agile.

Other companies provide their own process templates and can have these certified by Microsoft. For example, Sogeti has released a version of its Test Management Approach (TMap) methodology as a certified process template, downloadable from the Visual Studio Developer Center at http://msdn.microsoft.com/vstudio/aa718795.aspx.

When you create a team project with TFS, you choose the process template to apply, as shown in Figure 2.2.

Teams

Processes tend to prescribe team structure. Scrum, for example, has three roles. The Product Owner is responsible for the external definition of the product, captured in the product backlog, and the management of the stakeholders and customers. The Team of Developers is responsible for the implementation. And the Scrum Master is responsible for ensuring that the Scrum process is followed.

In Scrum, the team has three to nine dedicated members. Lots of evidence indicates that this is the size that works best for close communication. Often, one of the developers doubles as the Scrum Master. If work is larger than can be handled by one team, it should be split across multiple teams, and the Scrum Masters can coordinate in a scrum of scrums. A Product Owner can serve across multiple scrum teams but should not double as a Scrum Master.

In TFS, each team has a home page with data from the current sprint of its project, like an up-to-date burndown chart and the remaining, incomplete PBIs, as shown in Figure 2.3. Additionally, the team gets its own product backlog and a task board—both are available using the Web browser. To support larger projects with multiple teams, TFS enables the concept of master backlogs that consolidate each team's product backlog into a single view.[4]

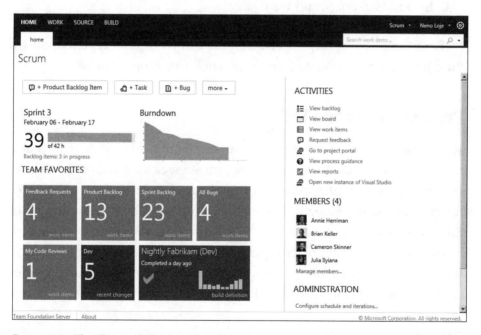

FIGURE 2.3: The tiles on the team's home page represent the team's current progress as well as favorite metrics, including work items, testing, source control, and the automated build and test results. Additionally, you can jump to all important views from this page.

In most cases, it is bad Scrum to use tooling to enforce permissions rather than to rely on the team to manage itself. Instead, it is generally better to assume trust, following the principle that "responsibility cannot be assigned; it can only be accepted."[5] TFS always captures the history of every work item change, thereby making it easy to trace any unexpected changes and reverse any errors.

Nonetheless, sometimes permissions are important (perhaps because of regulatory or contractual circumstances, for example). Accordingly, you can enforce permissions in a team project in four ways:

1. By role
2. By work item type down to the field and value
3. By component of the system (through the area path hierarchy of work items and the folder and branch hierarchy of source control)
4. By builds, reports, and team site

For example, you can set a rule on the PBI work item type that only a Product Owner can update PBIs. In practice, this is rarely done.

Process Cycles and TFS

A core concept of the convergent evolution discussed in Chapter 1 is iterative and incremental development. Scrum stresses the basis of iteration in empirical process control because through rapid iteration the team reduces uncertainty, learns by doing, inspects and adapts based on its progress, and improves as it goes.[6] Accordingly, Scrum provides the most common representation of the main macro cycles in a software project: the *release* and the *sprint* (a synonym for *iteration*), as shown in Figure 2.4. Scrum provides some simple rules for managing these.

Release
The release is the path from vision to delivered software. As Ken Schwaber and Jeff Sutherland explain in the *Scrum Guide:*

Release planning answers the questions, "How can we turn the vision into a winning product in the best possible way? How can we meet or exceed the desired customer satisfaction and Return on Investment?" The release plan establishes the goal of the release, the highest priority Product Backlog, the major risks, and the overall features and functionality that the release will contain. It also establishes a probable delivery date and cost that should hold if nothing changes.[7]

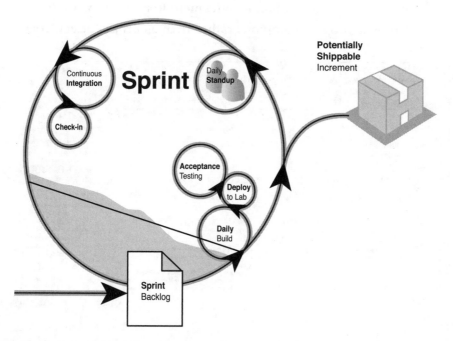

FIGURE 2.4: Software projects proceed on many interlocking cycles, ranging from the "code-edit-test-debug-check in" cycle, measured in minutes, to continuous integration, to daily testing cycles, to the sprint. These are views of both the process and the flow of data, automated by the process tooling.

The release definition is contained in the *product backlog,* which consists of requirements, unsurprisingly named *product backlog items,* as shown in Figure 2.5. Throughout the release, the Product Owner keeps the PBIs stack ranked to remove ambiguity about what to do next. As DeMarco and Lister have put it:

Rank-ordering for all functions and features is the cure for two ugly project maladies: The first is the assumption that all parts of the product are equally important. This fiction is preserved on many projects because it assures that no one has to confront the stakeholders who have added their favorite bells and whistles as a price for their cooperation. The same fiction facilitates the second malady, piling on, in which features are added with the intention of overloading the project and making it fail, a favorite tactic of those who oppose the project in the first place but find it convenient to present themselves as enthusiastic project champions rather than as project adversaries.[8]

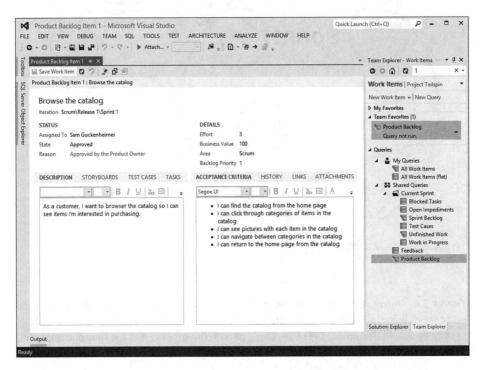

FIGURE 2.5: A product backlog item, shown here as accessed inside the VS IDE, can also be viewed from the Web Portal, Microsoft Excel, Microsoft Project, and many third-party plug-in tools available for TFS.

A common and useful practice is stating the PBIs, especially the functional requirements, as *user stories*. User stories take the form *As a <target*

customer persona>, I can <achieve result> in order to <realize value>. Chapter 3, "Product Ownership," goes into more detail about user stories and other forms of requirements.

Sprint

In a Scrum project, every sprint has the same duration, typically two to four weeks. Prior to the sprint, the team helps the Product Owner groom the product backlog, estimating a rough order of magnitude for the top PBIs. This estimation has to include all costs associated with completing the PBI according to the team's agreed-upon definition of *done.* The rough estimation method most widely favored these days is *Planning Poker,* adapted by Mike Cohn as a simple, fast application of what had been described by Barry Boehm as the Wideband Delphi Method.[9] Planning Poker is easy and fast, making it possible with minimal effort to provide estimates that are generally as good as those derived from much longer analysis. Estimates from Planning Poker get entered as story points in the PBI work item. Planning Poker is discussed further in Chapter 4, "Running the Sprint."

Another great practice is to define at least one acceptance test for each PBI. These are captured in TFS as test cases, a standard work item type. Defining acceptance tests early has three benefits:

1. They clarify the intent of the PBI.
2. They provide a *done* criterion for PBI completion.
3. They help inform the estimate of PBI size.

At the beginning of the sprint, the team commits to delivering a *potentially shippable increment* of software realizing some of the top-ranked product backlogs. The commitment factors the cumulative estimate of the PBIs, the team's capacity, and the need to deliver customer value in the potentially shippable increment. Then, only the PBIs committed for the current sprint are broken down by the team into tasks. These tasks are collectively called the *sprint backlog* (see Figure 2.6).

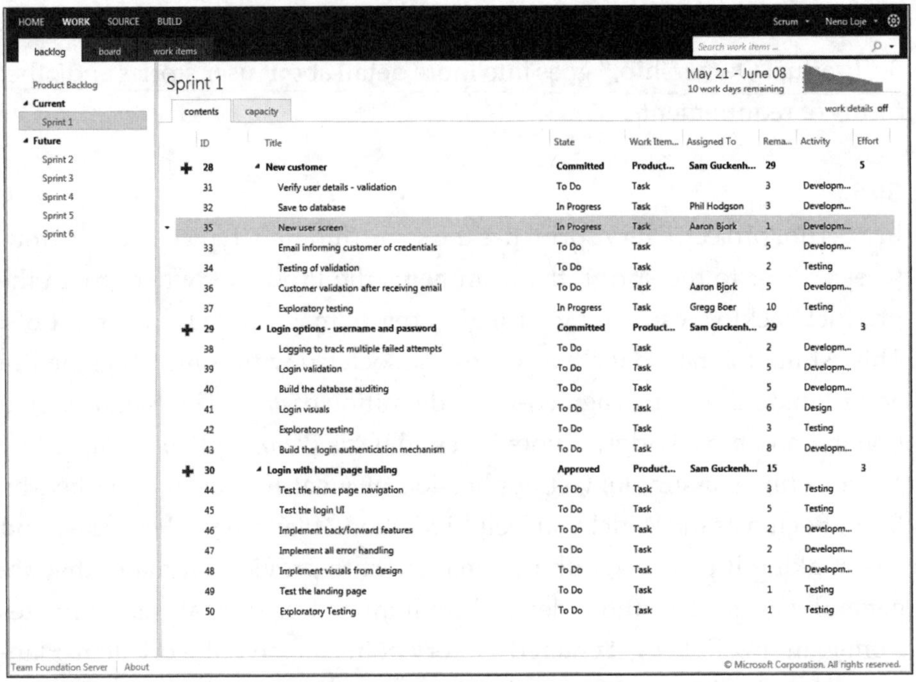

FIGURE 2.6: The sprint backlog, shown here as accessed from the Web Portal, consists of the tasks for the current sprint, grouped under the PBIs to which the team has committed.

Don't Confuse Product Backlog and Sprint Backlog

In our experience, the most common confusion around Scrum terminology is the use of the word *backlog* in two different instances. To some extent, the confusion is a holdover from earlier project management techniques. The product backlog holds only requirements and bugs deferred to future sprints and is the interface between the Product Owner, representing customers and other stakeholders, and the team. PBIs are assessed in story points only.

The *sprint backlog* consists of implementation tasks, test cases, bugs of the current sprint, and impediments and is for the implementation team. When working on a task, a team member updates the remaining hours on these tasks, but typically does not touch the PBI, except to mark it as ready for test or completed. Stakeholders should not be concerned with the sprint backlog, only with the PBIs.

Using tasks, the team lays out an initial plan for how to transform the selected PBIs into working software. Estimating each task's remaining hours helps the team verify the effort is not exceeding their capacity, as shown in Figure 2.7.

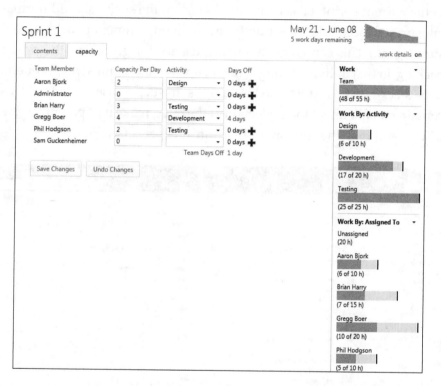

FIGURE 2.7: For each sprint the team sets its capacity. Each individual can identify primary activity and identify planned days off. The work pane compares available time against the estimated hours for the team, both for each team member and grouped at the level of activities like development or testing.

Handling Bugs

Bugs should be managed according to context. Different teams view bugs differently. Product teams tend to think of anything that detracts from customer value as a bug, whereas contractors stick to a much tighter definition.

In either case, do not consider a PBI done if there are outstanding bugs because doing so would create technical debt. Accordingly, treat bugs that are found in PBIs of the current sprint as simply undone work and manage them in the current iteration backlog.

In addition, you often discover bugs unrelated to the current PBIs, and these can be added to the product backlog, unless you have spare capacity in the current sprint. (The committed work of the sprint should normally take precedence, unless the bug found is an impediment to achieving the sprint goal.) This can create a small nuisance for grooming the product backlog, in that individual bugs are usually too fine-grained and numerous to be stack ranked against the heftier PBIs. In such a case, create a PBI as a container or allotment for a selection of the bugs, make it a "parent" of them in TFS, and rank the container PBI against its peers (see Figure 2.8).

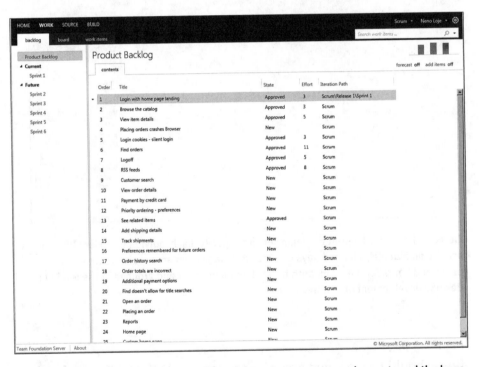

FIGURE 2.8: The product backlog contains the PBIs that express requirements and the bugs that are not handled in the current sprint. This can be accessed from any of the TFS clients; here it is shown in the VS IDE.

Avoiding Analysis Paralysis

A great discipline of Scrum is the strict timeboxing of the sprint planning meeting, used for commitment of the product backlog (the "what") and for initial task breakdown of the sprint backlog (the "how"). For a one-month sprint, the sprint planning meeting is limited to a day before work begins on the sprint. For shorter sprints, the meeting should take a proportionally shorter length of time.

Note that this does not mean that all tasks are known on the first day of the sprint. On the contrary, tasks may be added to the sprint backlog whenever necessary. Rather, timeboxing sprint planning means that the team needs to understand the committed PBIs *well enough to start* work. In this way, only 5% of the sprint time is consumed by planning before work begins. (Another 5% of the calendar, the last day of a monthly sprint, is devoted to review and retrospective.) In this way, 90% of the sprint is devoted to working through the sprint backlog.

Bottom-Up Cycles

In addition to the two macro cycles of release and sprint, TFS uses the two finer-grained cycles of check-in and test to collect data and trigger automation. In this way, with no overhead for the users, TFS can provide mechanisms to support both automating definitions of *done* and transparently collecting project metrics.

Personal Development Preparation

As discussed in Chapter 6, "Development," VS provides continuous feedback to the developer to practice test-driven development; correct syntax suggestions with IntelliSense; and check for errors with local builds, tests, and check-in policy reviews. These are private activities, in the sense that VS makes no attempt to persist any data from these activities before the developer decides to check in.

Check-In Cycle

The finest-grained coding cycle at which TFS collects data and applies workflow is the check-in (that is, any delivery of code by the developer from a private workspace to a shared branch). This cycle provides the first opportunity to measure *done* on working code. The most common Agile practice for the check-in cycle is continuous integration, in which every check-in triggers a team build from a TFS build definition. The team build gets the latest versions of all checked-in source from all contributors, provisions a build server, and runs the defined build workflow, including any code analysis, lab deployment, or build verification tests that have been defined in the build. (See Chapter 7, "Build and Lab," for more information.)

Continuous integration is a great practice, if build breaks are rare. In that case, it is a great way to keep a clean, running drop of the code at all times. The larger the project, however, the more frequent build breaks can become. For example, imagine a source base with 100 contributors. Suppose that they are all extraordinary developers, who make an average of only one build break per three months. With continuous integration, their build would be broken every day.

To avoid the frequent broken builds, TFS offers a form of continuous integration called *gated check-in*. Gated check-in extends the continuous integration workflow, in that it provisions a server and runs the team build *before* check-in. Only if the full build passes, *then* the server accepts the code as checked in. Otherwise, the check-in is returned to the developer as a shelveset with a warning detailing the errors. Chapter 9, "Lessons Learned at Microsoft Developer Division," describes how we use this at Microsoft.

In addition, prior to the server mechanisms of continuous integration or gated check-in, TFS runs *check-in policies* on the clients. These are the earliest and fastest automated warnings for the developer. They can validate whether unit tests and code analysis have been run locally, work items associated, check-in notes completed, and other "doneness" criteria met before the code goes to the server for either continuous integration or gated check-in.

Test Cycle

Completed PBIs need to be tested, as do bug fixes. Typically, team members check in code in small increments many times before completing a PBI. However, when a PBI is completed, a test cycle may start. In addition, many PBIs and bug fixes are often completed in rapid succession, and these can be combined into a single test cycle. Accordingly, a simple way to handle test cycles is to make them daily.

TFS allows for multiple team build definitions, and a good practice is to have a daily build in addition to the continuous integration or gated check-in build. When you do this, every daily "build details" page shows the increment in functionality delivered since the previous daily build, as shown in Figure 2.9.

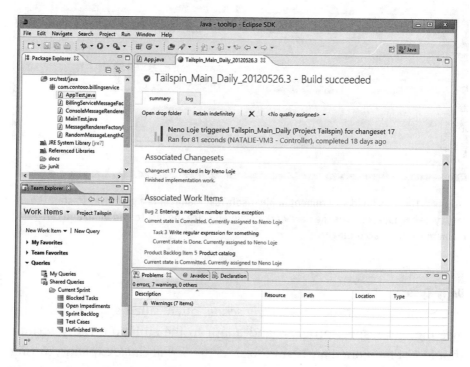

FIGURE 2.9: Every build has a "build details" page that serves as an automated release note, accessible from the dashboard or inside the IDE clients. In this case, it is shown inside Eclipse, as a team working with Java code would see.

In addition, Microsoft Test Manager (MTM, part of the VS product line) enables you to compare the current build against the last one tested to see the most important tests to run based on both backlog changes and new or churned code, as shown in Figure 2.10. (See Chapter 8, "Test," for more information.)

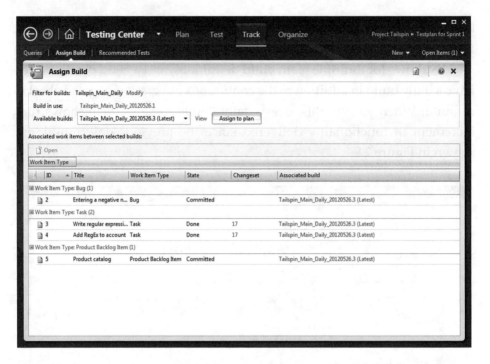

FIGURE 2.10: This build assignment in Microsoft Test Manager is a great way to start the test cycle because it shows the new work delivered since the last tested build and can recommend tests accordingly.

Daily Cycle

The Scrum process specifies a *daily scrum,* often called a "daily stand-up meeting," to inspect progress and adapt to the situation. Daily scrums should last no more than 15 minutes. As the *Scrum Guide* explains, during the meeting, each team member explains the following:

1. What has the team member accomplished since the last meeting?
2. What will the team member accomplish before the next meeting?
3. What obstacles currently impede the team member?

Daily scrums improve communications, eliminate other meetings, identify and remove impediments to development, highlight and promote quick decision making, and improve everyone's level of project knowledge.

Although TFS does not require daily builds, and the process rules do not mandate combining the daily and testing cycles, treating the daily cycle and test cycle as the same is certainly convenient. TFS helps considerably with preparation for the Scrum questions:

- As Figures 2.9 and 2.10 show, the automated release note of the "build details" page and the test recommendations of MTM help resolve any discrepancies in assumptions for question 1.
- The task board, shown in Figure 2.11, should align with question 2.
- The Open Impediments or Open Issues query, shown in Figure 2.12, should match question 3.

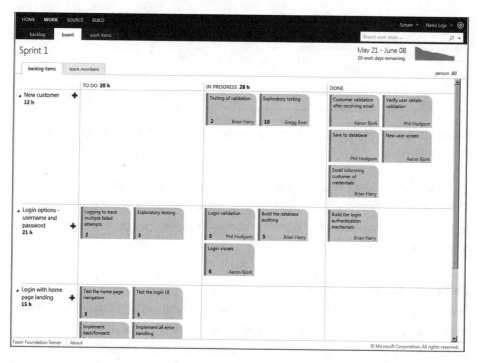

FIGURE 2.11: The TFS task board shows the progress of the sprint backlog visually grouped by PBI. Alternative queries allow different groupings, such as by team member.

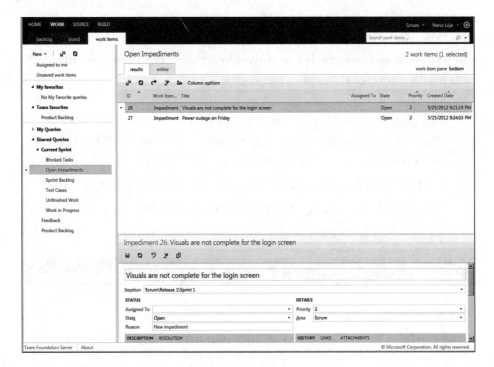

FIGURE 2.12: The Open Impediments query shows the current state of blocking issues as of the daily scrum.

These tools don't replace the daily scrum, but they remove any dispute about the data of record. In this way, the team members can focus the meeting on crucial interpersonal communication rather than on questions about whose data to trust.

Definition of *Done* at Every Cycle

For each of these cycles—check-in, test, release, and sprint—the team should have a common definition of *done* and treat it as a social contract. The entire team should be able to see the status of *done* transparently at all times. Without this social contract, it is impossible to assess technical debt and, accordingly, impossible to ship increments of software predictably.

With Scrum and TFS working together, every cycle has a done mechanism. Check-in has its policies and the build workflows, test has the test plans for the cycle, and sprint and release have work items to capture their done lists.

Inspect and Adapt

In addition to the daily 15 minutes, Scrum prescribes that the team have two meetings at the end of the sprint to inspect progress (the sprint review) and identify opportunities for process improvement (the sprint retrospective). Together, these should take about 5% of the sprint, or one day for a monthly sprint. Alistair Cockburn has described the goal of the retrospective well: "Can we deliver more easily or better?"[10] Retrospectives force the team to reflect on opportunities for improvement while the experience is fresh.

Based on the retrospective, the sprint end is a good boundary at which to make process changes. You can tune based on experience, and you can adjust for context. For example, you might increase the check-in requirements for code review as your project approaches production and use TFS check-in policies, check-in notes, and build workflow to enforce these requirements.

Task Boards

Scrum uses the sprint cadence as a common cycle to coordinate prioritization of the product backlog and implementation of the iteration backlog. The team manages its capacity by determining how much product backlog to take into the coming sprint, usually based on the story points delivered in prior sprints. This is an effective model for running an empirical process in complex contexts, as defined in Figure 1.3 in Chapter 1.

TFS includes an automated task board that visualizes the sprint backlog, as shown in Figure 2.11. It provides a graphical way to interact with TFS work items and an instant visual indicator of sprint status.

Automated task boards are especially useful for geographically distributed teams and scrums. You can hang large touch screens in meeting areas at multiple sites, and other participants can see the same images on their laptops. Because they all connect to the same TFS database, they are all current and visible. At Microsoft, we use these to coordinate Scrum teams across Redmond, Raleigh, Hyderabad, and many smaller sites.

Kanban

The history of task boards is an interesting study in idea diffusion. For Agile teams, they were modeled after the so-called *Kanban* (Japanese for "signboard") that Taiichi Ohno of Toyota had pioneered for just-in-time manufacturing. Ohno created his own model after observing how American supermarkets stocked their shelves in the 1950s.[11] Ohno observed that supermarket shelves were stocked not by store employees, but by distributors, and that the card at the back of the cans of soup, for example, was the signal to put more soup on the shelf. Ohno introduced this to the factory, where the card became the signal for the component supplier to bring a new bin of parts.

Surprisingly, only in the past few years have software teams discovered the value of the visual and tactile metaphor of the task board. And Toyota only recently looked to bring Agile methods into its software practices, based not on its manufacturing but on its observation again of Western work practices.[12] So, we've seen an idea move from American supermarkets to Japanese factories to American software teams back to Japanese software teams, over a period of 50 years.

In software practices, Kanban has become the name of more than the task board; it is also the name of an alternative process, most closely associated with David J. Anderson, who has been its primary proponent.[13] Where Scrum uses the team's commitments for the sprint to regulate capacity, Kanban uses work-in-progress (WIP) limits. Kanban models workflow more deterministically with finer state transitions on PBIs, such as Analysis Ready, Dev Ready, Test Ready, Release Ready, and so on. The PBIs in each such state are treated as a queue, and each queue is governed by a WIP limit. When a queue is above the WIP limit, no more work may be pulled from earlier states, and when it falls below, new work is pulled.

Kanban is more prescriptive than Scrum in managing queues. The Kanban control mechanism allows for continuous adjustment, in contrast to Scrum, which relies on the team commitment, reviewed at sprint boundaries. Kanban can readily be used inside the sprint boundaries to keep WIP low.

Fit the Process to the Project

Based on your project context and your retrospectives, you may choose to customize your process template. Ideally, this is a team decision, but certain stakeholders may have special influence. Even then, every team member should understand the rationale of the choice and the value of any practice that the process prescribes. If the value cannot be identified, it is unlikely that it can be realized. Sometimes the purpose might not be intuitive (certain legal requirements for example), but if understood can still be achieved.

As Barry Boehm and Richard Turner have described, it is best to start small:

> Build Your Method Up, Don't Tailor It Down
>
> Plan-driven methods have had a tradition of developing all-inclusive methods that can be tailored down to fit a particular situation. Experts can do this, but nonexperts tend to play it safe and use the whole thing, often at considerable unnecessary expense. Agilists offer a better approach of starting with relatively minimal sets of practices and only adding extras where they can be clearly justified by cost-benefit.[14]

Fortunately, TFS assumes that a team will "stretch the process to fit"—that is, take a small core of values and practices and add more as necessary (see Figure 2.13).

One of the tenets of the Agile Consensus is to keep overhead to a minimum. Extra process is waste unless it has a clear purpose whose return justifies the cost. Three common factors might lead to more steps or done criteria in the process than others: geographic distribution; required documentation; and governance, risk management, and compliance.

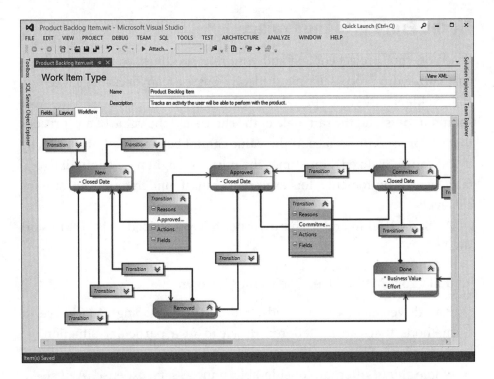

FIGURE 2.13: The Process Template Editor (in the TFS Power Tools on the VS Gallery) enables you to customize work item types, form design, and workflows.

Geographic Distribution

Most organizations are now geographically distributed. Individual Scrum teams of seven are best collocated, but multiple Scrum teams across multiple locations often need to coordinate work. For example, on VS, we are running scrums of scrums and coordinating sprint reviews and planning across Redmond, Raleigh, and Hyderabad, and several smaller sites, a spread of 12 time zones. In addition to TFS with large screens, we use Microsoft Lync for the video and screen sharing, and we record meetings and sprint review demos so that not everyone needs to be awake at weird hours to see others' work.

Tacit Knowledge or Required Documentation

When you have a geographically distributed team, it is harder to have spontaneous conversations than when you're all in one place, although instant messaging and video chat help a lot. When you're spread out, you cannot rely just on tacit knowledge. You can also use internal documentation to record contract, consensus, architecture, maintainability, or approval for future audit. Whatever the purpose, write the documentation for its audience and to its purpose and then *stop* writing. Once the documentation serves its purpose, more effort on it is waste. Wherever possible, use TFS work items as the official record so that there is a "single source of truth." Third-party products such as Ekobit TeamCompanion, shown in Chapter 4, can help by converting email into TFS work items for a visible and auditable record.

Governance, Risk Management, and Compliance

Governance, risk management, and *compliance* (GRC) are closely related terms that are usually considered together since the passage of the Sarbanes-Oxley Act of 2002 (SOX) in the United States. For public and otherwise regulated companies, GRC policies specify how management maintains its accountability for IT. GRC policies may require more formality in documentation or in the fields and states of TFS work items than a team would otherwise capture.

One Project at a Time Versus Many Projects at Once

One of the most valuable planning actions is to ensure that your team members can focus on the project at hand without other commitments that drain their time and attention. Gerald Weinberg once proposed a rule of thumb to compute the waste caused by project switching, shown in Table 2.1.[15]

TABLE 2.1: Waste Caused by Project Switching

Number of Simultaneous Projects	Percent of Working Time Available per Project	Loss to Context Switching
1	100%	0%
2	40%	20%
3	20%	40%
4	10%	60%
5	5%	75%

That was 20 years ago, without suitable tooling. In many organizations today, it is a fact of life that individuals have to work on multiple projects, and VS is much easier to handle now than it was when Weinberg wrote. In Chapter 6, I discuss how VS is continuing to help you stay in the groove despite context switching, but it is still a cognitive challenge.

Summary

As discussed in Chapter 1, in the decade since the Agile Manifesto, the industry has largely reached consensus on software process. Scrum is at its core, complemented with Agile engineering practices, and based on Lean principles. This convergent evolution is the basis for the practices supported by VS.

This chapter addressed how VS, and TFS in particular, enacts process. Microsoft provides three process templates with TFS: Scrum, MSF for Agile Software Development, and MSF for CMMI Process Improvement. All are Agile processes, relying on iterative development, iterative prioritization, continuous improvement, constituency-based risk management, and situationally specific adaptation of the process to the project. Microsoft partners provide more process templates and you can customize your own.

Core to all the processes is the idea of work in nested cycles: check-in, test, sprint, and release. Each cycle has its own definition of *done*, reinforced with tooling in TFS. The definitions of *done* by cycle are the best guards against the accumulation of technical debt and, thus, are the best aids in maintaining the flow of potentially shippable software in every sprint.

Consistent with Scrum, it is important to inspect and adapt not just the software but also the process itself. TFS provides a Process Template Editor to adapt the process to the needs of the project. The process design should reflect meaningful business circumstances and what the team learns as it matures from sprint to sprint.

Finally, inspect and adapt. Plan on investing in process and tooling early to improve the economics of the project over its life span. By following an Agile approach, you can achieve considerable long-term benefits, such as the development of high-quality and modifiable software without a long tail of technical debt. However, such an approach, and its attendant benefits, requires conscious investment.

The next chapter pulls back to the context around the sprint and discusses product ownership and the many cycles for collecting and acting on feedback. That chapter covers the requirements in their many forms and the techniques for eliciting them and keeping them current in the backlog.

Endnotes

1. Alistair Cockburn coined the phrase *stretch to fit* in his Crystal family of methodologies and largely pioneered this discussion of context with his paper "A Methodology per Project," available at http://alistair.cockburn.us/crystal/articles/mpp/methodologyperproject.html.

2. Ken Schwaber and Jeff Sutherland, *Scrum Guide*, February 2010, available at www.scrum.org/scrumguides/.

3. www.sei.cmu.edu

4. See Gregg Boer's blog, http://blogs.msdn.com/b/greggboer/archive/2012/01/27/tfs-vnext-configuring-your-project-to-have-a-master-backlog-and-sub-teams.aspx.

5. Kent Beck with Cynthia Andres, *Extreme Programming Explained: Embrace Change, Second Edition* (Boston: Addison-Wesley, 2005), 34.

6. Mentioned in the *Scrum Guide,* and discussed in somewhat greater length in Ken Schwaber and Mike Beedle, *Agile Software Development with Scrum* (Upper Saddle River, NJ: Prentice Hall, 2001), 25.

7. *Scrum Guide,* 9.

8. Tom DeMarco and Timothy Lister, *Waltzing with Bears: Managing Risk on Software Projects* (New York: Dorset House, 2003), 130.

9. Mike Cohn, *Agile Estimating and Planning* (Upper Saddle River, NJ: Prentice Hall, 2005).

10. Cockburn, *op. cit.*

11. Ohno, *op. cit.,* 26.

[12] Henrik Kniberg, "Toyota's Journey from Waterfall to Lean Software Development," posted March 16, 2010, at http://blog.crisp.se/henrikkniberg/2010/03/16/1268757660000.html.

[13] David J. Anderson, *Kanban, Successful Evolutionary Change for Your Technology Business* (Seattle: Blue Hole Press, 2010). This control mechanism is very similar to the drum-buffer-rope described by Eli Goldratt in *The Goal.*

[14] Barry Boehm and Richard Turner, *Balancing Agility with Discipline: A Guide for the Perplexed* (Boston: Addison-Wesley, 2004), 152.

[15] Gerald M. Weinberg, *Quality Software Management: Systems Thinking* (New York: Dorset House, 1992), 284.

3

Product Ownership

The single hardest part of building a software system is deciding precisely what to build.[1]

—Frederick Brooks, *The Mythical Man-Month*

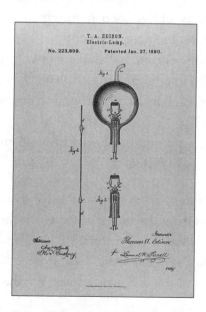

FIGURE 3.1: Edison patented the light bulb in 1880, but it has gone through more design change in the past 20 years than in the prior 100 years. The compact fluorescent at the right is just one of the unforeseeable evolutions of the original.[2]

THE PRECEDING CHAPTER FOCUSED heavily on what happens inside the cycle of the sprint and how the team can manage tasks and activities with Team Foundation Server (TFS). Of course, the sprint starts with a product backlog, and on the first day, the team commits to implementing the tasks for the most important product backlog items (PBIs) of that backlog.

Now we pull the lens back and look at the product backlog: its creation, maintenance ("grooming"), and the feedback cycles around it. Continuous feedback is as important a part of "inspect and adapt" as the internal team practices are. Although I discuss several techniques in an order, I don't mean that you apply these feedback practices only once or sequentially. Continuous feedback reduces uncertainty, keeps you on course, and almost certainly produces a result most fit for purpose.

What Is Product Ownership?

Frederick Brooks wrote the opening quote of the chapter in the 1960s, based on his experience at IBM. For the next 40 years, it was commonplace to blame software project failure on poorly understood requirements and, entertainingly, on customers not knowing their requirements.

More recently, Agile practices, notably Scrum, have taken a two-prong approach to the requirements problem. First, by creating small batches and frequent iteration, the team gets rapid feedback and course correction. That's the idea of the short sprint.

Second, Scrum (similar to XP) defines a unique authority to avoid ambiguity and randomization. As the *Scrum Guide* puts it:

> The Product Owner is the one and only person responsible for managing the Product Backlog and ensuring the value of the work the Team performs. This person maintains the Product Backlog and ensures that it is visible to everyone. *Everyone knows what items have the highest priority, so everyone knows what will be worked on.*[3] [Emphasis added.]

Having an authority on the product backlog is great for helping the Scrum team execute, but getting the product backlog right and keeping it in the right shape remains complex work. This chapter covers some techniques for that. Let's start with the problems a good product backlog solves.

The Business Value Problem: Peanut Butter

In 2006, the *Wall Street Journal* published a leaked email from Yahoo! under the title "Yahoo Memo: The 'Peanut Butter Manifesto.'"[4] In it, Brad Garlinghouse, a Yahoo! senior vice president, complained of three gaps in Yahoo!'s business approach:

"1. We lack a focused, cohesive vision for our company.

   I have heard our strategy described as spreading peanut butter across the myriad opportunities that continue to evolve in the online world. The result: a thin layer of investment spread across everything we do and thus we focus on nothing in particular.

2. We lack clarity of ownership and accountability.

3. We lack decisiveness."

Peanut butter was a term in widespread use outside of Yahoo! too, because it is a pervasive problem that affects businesses in general and software teams in particular. In the absence of clear prioritization, teams default to what they know best, not necessarily what is best for the business or its customers. This is the waste of overproduction described previously in Table 1.1.

The Customer Value Problem: Dead Parrots

It is tempting to say that a Product Owner just needs to make sure we give the customers what they ask for. However, customer requests aren't always clear. Consider a Monty Python sketch, *The Pet Shoppe,* in which a man goes to a pet store to return a parrot he bought (see Figure 3.2). He did not specify that the parrot must be alive, so the pet dealer sold him a dead one. The sketch is hilarious because it reveals such a frequent misunderstanding.

In Monty Python, a dishonest pet dealer exploits the misunderstanding. In everyday software teams, statements such as "You didn't tell me *X*," "The customer didn't specify *X*," and "*X* didn't show up in our research" are usually honest symptoms of failing to consider the customer's context.

Python (Monty) Pictures LTD

FIGURE 3.2: The Pet Shoppe customer: I wish to complain about this parrot what I purchased not half an hour ago from this very boutique.
Owner: Oh yes, the, uh, the Norwegian Blue: What's, uh … What's wrong with it?
Customer: I'll tell you what's wrong with it, my lad. 'E's dead, that's what's wrong with it![5]

The Scope-Creep Problem: Ships That Sink

One of Sweden's greatest tourist attractions is the *Vasa*, a warship that launched in 1628 and sank a mile from port in calm weather. The *Vasa* was built to be the most powerful and impressive vessel of its day to prove Sweden's new military might, with every armament and ornament the king ordered. Unfortunately, all the accoutrements made the ship keel over when she tried to sail (see Figure 3.3).

It is easy to get cocky about the foolish Swedish king, but almost every modern weapon system suffers the same fate of scope creep. Long procurement cycles, the lack of prompt feedback, and the ability of too many stakeholders to pile on requirements are problems as common today as 400 years ago.

The Perishable Requirements Problem: Ineffective Armor

Another lesson that is unfortunately all too visible in recent military history is that requirements are perishable. The U.S. and NATO forces entered the recent Middle East wars with armored vehicles designed to withstand confrontational attacks from heavy artillery in a European war. Unfortunately, the blasts they faced came from improvised explosive devices (IEDs) triggered by cell phones, and the armor proved useless.

FIGURE 3.3: The *Vasa* was so well built that the construction survived three centuries underwater and it has now been fully restored. Unfortunately, its bloated requirements made the ship too top-heavy to sail.[6] It's a vivid image of scope creep.

This fatal history plays out to the fallacy that we can "just get the requirements right." Requirements are not static, but constantly change. In the context of modern software, there are many aspects to this pattern:

- **The business environment or problem space changes.** Competitors, regulators, customers, users, technology, and management all have a way of altering the assumptions on which your requirements are based. If you let too much time lapse between the definition of requirements and their implementation, you risk discovering that you're "fighting the last war."

- **The knowledge behind the requirements becomes stale.** When an analyst or team is capturing requirements, knowledge of the requirements is at its peak. The more closely you couple the implementation to the requirements definition, the less you allow that knowledge to decay.

- **There is a psychological limit to the number of requirements that a team can meaningfully consider in detail at one time.** The smaller you make the batch of requirements, the more attention you get to quality design and implementation. Conversely, the larger you allow the requirements scope of an iteration to grow, the more you risk confusion and carelessness.

- **The implementation of one sprint's requirements influences the detailed design of the requirements of the next sprint.** Design doesn't happen in a vacuum. What you learn from one iteration enables you to complete the design for the next.

Scrum Product Ownership

Figure 1.3 showed the most well-known view of Scrum, a drawing that focuses on the core execution work of the Scrum team of 7±2 members, working in sprints typically of two to four weeks. Key to that picture is the central notion of a product backlog that contains the best current under-standing of what the product is intended to do. From this, the sprint back-logs get started.

In Scrum, the *Product Owner* ensures that the product backlog is well maintained ("groomed" in typical Scrum terminology), for which the Prod-uct Owner engages the whole team and all the relevant stakeholders. Let's step back and look at the broader context of the Product Owner's work in Figure 3.4.

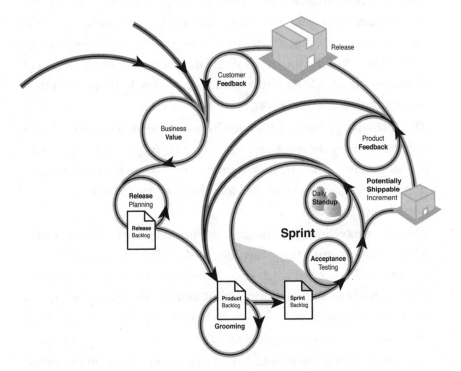

FIGURE 3.4: Many cycles outside the sprint execution influence the product backlog.

Many cycles of activity around the sprint feed the product backlog. The next sections discuss these in detail.

Release Planning

The Product Owner drives release planning to create the initial product backlog. The goal is to wrestle ambiguous, often conflicting inputs into a clear release vision and an initial stack rank of requirements to begin the first sprints.

Release planning is the best time to form a high-functioning team with shared context. When everyone on the team has the hands-on experience of articulating business and customer value, makes choices in priority, and airs points of view in a safe environment, the team can accelerate its growth through *forming-storming-norming-performing*.[7] Inside Microsoft product divisions, we use release planning not only to create the release vision, but also to reorganize the leadership and teams around that vision. In this way, the decisions governing release priorities and formal organizational structure inform each other.

Timebox release planning just as you would timebox the execution sprints. Use two- to four-week increments, with a clear backlog for each increment, and inspect and adapt the results. The release plan goals are a credible vision, enough of a product backlog to start execution sprints, and a well-formed team.

Business Value

Business strategy is hard. If it weren't, we wouldn't see so many companies struggle with it in every annual report. In nearly every case I have seen, there are many lenses that apply to business strategy, and they don't all focus in the same direction. Conflicts are typical among time to market, innovation, growing new segments, deepening share in existing segments, developing business partners, improving margins, addressing competitive threats, and many more. There are never crystal-ball answers.[8]

Customer Value

Understanding customer value isn't necessarily easier than business value, but it does have the advantage that you can use many mechanisms to elicit feedback. The Web has made it very easy to get huge volumes of feedback, but that volume has made it only more important that you balance your knowledge of whom you are serving (that is, whose feedback you want). As in all discussions, it's not always the loudest voice that is the most important or representative.

Be Clear About the Customer

To get clear goals for a project, you need to know the intended users. Start with recognizable, realistic, appealing *personas.* By now, personas have become commonplace in usability engineering literature, but before the term *personas* became popular there, the technique had been identified as a means of product definition in market research. Geoffrey Moore described the technique well:

> The place most . . . marketing segmentation gets into trouble is at the beginning, when they focus on a target market or target segment instead of on a target customer… We need something that feels a lot more like real people… Then, once we have their images in mind, we can let them guide us to developing a truly responsive approach to their needs.[9]

Understand the Pain Points

Often, the goals are chosen to address *pain points* (that is, issues that the user faces with current alternatives, which the new solution is intended to solve). When this is true, you should capture the pain points with the goals. At other times, the goals are intended to capture exciters. Be sure to tag these as well so that you can test how much delight the scenario actually brings.

Distill a Clear Vision Everyone Can Cite

Except in the smallest start-ups, the Product Owner will be a key stakeholder but not an owner of the business strategy. Nonetheless, the Product

Owner is responsible for condensing the strategy into a release vision that every stakeholder can understand.

A sign of a successful vision statement is that all project team members can recite it from memory and connect their daily work to it. A useful format for thinking about the key values of such a strategic project, and hence the vision statement, is the "elevator pitch."[10] It captures the vision crisply enough that the customer or investor can remember it from that short encounter. Moore invented a succinct form for the elevator pitch, as illustrated in Table 3.1.

TABLE 3.1: Release Vision Elevator Pitch

For	(the target customer segment only)
Who are dissatisfied with	(the current…alternative)
Our solution is a	(product category)
That provides	(key problem-solving capability)
Unlike	(the product alternative)
We have assembled	(key requirements for your solution)

User Story Form

The most common form for capturing requirements in the product backlog is a user story, as popularized by Mike Cohn in his book *User Stories Applied: For Agile Software Development.*[11] User stories take the following form:

As a <target customer persona>,
I can <achieve result>
In order to <realize value>

This useful short form can describe functional requirements at both coarse and fine levels. It works well because it keeps the focus on the customer persona and the value to be achieved. User stories can and should serve as the basis of acceptance tests to verify the "doneness" of the corresponding functionality.

Scale

It is important to think of PBIs at multiple levels of granularity. For broad communication, prioritization, and initial estimation (see Planning Poker in the next chapter), you need a coarse understanding that is easy to grasp. On the other hand, for implementation of a PBI within the current iteration, you need a much more detailed understanding. Indeed, the ultimate PBI definition is the associated test case (see Chapters 6 and 8, "Development" and "Test," respectively).

At the fine level of the product backlog, it is important that user stories

- Be small enough for a single sprint, yet
- Be large enough to convey value that a product owner can assess

Often, this is finer-grained than the customer value needed to describe a release, and the result is a hierarchy in which *epics* are the largest-grained stories, and these contain *themes* that in turn contain user stories. There is no "one size fits all" prescription here. Regardless of the scale, the user-story form is a great convention to focus the appropriate PBIs on customer value. In Chapter 9, "Lessons Learned at Microsoft Developer Division," I describe how we have done this at Microsoft.

Exciters, Satisfiers, and Dissatisfiers: Kano Analysis

Not all user stories are made alike. It is easy to focus on requirements of a solution that make users enjoy the solution and achieve their goals. You can think of these as *satisfiers*. When the goals are important and the scenario compelling enough to elicit a *"Wow!"* from the customer, we can call the scenario an *exciter.*

At the same time, potential attributes of a solution (or absence of attributes) can really annoy users or disrupt their experience. These are *must-haves if present or dissatisfiers if absent.* Customers just take them for granted. Dissatisfiers frequently occur because qualities of service haven't been considered fully. "The system's too slow," "Spyware picked up my ID," "I can no longer run my favorite app," and "It doesn't scale" are all examples of dissatisfiers that result from the corresponding qualities of service not being addressed.

Exciters are a third group of scenarios that delight the customer dispro-
portionately when present. Sometimes they are not described or imagined
because they may require true innovation to achieve. However, sometimes
they are simple conveniences that make a huge perceived difference. For a
brief period, minivan manufacturers competed based on the number of
cupholders in the backseats, then on the number of sliding doors, then on
backseat video equipment, and now on the navigational electronics. All
these pieces of product differentiation were small, evolutionary features,
which initially came to the market as exciters and over time came to be recognized as must-haves.

A useful technique called Kano analysis (named for its inventor) plots
exciters, satisfiers, and dissatisfiers on the same axes, as illustrated in Figure 3.5. The x-axis identifies the extent to which a scenario or quality of
service is implemented, and the y-axis plots the resulting customer satisfaction.[12]

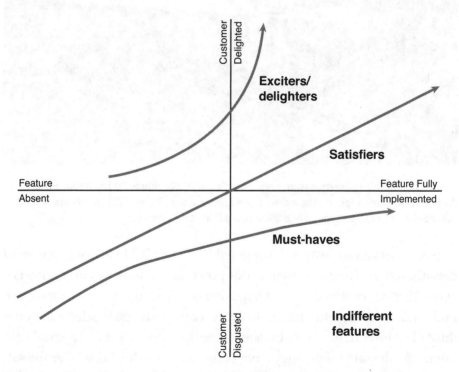

FIGURE 3.5: The x-axis shows the extent to which different solution requirements are implemented; the y-axis shows the resulting customer response.

Applying Kano Analysis

Although conceived as a quantitative technique, Kano analysis is most effective as a means to a structured conversation. At Microsoft, we hold software design reviews with customers such as the one shown in Figure 3.6.

FIGURE 3.6: In this software design review at Microsoft, Stephanie Cuthbertson, a Group Program Manager, is facilitating a discussion among Visual Studio (VS) customers around potential areas of investment while the product team takes notes.

The charts on the wall are formatted like Table 3.2 to measure pain and dissatisfaction. The rows are a list of potential customer pain points. For every 15 rows, customers are given five green dots and five red dots to use in the importance columns. In this way, each participant selects the one-third most important, one-third least important, and one-third neutral pain points. At the same time, they have unlimited blue dots to answer the satisfaction and approval columns.

TABLE 3.2: Using Kano Analysis to Understand Customer Pain

Pain Described	Importance to Your Business		Are You Satisfied with Your Current Solution?			Is the Proposed Solution Heading in the Right Direction?			Why?
	Most important third	Least important third	Yes	No	Don't know	Yes	No	Don't Know	

The goal of the wall charts is to focus conversation on areas of disagreement or puzzlement. Sometimes obvious patterns emerge that do not need much discussion:

- A cluster of least important means "Don't waste your time." The same applies to a cluster of Yes for currently satisfied.
- A cluster of most important, along with No for currently satisfied and Yes for right direction, is an obvious investment area.

In contrast, areas of disagreement reveal the most interesting insights. For example, you might see green and red next to each other. For example, customers with regulatory concerns might rate something very important that unregulated customers don't care about. Or you might discover that there is an area of high importance and low satisfaction, where your proposal is heading in the wrong direction. That's an obvious time to rethink.

We try to do these reviews with customers whenever needed, both in person, as shown in Figure 3.6, and via Lync or Skype. (In all cases, we broadcast and record the sessions for remote participants and later reviewers.) We've found that it is important to develop communities of participants who share sufficient common business context yet hold diverse-enough opinions to yield a rich discussion. When the business interests and context are too diverse, we split the participants into parallel groups.

Although Kano analysis is widely used as a quantitative technique, we achieve the best results when we use the numbers strictly as an impetus to discussion. We capture the insights of the discussion, and then throw away the numbers.

Design Thinking

While business value and customer value are key inputs, effective release planning has to transform the data into key insights. Tim Brown, CEO of Ideo and author of *Change by Design,* has a simple picture of the forces at play, shown in Figure 3.7.[13]

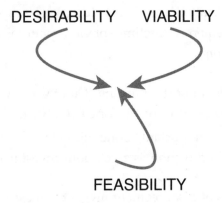

DESIRABILITY   VIABILITY

FEASIBILITY

FIGURE 3.7: Tim Brown distills three successful forces of design that apply to release planning: desirability, viability, and feasibility.

The forces Brown identifies are as follows:

- **Feasibility:** Can the desired product be built within the business constraints (time, cost, technology, quality expectations, and so on)? In other words, would the proposed solution be *usable* and *possible?*
- **Viability:** If built, would the proposed product make sense? If commercially available alternatives do the same thing as well or better, then probably not. If there aren't good alternatives, what would make the proposed product *useful* and *worth building?*

- **Desirability:** We all live and work in marketplaces with lots of
  options. What makes this particular solution the most *desirable* one?
  Especially among consumer products, it is easy to see how certain
  products capture the imagination of the market and others become
  also-rans. In the business world, criteria may be different and tasks
  less volatile, but the same dynamics apply.

The intent of Brown's design thinking is to foster rapid ideation and
expansive thinking, not to condemn visions with analysis paralysis. In
Microsoft, we use paper and pen at this stage to do *paper prototyping*, literally the manual sketching of as many ideas as possible (often hundreds) as
quickly as possible (often in five-minute cycles). We also do this together
as a team exercise, both to leverage the wisdom of the crowd and to help
form more cohesive teams. Figure 3.8 shows sample output from such an
exercise by the Visual Studio Ultimate team at Microsoft.

FIGURE 3.8: Hundreds of paper prototypes hanging in a hallway indicate the rapid ideation
nature of the exercise. There are many, many attempts to shape each idea and many people
who participate in each one.

Storyboards

Once an idea looks promising, it is often worth fleshing out the detailed interaction flow, especially when you have rich data and state in the solution being designed. Wireframes and storyboards can do this. Across an epic, you might have one screen per user story, and test that the user stories hang together as a coherent experience. Figure 3.9 is an excerpt of such a storyboard. Figure 3.10, in turn, is a single frame drawn to highlight key points.

As you can see in Figures 3.9 and 3.10, we often use PowerPoint for storyboarding at Microsoft. This is an example of an internal practice that we used successfully, refined through user feedback and testing against market alternatives, and then built into VS 2012.

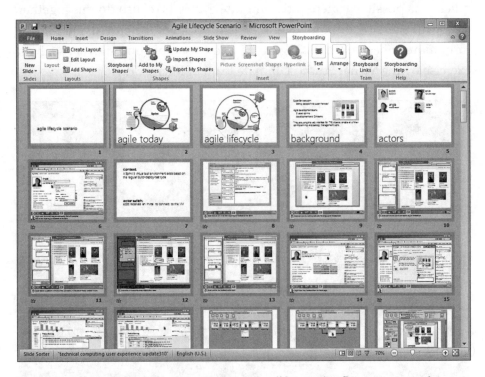

FIGURE 3.9: A storyboard is used to assess the overall interaction flow across an epic.

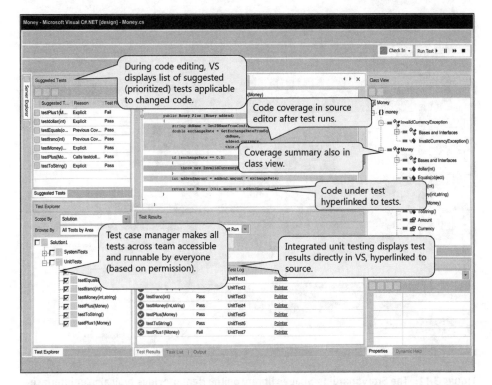

FIGURE 3.10: One wireframe illustrates the key points of an interaction. It is worth noting that this particular wireframe was drawn in 2004. It is not a "spec" in the traditional sense. Not all the user stories were implemented until VS 2010, and when they were, the implementation often improved on the ideas in the drawing. (See Chapters 6 and 8 for the description of what was implemented.)

PowerPoint Storyboarding adds a storyboarding ribbon to PowerPoint (as shown in Figure 3.11). When you create a storyboard, you can build up each slide from a library of commonly used shapes for different application types, and additional shapes are available through the VS Gallery. You can use the standard features of PowerPoint for shapes and apply animations to simulate mouse or touch actions, such as dragging and dropping or clicking on a control. You can share the resulting presentation as a stand-alone file, so that the recipient does not need any extra software in order to open or present the storyboard.

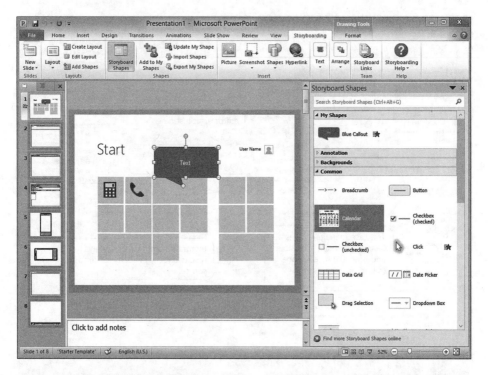

FIGURE 3.11: The Storyboarding Shapes library on the right provides typical user interface elements for all common application types. You can store your own, customized shapes in the "My Shapes" section at the top, or download additional shapes from the VS Gallery using the link at the bottom.

Storyboards typically represent product backlog items. Figure 3.12 shows how storyboards can be linked with work items in TFS (product backlog items or epics). Use the SharePoint-based project portal to store the storyboard files, a good practice anyway, and link to them there.

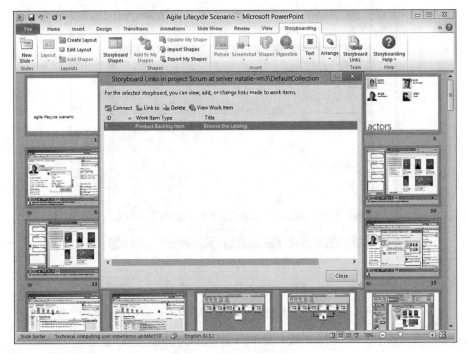

FIGURE 3.12: Storyboards can be linked with work items in TFS, making it easy to navigate from a product backlog item (or epic) to the corresponding storyboard.

Customer Validation

Storyboards are great ways to quickly make your hypotheses testable, but they are only assumptions until tested. It is essential that customers and stakeholders can "inspect and adapt" the intended product and participate with the product team.

Early in a project, this validation can be done in design reviews or contextual interviews with scenarios as lists and then as wireframes. Storyboards and live functionality, as it becomes available, can also be tested in a usability lab, as shown in Figure 3.13.

FIGURE 3.13: This is a frame from the streaming video of a usability lab. The bulk of the image is the computer screen as the user sees it. The user is superimposed in the lower right so that observers can watch and listen to the user working through the lab assignments.

There are three keys to making a feedback effective:

1. Create a trusting atmosphere in which the user knows that the software is being tested, not the user.
2. Have the user think out loud continually so that you can hear the unfiltered internal monologue.
3. Don't "lead the witness"—that is, don't interfere with the user's exploration and discovery of the software under test.

Of course, not everyone has a specialized room outfitted with one-way mirrors and video recording that enable spectators to watch behind the glass or over streaming video. Fortunately with VS 2012, you don't need the special facility. We have put the usability lab into the software, so that you can get the same kind of feedback from any customer with a normal laptop or tablet with a microphone. VS 2012 does this through a new work item type called a *Feedback Request,* as shown in Figure 3.14.

FIGURE 3.14: Feedback Requests let you specify the recipients, instructions on how to access or install (if applicable) the application, and the items where you want the stakeholders to focus their feedback.

When you create a feedback request in TFS, the server prepares an editable email for you to send to the individual or groups of stakeholders you invite for feedback. The feedback request will contain instructions on how to access or install the latest version of the software and what feedback should be provided.

When you click Send, TFS will generate an email like the one shown in Figure 3.15. The first link launches the *Feedback Client for TFS* and immediately starts the feedback session, whereas the second link downloads and installs the required client from the Microsoft Download Center. You can edit this email with whatever additional information you would like to add before sending.

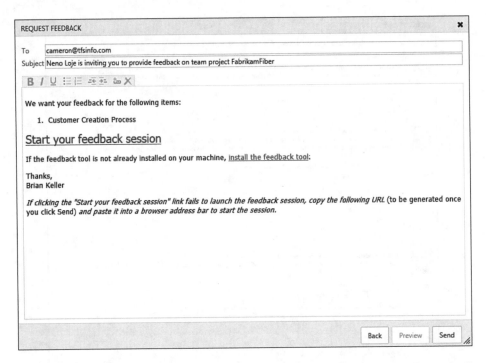

FIGURE 3.15: When you click Preview on the previous screen, you see and can edit the email that will be sent to the stakeholders in order to request their feedback.

When the user receives the email and starts the feedback session, the *Feedback Client* launches, as shown in Figure 3.16. Think of this as the distributed usability lab. The *Feedback Client* guides the user through three steps.

The first panel provides instructions on how to access the version to test. The second panel collects the actual feedback. The third panel allows the user to submit the feedback with an overall rating. This submission will create a *Feedback Response* work time in TFS as a child of the original request on which the items of feedback will be attached.

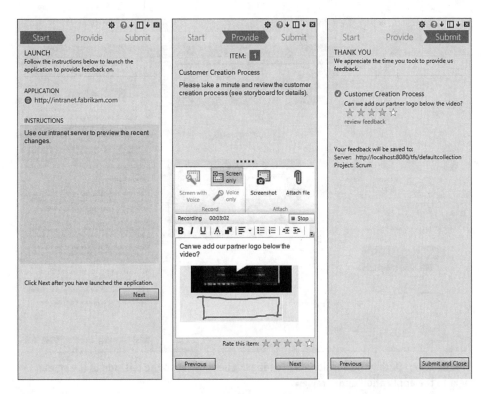

FIGURE 3.16: The TFS Feedback Client guides the stakeholder through a feedback session, from launching the application, to commenting and recording notes, to submitting the responses.

During the feedback session, the middle panel docks next to the application under review, as shown in Figure 3.17. The user can use the Feedback Client panel to comment, add screenshots, record audio or video, or add attachments.

TFS collects the Feedback Responses automatically and groups them as children of the appropriate Feedback Requests, as shown in Figure 3.18. You can watch for new ones by adding the Feedbacks query as a team favorite and putting a tile with the number of new feedbacks on the team's home page as well. All of this ties the communication with stakeholders directly into the product backlog and lets you continuously groom PBIs and engage your customers.

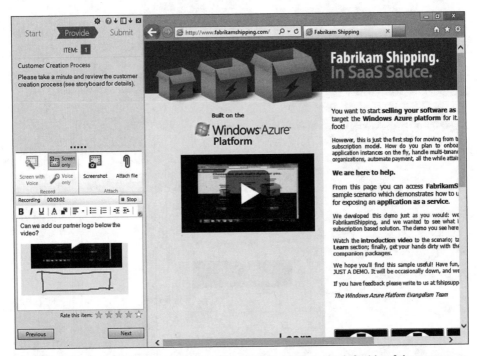

FIGURE 3.17: During the session, the Feedback Client docks to the left side of the screen next to the application under review.

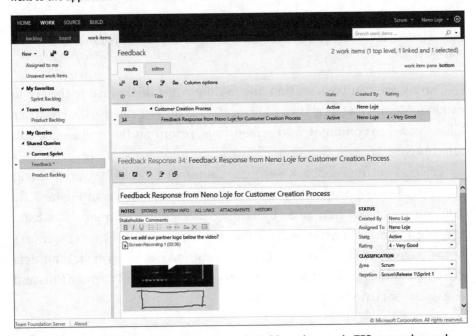

FIGURE 3.18: Feedback Responses from the stakeholders show up in TFS as regular work items under the Feedback Request.

Besides this explicit workflow where feedback is requested by the team, stakeholders can download and start the Feedback Client and provide voluntary feedback at any time. Those feedback responses can then be evaluated by the team and lead to new PBIs or Bugs, which are then linked to the source feedback response work items in TFS, from which they originated (see Figure 3.18).

Qualities of Service

Not all product backlog items are user stories or epics and themes made up solely from user stories. They need to be understood in the context of qualities of service (QoS). (QoS are sometimes called nonfunctional requirements or quality attributes, but because these terms are less descriptive, I stick to QoS here. Sometimes they're called *'ilities*, which is a useful shorthand.)

QoS are appropriately treated in two different ways. Those attributes that always apply to every PBI belong on your definition of *done*. For example, in Microsoft, all functionality must go through a security review that includes threat modeling and protections for personally identifiable information (PII). Both the security review of the planned implementation and the security test of the actual implementation are on our definition of *done*.

On the other hand, some QoS are quite specific and should be treated as PBIs. For example, the performance requirement that "for 95% of orders placed, confirmation must appear within three seconds at 1,000-user load" is a specific performance QoS about a scenario of placing an order. That would be a new PBI.

Not all QoS apply to all systems, but you should know which ones apply to yours. Often QoS imply large architectural requirements or risk, so they should be negotiated with stakeholders early in a project.

There is no definitive list of all the QoS that you need to consider. There have been several standards, but they tend to become obsolete as technology evolves.[14] For example, security and privacy issues are not covered in many major standards, even though they are the most important ones in many modern systems.[15]

The following four sections list some of the most common QoS to consider on a project.

Security and Privacy

Unfortunately, the spread of the Internet has made security and privacy every computer user's concern. These two QoS are important for both application development and operations, and customers are now sophisticated enough to demand to know what measures you are taking to protect them. Increasingly, they are becoming the subject of government regulation. The two common definitions are:

- **Security:** The ability of the software to prevent access and disruption by unauthorized users, viruses, worms, spyware, and other agents
- **Privacy:** The ability of the software to prevent unauthorized access or viewing of PII

Performance

Performance is most often noticed when it is poor. In designing, developing, and testing for performance, it is important to differentiate the various QoS that influence the end experience of overall performance:

- **Responsiveness:** The absence of delay when the software responds to an action, call, or event
- **Concurrency:** The capability of the software to perform well when operated concurrently with other software
- **Efficiency:** The capability of the software to provide appropriate performance relative to the resources used under stated conditions
- **Fault tolerance:** The capability of the software to maintain a specified level of performance in cases of software faults or of infringement of its specified interface
- **Scalability:** The ability of the software to handle simultaneous operational loads

User Experience

Even though the term *easy to use* has become a cliché, a significant body of knowledge has grown around design for user experience:

- **Accessibility:** The extent to which individuals with disabilities have access to and use of information and data that is comparable to the access to and use by individuals without disabilities

- **Attractiveness:** The capability of the software to be attractive to the user

- **Compatibility:** The conformance of the software to conventions and expectations

- **Discoverability:** The ability of the user to find and learn features of the software

- **Ease of use:** The cognitive efficiency with which a target user can perform desired tasks with the software

- **World readiness:** The extent to which the software can be adapted to conform to the linguistic, cultural, and conventional needs and expectations of a specific group of users

Manageability

Most modern solutions are multitier, distributed, service-oriented, and often cloud-hosted. The cost of operating these applications often exceeds the cost of developing them by a large factor, yet few development teams know how to design for operations. Appropriate QoS factors to consider include the following:

- **Availability:** The degree to which a system or component is operational and accessible when required for use. Often expressed as a Service Level Agreement (SLA) with a probability. This is cited as "nines," as in "three nines," meaning 99.9% availability, or a maximum of 40 minutes downtime per month.

- **Recoverability:** The capability of the software to reestablish a specified level of performance and recover the data directly affected in the case of a failure. This is typically stated as mean time to recover (MTTR), in minutes. An MTTR of 5:00 minutes means that the service can be restored in five minutes.

If you're consuming services, the previous two QoS are probably all you care about. If you're also building services, you may care about some of these as well:

- **Reliability:** The capability to maintain a specified level of performance when used under specified conditions (often stated as mean time between failures [MTBF]).

- **Installability and uninstallability:** The capability to be installed in a specific environment and uninstalled without altering the environment's initial state.

- **Maintainability:** The ease with which a software system or component can be modified to correct faults, improve performance or other attributes, or adapt to a changed environment.

- **Monitorability:** The extent to which health and operational data can be automatically collected from the software in operation.

- **Operability:** The extent to which the software can be controlled automatically in operation.

- **Portability:** The capability of the software to be transferred from one environment to another.

- **Testability:** The degree to which a system or component facilitates the establishment of test criteria and the performance of tests to determine whether those criteria have been met.

- **Serviceability:** The extent to which operational problems can be corrected in the software without disruption. Microsoft Update is an example of a system that delivers weekly updates to hundreds of millions of customers for servicing.

- **Conformance to standards:** The extent to which the software adheres to applicable rules.

- **Interoperability:** The capability of the software to interact with one or more specified systems.

What makes a good QoS requirement? As with user stories, QoS requirements need to be explicitly understandable to their stakeholder audiences, defined early, and when planned for a sprint, they need to be testable. You may start with a general statement about performance, for example, but in the sprint you need specific targets on specific transactions at specific load.

If you cannot state how to test satisfaction of the requirement when it becomes time to assess it, you cannot measure the completion.

How Many Levels of Requirements

In the early days of Agile, a widely espoused belief held that a user story needed to fit on a single 3×5 card and that the product backlog should consist of a flat list of user stories. Although this is great if you have fewer than 100 user stories, many teams find that they need to scale into large-grained requirements. The typical terminology is that themes contain user stories and epics contain themes.

The four key elements in determining the appropriate granularity of requirements are as follows:

1. Do they communicate effectively to the stakeholders and allow for the feedback loops described earlier?
2. Are they clear enough to allow acceptance tests?
3. Are they discrete enough to be implemented in a sprint? If not, do their children fit cleanly into sprints with discrete acceptance tests?
4. Are there few enough requirements at this granularity that they can meaningfully be stack ranked?

Our experience on VS is that we need three levels of requirements, which we call *scenarios* (for epics), *experiences* (for themes), and *features*, which are typically user stories or QoS. (See Chapter 9 for more detail.) TFS makes it easy to track progress at all the levels, so that teams and stakeholders can focus on dashboards appropriate to their needs.

Work Breakdown

One of the practical aspects of PBIs at the level of user stories is that they are both requirements objects and units of work breakdown. Accordingly, they form a great level for measuring *done* and for forming the social contract around the sprint. Figure 3.19 shows a view in Excel of the PBIs broken down by the team into tasks, along with the status of each.

This multiple value does not mean that coarser-grained requirements should be treated as units of work breakdown, however. It is completely normal that a single user story will roll up into multiple themes or epics. For example, consider a user story to the effect of "As a registered user of this site, I can log in once and stay logged in so that I'm not distracted by multiple requests for credentials." There are probably dozens of experiences whose flows include a login somewhere, and whose "doneness" might require the login to be working, but that doesn't mean that login should be implemented multiple times.

This distinction between the natural requirements structure and the work breakdown structure directly contradicts historical practices that depended on well-formed hierarchies, often based on the Project Management Body of Knowledge (PMBOK) and Microsoft Project. This distinction between hierarchy for work breakdown and a network for requirements may be hard for traditional product managers to come to terms with, although TFS can greatly simplify the reporting.

Remember the execution contract with the team is the sprint and the user stories or other PBIs taken into the sprint. The Product Owner needs to ensure that the sequencing makes sense and that the rollup into the whole experience comes together.

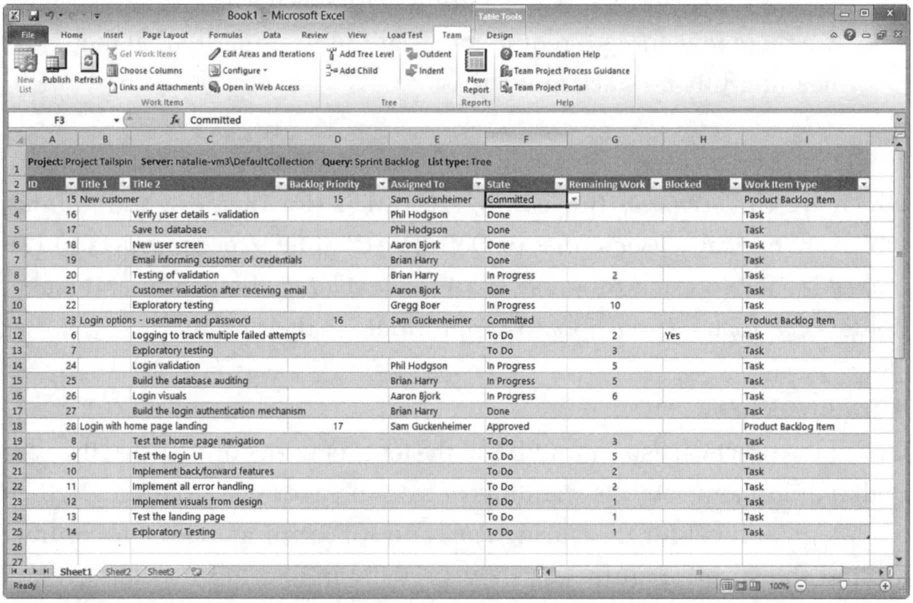

Project: Project Tailspin Server: natalie-vm3\DefaultCollection Query: Sprint Backlog List type: Tree

ID	Title 1	Title 2	Backlog Priority	Assigned To	State	Remaining Work	Blocked	Work Item Type
15	New customer		15	Sam Guckenheimer	Committed			Product Backlog Item
16		Verify user details - validation		Phil Hodgson	Done			Task
17		Save to database		Phil Hodgson	Done			Task
18		New user screen		Aaron Bjork	Done			Task
19		Email informing customer of credentials		Brian Harry	Done			Task
20		Testing of validation		Brian Harry	In Progress	2		Task
21		Customer validation after receiving email		Aaron Bjork	Done			Task
22		Exploratory testing		Gregg Boer	In Progress	10		Task
23	Login options - username and password		16	Sam Guckenheimer	Committed			Product Backlog Item
6		Logging to track multiple failed attempts			To Do	2	Yes	Task
7		Exploratory testing			To Do	3		Task
24		Login validation		Phil Hodgson	In Progress	5		Task
25		Build the database auditing		Brian Harry	In Progress	5		Task
26		Login visuals		Aaron Bjork	In Progress	6		Task
27		Build the login authentication mechanism		Brian Harry	Done			Task
28	Login with home page landing		17	Sam Guckenheimer	Approved			Product Backlog Item
8		Test the home page navigation			To Do	3		Task
9		Test the login UI			To Do	5		Task
10		Implement back/forward features			To Do	2		Task
11		Implement all error handling			To Do	2		Task
12		Implement visuals from design			To Do	1		Task
13		Test the landing page			To Do	1		Task
14		Exploratory Testing			To Do	1		Task

FIGURE 3.19: Using Excel as the client on TFS, the team can see the hierarchy of PBIs to tasks, effectively the PBIs in their dual role as both agreed requirements and work breakdown hierarchy with the status of each task.

Summary

Like Chapter 1, "The Agile Consensus," this is an outside-in chapter to describe product ownership in the Agile Consensus. I broadened the perspective of the project to include the creation, grooming, and feedback on the product backlog. VS 2012 has made it easy to groom the product backlog continuously and we have glimpsed here at the tools that can help you.

Among the most important Agile discoveries of the past decade is the ability to scale Agile practices to the very large and the ability to draw feedback into product ownership as readily as into the execution sprints. I hope I convinced you.

In the remaining chapters, we delve into running the project using VS and TFS. There, I assume that these concepts are familiar and that you're itching to see examples. In Chapter 9, we return to some of the topics explored in this chapter and discuss the lessons learned from applying these practices to our own teams within Microsoft. In Chapter 10, "Continuous Feedback," you will see how product ownership fits more completely into a life cycle of continuous feedback.

Before we get that far, let's look at running the Sprint in the next chapter.

Endnotes

[1] Frederick P. Brooks, Jr., *The Mythical Man-Month: Essays on Software Engineering, Anniversary Edition* (Boston: Addison-Wesley, 1995), 199.

[2] United States Patent and Trademark Office and http://genet.gelighting.com/LightProducts/Dispatcher?REQUEST =PHOTOGALLERY&PRODUCTCODE=85383&SELECTED= Package Photo&COLOR=Yes.

[3] *Scrum Guide*, 7.

[4] "Yahoo Memo: The 'Peanut Butter Manifesto'," *Wall Street Journal*, November 18, 2006, available at http://online.wsj.com/public/ article/SB116379821933826657-0mbjXoHnQwDMFH_PVeb_ jqe3Chk_ 20061125.html.

5   Monty Python's Flying Circus, "The Dead Parrot Sketch," available on The 16-Ton Monty Python DVD Megaset, Disc 3 (A&E Home Video, 2005).

6   http://mobile.vasamuseum.com/Default.aspx?s=84&p=3817 and www.mmk.su.se/~magnuss/images/vasa-hull2.jpg

7   Bruce Tuckman, "Developmental Sequence in Small Groups," *Psychological Bulletin* 63:6 (1965): 384–99.

8   In fact, there is a growing consensus among economists that accurate long-term business strategy is as elusive as accurate long-term weather forecasting. See Beinhofer, *The Origins of Wealth.*

9   Geoffrey A. Moore, *Crossing the Chasm: Marketing and Selling High-Tech Products to Mainstream Customers* (New York: HarperCollins, 2002), 93–4.

10   Adapted from Moore, 154.

11   Mike Cohn, *User Stories Applied: For Agile Software Development* (Boston: Addison-Wesley, 2004).

12   N. Kano, N. Seraku, F. Takahashi, and S. Tsuji, "Attractive quality and must-be quality," originally published in "Hinshitsu" (Quality), *The Journal of the Japanese Society for Quality Control,* XIV:2 (1996): 39–48, April 1984, translated in *The Best On Quality,* edited by John D. Hromi. Volume 7 of the Book Series of the International Academy for Quality (Milwaukee: ASQC Quality Press, 1996).

13   Tim Brown, *Change by Design* (New York: HarperCollins, 2009), 19. Also discussed at www.ideo.com/cbd.

14   For example, ISO/IEC 9126/2001 and IEEE Std 610.12-1990, from which many of these examples are drawn. Section 504 of the Rehabilitation Act, 29 U.S.C. § 794d, is available from www.usdoj.gov/crt/508/508law.html.

15   They are beginning to show up in weak form from the Payment Card Industry Security Standards Council, www.pcisecurity-standards.org.

4

Running the Sprint

The deficiencies of the theory of the project and of the theory of
management reinforce each other and their detrimental effects
propagate through the life cycle of a project. Typically, customer
requirements are poorly investigated at the outset, and the
process of requirement clarification and change leads disruption
in the progress of the project. The actual progress starts to drift
from the plan, the updating of which is too cumbersome to be
done regularly. Without an up-to-date plan, the work
authorization system transforms to an approach of informal
management. Increasingly, tasks are commenced without all
inputs and prerequisites at hand, leading to low efficiency or
task interruption and increased variability downstream.
Correspondingly, controlling by means of a performance
baseline that is not based on the actual status becomes ineffective
or simply counterproductive. All in all, systematic project
management is transformed to a facade, behind which the job
actually gets done, even if with reduced efficiency and lessened
value to the customer.[1]

—L. Koskela and G. Howell, "The Underlying Theory
of Project Management Is Obsolete"

UNLV Special Collections

FIGURE 4.1: Without transparent data, project management can descend into a game of hedging bets based on partial information and divergent perspectives of stakeholders. Poker is a good metaphor for this pattern.

THE PRECEDING CHAPTER ADDRESSED the grooming of the product backlog. This chapter and the following four focus on implementing the requirements taken from the product backlog into the sprint.

First, let's cover some concepts that are core to the Agile Consensus:

- Empirical over defined process control
- Scrum mastery
- Team size
- Rapid estimation
- Descriptive rather than prescriptive metrics
- Multiple dimensions of project health

Empirical over Defined Process Control

In the 1970s, 1980s, and 1990s, the "iron triangle" was an icon of project management based on the defined process control paradigm.[2] The iron triangle is the notion that a project manager can work with only three variables: *time, functionality,* and *resources* (including people, who are reduced to units of production). In the past ten years, *quality* was acknowledged as a fourth dimension, making a tetrahedron, as shown in Figure 4.2.

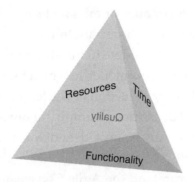

FIGURE 4.2: The iron triangle (or tetrahedron) treats a project as a fixed stock of work, in classic defined process terms. To stretch one face of the tetrahedron, you need to stretch the others.

In *Rapid Development,* Steve McConnell summarizes the iron triangle as follows:

> To keep the triangle balanced, you have to balance schedule, cost, and product. If you want to load up the product corner of the triangle, you also have to load up cost or schedule or both. The same goes for the other combinations. If you want to change one of the corners of the triangle, you have to change at least one of the others to keep it in balance.[3]

According to this view, a project has an initial stock of resources and time. Any change to functionality or quality requires a corresponding increase in time or resources. You cannot stretch one face without stretching the others because they are all connected.

Although widely practiced, this paradigm is a counterproductive model. Think of your project as a pipe intended to deliver a smooth flow of value. The iron triangle is like a cross-section at a particular point in the pipe. So long as there is a kink in the pipe downstream, expanding the pipe section upstream won't help.

Most of us have experienced this in spades. Pouring water into a sink with a clogged drain doesn't clear the drain. Eventually the sink overflows, your feet get wet, and your floor gets ruined. Similarly, if builds are broken, adding code only creates technical debt until the builds are fixed. If debt is accumulating in the form of bugs or missing tests, adding debt only raises risk and creates exponentially more handling later.

Scrum is a very pleasant antidote to iron-triangle thinking. The iron triangle assumes a defined process model, in which there are no opportunities for improvements in flow or reduction of waste. Scrum and the Agile Consensus, on the other hand, assume an empirical model, in which the small batches done in sprints are inspected and the process is adapted for improvement continually.

Teams following Scrum and the Agile Consensus have demonstrated experiences that pleasantly contradict the iron triangle. For example, in iron-triangle thought, a stringent definition of *done* may appear to require extra resources or time because it mandates more up-front activity. In practice, it shortens time to delivery because it prevents the accumulation of technical debt elsewhere in the pipe. To extend the analogy of the sink, imagine replacing the drain with clear glass so that you can always see the rate of flow and always clear any blockage as soon as it occurs.

Scrum Mastery

Nowadays, there are more Scrum Master courses than most Scrum teams have fingers to count them on. It was tempting to position this chapter as reading for the Scrum Master to make a nice parallel with Chapter 3, "Product Ownership." Yet mastery of Scrum is really for the whole team, not just a designated individual. The Scrum Master does very little when the team is functioning well, other than make sure that the rules of Scrum are being followed. Accordingly, on most high-functioning teams, being a Scrum Master is a very part-time role.

We have already covered most of the rules of Scrum. If you're not familiar with the rest, I'll give you a very quick recap of the *Scrum Guide*.[4] There are timeboxed *sprints,* usually two to four weeks, usually of equal length. The first and last days of the sprint are special. The first day is sprint planning, which is broken into two halves. The morning is a review of the top of the product backlog with the Product Owner, including rapid estimation as discussed later, with a goal of committing to the right set of product backlog items (PBIs) for the sprint. The afternoon is a discussion of how to build the chosen PBIs and with a goal of fleshing out the initial set of tasks in the iteration backlog.

The last day has a sprint review and a sprint retrospective. These form a scheduled time to inspect and adapt. The sprint review focuses on the output of the sprint, including the team's live demonstration of the delivered software relative to the PBIs committed. The sprint retrospective, as the name suggests, is an explicit opportunity for the team to inspect the process followed during the sprint and adapt it to improve the next sprint.

On the other days of the sprint, there is a 15-minute daily scrum (also known as the daily stand-up meeting). It is not a status meeting. As made clear in Chapter 2, "Scrum, Agile Practices, and Visual Studio," your status should be visible to everyone in Team Foundation Server (TFS), and you don't need a meeting to ask each other if you meant what you typed. This is a daily planning meeting for the team, affording them the opportunity to create a plan for the next 24 hours. The focus is on looking ahead, not behind (unlike many conventional status meetings). By sticking to these simple meetings, Scrum keeps 90% of the team time scheduled on task and limits 10% to communication overhead (2 days out of 20).

Team Size

Scrum specifies a team size of 7±2. There's no magic here. That's how large a group you can put together and still have everyone talk to each other regularly. As projects get larger, you need to split the teams. As you accumulate more teams, you need to introduce coordination. The good news is that TFS can do the bookkeeping for you of tracking integrations and dependencies across multiple teams' backlogs. In Chapter 9, "Lessons Learned at Microsoft Developer Division," I describe how we do this at Microsoft.

Rapid Estimation (Planning Poker)

This is the usually the time where the boss (pointy-haired or otherwise) gets squeamish, so some explanation is in order. Planning Poker is the estimation technique that has matured over time with Scrum. Planning Poker estimates PBIs in units of story points. By convention, a story point estimate is usually a number from the Fibonacci series: 1, 2, 3, 5, 8, 13, 21, 34, with values allowed for 0 and ?, as well.[5] In this way, the estimates are suitably spread out, and they obey simple addition. For example, *big 13 costs as much as the 2, 3, 3, and 5 together. Is it really worth it?*

Story points are intentionally not units of implementation such as hours. Their sole purpose is to allow tradeoffs among user stories in the product backlog. In practice, hours tend to lead to debates of whether we mean "ideal hours" free of distraction or "actual hours," including overhead tasks. And by keeping user stories compared with user stories, the team does not have to waste time on detailed estimation to decide what part of the backlog to accept into the sprint.

In Planning Poker, every "player" (that is, estimator) has a deck of cards marked with valid story point estimates (Fibonacci numbers), as shown in Figure 4.3. In each hand, the dealer selects a PBI, and every player puts a card from his or her hand face down. When all players have put their cards face down, the dealer, often the Product Owner, says, "Show!"

At this point, differences in the estimates are discussed. If players agree through the discussion, the dealer records the estimate and chooses the next PBI. Otherwise, the players redraw cards for this PBI. The dealer has the privilege to declare the discussion finished and to average the current estimates for the PBI and record the average.

Planning Poker is extraordinarily effective because it plays to at least four human cognitive strengths:

1. **Comparison of quantities:** We are very good at making approximate judgments about how much bigger or smaller one pile of fruit is than another, without counting or weighing. Unlike time estimates, story points may be added together to see the size of several items simultaneously. Time estimates often overlap when work is executed nonsequentially, whereas story points do not.

2. **Rapid cognition:**[6] Very often, the conclusion you draw in two seconds is indeed your best, especially where you have expertise, and with more time you only talk yourself into inferior results through further analysis. Quick judgments rely on a different and more reliable neural pathway than long analyses. The rapid pace of Planning Poker does not give you time to do the double-talk.

3. **Wisdom of crowds:**[7] Every hand of the game is effectively a prediction market among experienced players, who are judging individually. To the extent that any one estimate is off, the law of large numbers tends to average out the roughness of the estimates.

4. **Inspect and adapt:** The team gets better with every round. "Last time we saw one of these widgets, we estimated 5 but it took 8, so we should call this an 8." Of course, this is part of the team's storming-norming-forming-performing.

FIGURE 4.3: In Planning Poker, every player has a deck marked with the same Fibonacci numbers for estimation.[8]

At the conclusion of a sprint, you can measure the story points achieved. This is your team's *velocity*. (Velocity = story points achieved to the definition of *done* in the sprint.) This gives you a basis for estimating the capacity of the next sprint. Obviously, you can make adjustments for calendar issues, absences, team changes, and so on.

A frequent objection to Planning Poker is the seeming arbitrariness of story points as a size measure. In fact, story points are optimized for rapid estimation, as discussed earlier, and at the conclusion of a sprint can be converted into observable units of work. Consider a simple example. Imagine you have a team of seven, who completed a sprint of 20 workdays (4 weeks x 5 days), and delivered 140 story points. The team's velocity is 140 story points, *averaging* 1 story point per team member per day (7 x 20 = 140).

Don't stretch this too far. The purpose of story-point estimation is to allow the team to examine the highest stack-ranked PBIs and to make a commitment for the coming sprint, nothing more or less. Do not create reward systems out of story points. Do not use story points for comparisons across teams. If someone outside the team becomes enamored with a conversion of story points to time worked, it is likely that the estimation will no longer be as effective, as you'll see in Figure 4.5 later in this chapter.

TFS calculates the velocity based on the user story points entered and shows a velocity chart for the current and previous sprints in the upper-right corner of the product backlog. The chart can be enlarged by clicking on it, as shown in Figure 4.4. Changes to PBIs are reflected immediately.

When you prioritize the product backlog, TFS uses velocity and your story point estimates to provide a rough view of how many sprints will be needed for the top-ranked PBIs. The sprints are shown as forecast lines overlain on product backlog, as shown in Figure 4.5.

A Contrasting Analogy

Remember your school days and the ritual of "picture day," when you would have to dress up, your parents would overpay, a photographer would come to take your picture, and a month later the teacher would hand out prints that you hated anyway.

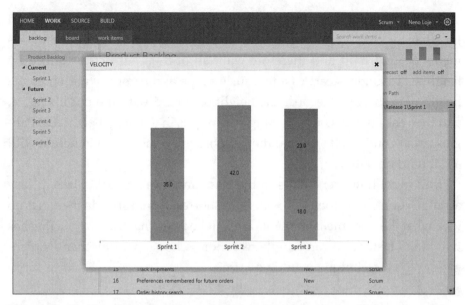

FIGURE 4.4: The Velocity chart on the upper-right corner of the product backlog shows the amount of user story points delivered (in green) and in progress (in blue) of the current and past sprints. Changes to PBIs are immediately reflected.

Forecast	Order	Title	State	Effort	Iteration Path
	1	Login with home page landing	Approved	3	Scrum\Release 1\Sprint 1
Sprint 2	2	Browse the catalog	Approved	3	Scrum
	3	View item details	Approved	5	Scrum
	4	Placing orders crashes Browser	New	2	Scrum
Sprint 3	5	Login cookies - silent login	Approved	3	Scrum
Sprint 4	6	Find orders	Approved	11	Scrum
	7	Logoff	Approved	5	Scrum
	8	RSS feeds	Approved	8	Scrum
	9	Customer search	New		Scrum
	10	View order details	New		Scrum
	11	Payment by credit card	New		Scrum
	12	Priority ordering - preferences	New		Scrum
	13	See related items	Approved		Scrum
	14	Add shipping details	New		Scrum
	15	Track shipments	New		Scrum
	16	Preferences remembered for future orders	New		Scrum
	17	Order history search	New		Scrum
	18	Order totals are incorrect	New		Scrum
	19	Additional payment options	New		Scrum

FIGURE 4.5: TFS automatically overlays the horizontal forecast lines on the product backlog to show, based on expected velocity, how many PBIs can be done in the coming sprints.

Consider two photographers, whom we will name Dr. Pangloss and Jonathan Swift. Both photographers want to minimize unnecessary adjustments of the tripod and therefore want all of their subjects arranged by height. Dr. Pangloss carries a measuring tape and carefully measures the height of each pupil, records the height on a card with the pupil's name, and then asks the teacher to arrange the pupils in a line by height. Dr. Pangloss can proudly tell you that the 30 subjects average 1.5m in height with a standard deviation of .2m.

Mr. Swift, however, walks in the class and announces, "Class, please arrange yourselves along this wall from shortest to tallest." Mr. Swift has no idea what the class measurements are, but he finds that this way he finishes two hours faster and can handle two more schools per day than Dr. Pangloss. Whose technique would you use?

Use Descriptive Rather Than Prescriptive Metrics

Often, there are tacit or even explicit assumptions about the "right" answers to metrics. These expectations can determine how individuals are recognized or not recognized for their performance. Developers are praised for completing tasks on time. Testers are praised for running lots of tests or finding lots of bugs. Hotline specialists are praised for handling lots of calls and marking them resolved. Everyone is praised for keeping billable hours up. And so on. Unfortunately, using metrics to evaluate individual performance is often horribly counterproductive, as Robert Austin describes:

> When a measurement system is put in place, performance measures begin to increase. At first, the true value of an organization's output may also increase. This happens in part because workers do not understand the measurement system very well early on, so their safest course is to strive to fulfill the spirit of the system architects' intentions. Real improvement may result as well, because early targets are modest and do not drive workers into taking severe shortcuts. Over time, however, as the organization demands ever greater performance measurements, by increasing explicit quotas or inducing competition between coworkers, ways of increasing measures

that are not consistent with the spirit of intentions are used. Once one group of workers sees another group cutting corners, the "slower" group feels pressure to imitate. Gradually, measures fall (or, more accurately, are pushed) out of synchronization with true performance, as workers succumb to pressures to take shortcuts. Measured performance trends upward; true performance declines sharply. In this way, the measurement system becomes dysfunctional.[9]

These are *prescriptive* metrics. They can have unforeseen side effects. There is a well-identified pattern of organizational behavior adapting to fit the expectations of a prescriptive measurement program, as shown in Figure 4.6. Typically, a metrics program produces an initial boost in productivity, followed by a steep return to the status quo ante but with different numbers. For example, if bug find and fix rates are critically monitored, bug curves start conforming to desirable expectations.

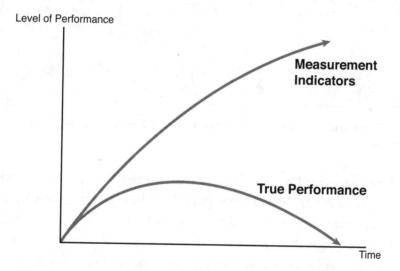

FIGURE 4.6: This graph summarizes the common experience with prescriptive, one-dimensional metrics programs. Performance shoots up early in accord with management aspirations, and the numbers get better and better, but the desired effect tapers off quickly.

Consider some examples of prescriptive metric misuse:

- Imagine measuring programmer productivity based on lines of code written per day. An individual has a choice of calling a framework method (perhaps 5 lines with error handling) or of copying 200 lines of open source sample code. Which one gets rewarded? Which one is easier to maintain, to code-review, to security-review, to test, and to integrate? Or similarly, the individual has the chance to refactor three overlapping methods into one, reducing the size of the code base. (Now ask the same questions.)

- Imagine rewarding programmers based on number of bugs fixed. This was once the subject of a Dilbert cartoon, shown in Figure 4.7, which ended with Wally saying, "I'm going to write me a new mini-van this afternoon."[10]

FIGURE 4.7: Prescriptive metrics distort behavior, as captured in this classic Dilbert comic strip.

- Imagine rewarding the team for creating tests and code to achieve 90% code coverage. Do they spend their time writing complex test setups for every error condition, or easily comment out the error-handling code that tests aren't able to trigger? After all, if the tests cannot invoke those conditions, how important can they be? (Not very, until a customer encounters them.)

- Imagine measuring testers based on the number of bugs found. Do they look for easy-to-find, overlapping, simple bugs or go after significant ones that require setting up complex customer data and configurations? Which approach gets rewarded? Which one yields more customer value?

Each example leads to obvious dysfunction—discouraging reuse and maintainability, encouraging buggy check-ins, reducing error handling, and discouraging finding the important bugs. Other dysfunctions from misuse of prescriptive metrics are less obvious but equally severe. People who don't get the best scores will be demoralized and face the choice of gaming the numbers or leaving the team.

Prevent Distortion

At the root of the distortion is the prescriptive, rather than descriptive, use of these metrics. This problem has at least four causes. First, the metrics are only approximations of the business objective, such as customer satisfaction or solution marketability. The team aims to deliver customer value, but that cannot be counted easily on a daily basis. So the available metrics, such as task completion, test pass rate, or bug count, are imperfect but easily countable proxies.

Under the Agile Consensus, you give credit only for potentially shippable increments to the agreed definition of *done*.[11] With sprints of two to four weeks and assessment at the end of the iteration, this practice allows for intervals of project monitoring at iteration boundaries. Treat all interim measurements as hypothetical until you can assess delivery of working scenarios at known qualities of service.

Second, the measurements are made *one dimension at a time.* The negative consequences of a one-dimensional view are dramatic. If you're measuring only one dimension at a time and are prescribing expected results, behavioral distortion is a natural consequence. Most experienced project managers know this. However, gathering data from multiple sources at the same time in a manner that lends itself to reasonable correlation is historically very difficult without suitable tooling.

Third, when applied to individuals, metrics create all sorts of disincentives, as illustrated in the previous examples. Keep the observations, even descriptive ones, at the team level.

Fourth, variation is normal. Don't reward the most prolific coder or highest-count bug finder. Expect the numbers to show variance, and don't punish cases of in-control variance. Instead, reward a team based on customer-deliverable units of functionality and make the assessment cycle frequent.

Avoid Broken Windows

In Chapter 3, I discussed the importance of the definition of *done*, agreed and respected by the team. A risk exists that, despite such definition, teams let undone work escape from the sprint without accounting for the remaining debt in the backlog. Sometimes this is a side effect of the misuse of metrics, where team members are effectively punished for being transparent. An example might be the vice president's innocent question, "Why is this team reporting so many more bugs and issues than that team?" Nonetheless, don't shy away from the transparency. Use it as an opportunity to educate.

Every time you defer resolving or closing a bug, you impose additional future liability on the project for three reasons: The bug itself will have to be handled multiple times, someone (usually a developer) will have a longer lag before returning to the code for analysis and fixing, and you'll create a "broken windows" effect. The broken windows theory holds that in neighborhoods where small details, such as broken windows, go unaddressed, other acts of crime are more likely to be ignored. Cem Kaner, software testing professor and former public prosecutor, describes this well:[12]

> The challenge with graffiti and broken windows is that they identify a community standard. If the community can't even keep itself moderately clean, then: (1) Problems like these are not worth reporting, and so citizens will stop reporting them. (We also see the converse of this, as a well-established phenomenon. In communities that start actually prosecuting domestic violence or rape, the reported incidence of these crimes rises substantially—presumably, the visible enforcement causes a higher probability of a report of a crime, rather than more crime). In software, many bugs are kept off the lists as not worth reporting. (2) People will be less likely to clean these bugs up

on their own because their small effort won't make much of a difference. (3) Some people will feel it is acceptable (socially tolerated in this community) to commit more graffiti or to break more windows. (4) Many people will feel that if these are tolerated, there probably isn't much bandwidth available to enforce laws against more serious street crimes.

Similarly, in projects with large bug backlogs, overall attention to quality issues is likely to decline. This is one of many reasons to keep the bug backlog as close to zero as possible.

Answering Everyday Questions with Dashboards

One of the principles of the Agile Consensus is transparency. Because software projects have many interacting dimensions, any of them can be relevant. Looking at these dimensions helps you see the whole story and provides an opportunity for early discovery of exceptions and bottlenecks that need course corrections.

TFS uses a team portal with a series of dashboards to present the data. The examples that follow are taken from the standard Agile project template that is installed with TFS. There are five dashboards designed to help the team run the sprint, plus a sixth (*My* Dashboard) that each user can personally customize. Because the Web parts of these dashboards are Excel graphs or TFS queries, no special skills are needed for customization.

"*Five* dashboards," I imagine some readers asking. "Don't you just need a burndown chart for the Scrum team?" Actually, you need more, precisely to understand the multiple dimensions of project health:

- **Burndown** focuses on showing the rate and quantity of completed items.
- **Quality** examines several dimensions of quality simultaneously to help you spot anomalies not represented by the reported work.
- **Bugs** drills more specifically into bug trends to provide an early warning against accumulating technical debt.

- **Test** looks at the relationships of test activity planned to executed, and test results to product backlog. This is a key indicator to achieving "Done Done" on the PBIs.

- **Build** is like the EKG for the project. It's there to ensure that the build automation is acting as the effective heartbeat for the project and to warn of problems, such as broken build verification tests (BVTs) or incomplete test lab deployments.

Burndown

The purpose of the Burndown dashboard, as shown in Figure 4.8, is to give the team a view of progress against the sprint plan from the standpoint of the sprint backlog and the chosen PBIs.

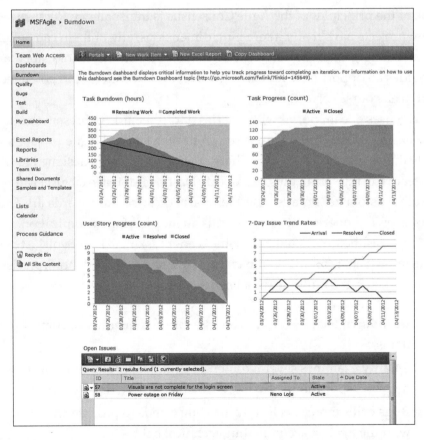

FIGURE 4.8: The Burndown dashboard provides the perspective of the PBIs, tasks, and impediments.

The middle-left chart on this dashboard is a picture of how quickly the team is working through the PBIs that have been taken into the sprint. It is essential that there be a smooth flow to closure. An antipattern to watch for is a big bulge in the resolved band in the middle, indicating that PBIs are not getting closed (that is, test and carried to done), which is a sign that the team is allowing technical debt to build up during the sprint.

The top two charts are sprint burndown charts. These are the icons of tracking tasks in Scrum. The left one shows hours, and the right one shows the count of tasks to complete. This example is typical, in that the team discovers additional work in the first few days of the sprint, forcing both remaining work and total work (the top line) to rise. As the sprint progresses, work completion accelerates, and the team hits the completion date on time.

The middle-right chart looks at impediments, called *issues* in this process template. Although new impediments arise throughout the sprint, they are getting handled promptly. It shows the seven-day arrival (that is, newly active), resolved, and closed rates, to smooth out variation for days of the week. The number of arriving issues is below the line showing issues getting closed, but there are still two open issues currently, as shown by the query at the bottom of the page. The antipattern to watch for here is the buildup of active issues that are not getting closed. Not only is this debt, but it can also be actively blocking progress on the current sprint backlog.

Quality

Quality has many dimensions, as discussed earlier, and they interact subtly. The Quality dashboard pulls together the key indicators so that you can look at key correlations or discrepancies, all in one place, as shown in Figure 4.9. In turn, more detail is provided for each of the areas on the three subsequent dashboards, as shown in Figures 4.10, 4.11, and 4.12 in the sections that follow.

The upper-left chart tracks the overall progress of test cases in the sprint, as they progress from not run, to blocked, to failed, to passed. In this example, there is an initial period of blocked test plans, which might be related to the status of builds in the upper-right chart.

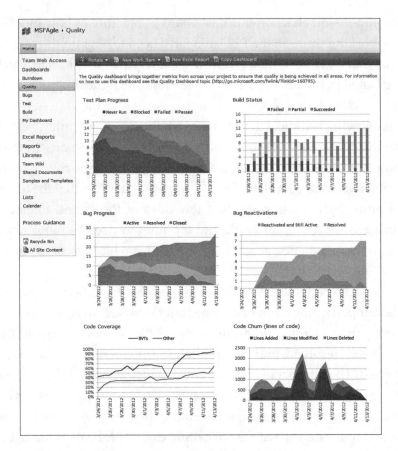

FIGURE 4.9: The Quality dashboard summarizes the many engineering perspectives on progress toward the potentially shippable increment of the sprint.

Every day's builds are shown. Note that for the first half of the sprint, more than half the builds fail or only partially succeed. A partially successful build is one that might succeed at compilation but fail at subsequent steps such as deployment or BVTs. That could explain why many test plans were blocked; they could be waiting on successful builds.

The middle two charts look at bugs. On the left, you see total bugs in the sprint as they progress from active to resolved and then to closed. Note that the sprint finished with five bugs resolved not closed, so they need to go on the product backlog for handling in subsequent sprints.

The right chart tracks bug reactivations. This is a key early-warning indicator. Bug reactivations are bugs whose state went from active to resolved and back to active. In other words, they had fixes checked in that turned out not to be fixes. This can be a huge source of waste, for many reasons. Obviously, these bugs go through repeated handling, forcing team members to switch contexts unnecessarily. More subtly, they are a sign of misdiagnosis, crossed communication, or sloppy practices, such as inadequate unit testing. In this example, no more than two bugs are reactivated and still active at any time. If you see this lower line climb in your sprint, it is a definite sign of team dysfunction, and you should investigate the cause immediately.

The third row looks at code coverage and code churn. Code coverage is the percentage of code exercised by testing. By itself, it is not a very meaningful number, but its trend can be. As you can see in this example, a sudden dip occurs in the code coverage from BVTs, which could be a warning that BVTs aren't running or that new code is missing tests. Sure enough, it corresponds to a spike in code churn (that is, the newly added code, on the right), but the BVTs quickly catch up.

An antipattern to watch for is a dip in code coverage and a rise in code churn *without* the subsequent recovery in code coverage. That combination often indicates that the tests are stale and the new code is going untested.

Bugs

The Bugs dashboard repeats the bug trend chart from the Quality dashboard and drills into more detail, as shown in Figure 4.10. It shows the seven-day arrival (that is, newly active), resolved, and closed rates, to smooth out variation for days of the week. It also breaks out the trend chart by priority as well as the active bugs by assignment (it uses different shares of blue to indicate the priorities) and shows a query of the individual bugs that are currently active.

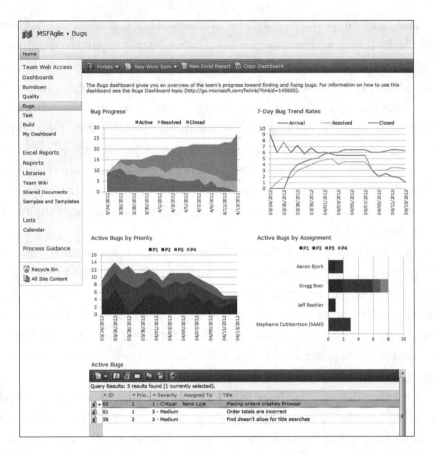

FIGURE 4.10: The Bugs dashboard drills into additional detail on the bug trends and queries for the currently active bugs.

Test

The Test dashboard is designed to provide insight into the key aspects of test activity, as shown in Figure 4.11.

The upper-left chart shows the same Test Plan Progress chart as on the Quality dashboard to provide the overall view of how well testing as a whole is proceeding. The upper-right chart is a trend of test case readiness (that is, how many of the test cases are ready to run). If test cases are stuck in design, you clearly have a problem of prioritization of the backlog of test tasks.

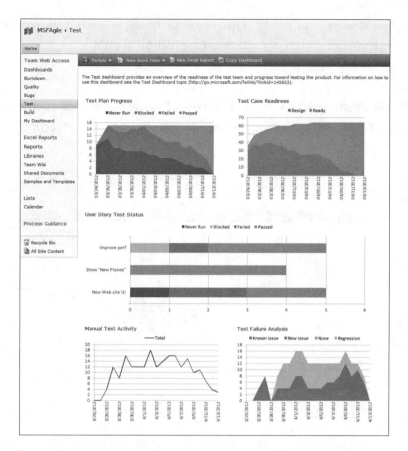

FIGURE 4.11: The Test dashboard offers several lenses on test progress toward the done-ness of the potentially shippable increment and gives you the opportunity to look for early-warning signs of issues that might surface.

The middle chart, User Story Test Status, is my favorite of all the dashboard charts. Each row is a PBI that has been taken into the sprint. The total length of the bar indicates the number of test cases for that PBI, and the colors show the last test result for each test case. In this example, for the third story ("New Web site UI"), there is one test case that has never been run, two that are failing, and two that are currently passing.

The lower-left chart shows how many test results have been collected by manual testing. Use this chart to watch for manual testing continuing to rise indefinitely (indicating that no tests are getting automated). The lower-right chart breaks out the reasons for test-run failures. Use this one to watch for the antipatterns of rising regressions or rising known issues, either of which is a warning sign of accumulating technical debt.

Build

The Build dashboard, shown in Figure 4.12, repeats the code metrics from the Quality dashboard and provides details for each of the recently completed builds.

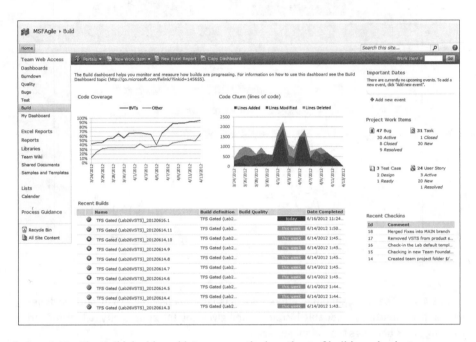

FIGURE 4.12: The Build dashboard lets you see the heartbeat of builds and select any one.

Choosing and Customizing Dashboards

The dashboards previously discussed are the standard ones that are installed for a team project using the MSF for Agile process template. The pages are rendered by Microsoft SharePoint Server, and the parts are a combination of graphs from Microsoft Excel services and queries from Team Web Access.

Of course, you can customize all of these at three levels:

1. There is a My Dashboard page for every user in every team project.

2. Any team member with project admin rights can customize all the dashboards with new queries or new data-bound Excel worksheets or queries.

3. You can customize your own process template so that all your projects have a customer set of dashboards to your specification.

Because the dashboards rely on SharePoint Enterprise, you need to have a full TFS installation (Advanced, not Basic configuration), and your team members need SharePoint Enterprise client access licenses (CALs). (If you install TFS with the Basic configuration option, you skip SharePoint and SQL Server Reporting Services and will not get the dashboards.)

For simple reporting scenarios, it's easy to create a standard work item query in VS and convert it to an Excel report, as shown in Figure 4.13.

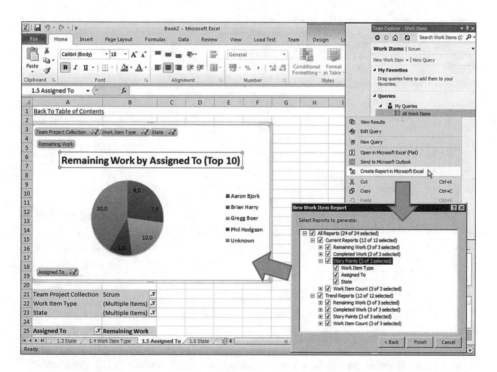

FIGURE 4.13: Team Explorer in the Visual Studio IDE will convert work item queries into an Excel workbook, with each sheet of a workbook showing a different report. The so-called *current* reports show the slice of current data and *trend* reports show the time series of historical data.

Querying Data Using the Open Data Protocol

You can also access all of the work item data inside of TFS by using the Open Data Protocol (OData) standard from www.odata.org. OData support for TFS can be added by downloading a plug-in.[13]

Using Microsoft Outlook to Manage the Sprint

In addition to the tools provided directly by TFS in Team Web Access, SharePoint, Excel, and the VS IDE, the company Ekobit has produced a product called TeamCompanion that lets you manage the sprint from Microsoft Outlook, as shown in Figure 4.14. TeamCompanion started with the easy unification of email and TFS work items, and it has grown into a richly capable client for TFS to help the team see the status of its sprints.

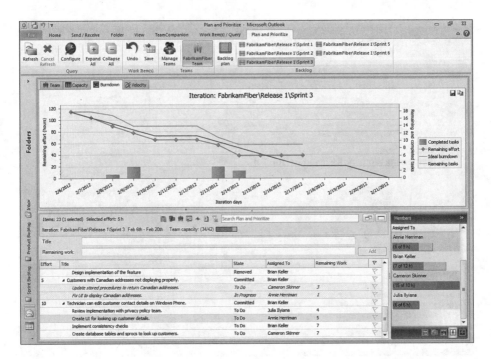

FIGURE 4.14: TeamCompanion from Ekobit connects Microsoft Outlook to TFS and enables you to monitor the sprint backlog and status there.

Summary

This chapter covered monitoring and managing the sprint using TFS and assuming development and testing practices from VS Ultimate. The next chapters drill into those practices.

This chapter started by reviewing the difference between defined and empirical process control and reviewed basic practices of Scrum for running a sprint. Some time was spent on Planning Poker because its rapid estimation makes a huge difference in eliminating waste for teams that use more-complicated estimation.

The next section extended the discussion of empirical process control to the difference between prescriptive and descriptive metrics. Using descriptive metrics sheds enormous light on the workings of the sprint, without the Dilbertesque side effects of prescriptive metrics. TFS reports and dashboards are designed to help you see that light and recognize early warnings when they occur.

This chapter also covered lots of "Scrumdamentals," such as meetings, team size, Planning Poker, and maintaining the definition of *done*. I don't intend this chapter to replace reading the *Scrum Guide,* which is a quick 20 pages and the definitive reference. Instead, I see this as a practical complement that puts the *Scrum Guide* rules into action with examples.

Chapter 5, "Architecture," and Chapter 6, "Development," focus heavily on the VS Ultimate IDE. Chapter 5 delves into Agile architectural practices, notably working with existing assets and ensuring that you get clean and stay clean. Chapter 6 focuses on everyday Agile development. All of these are in the context of the discussion here: one team, one backlog, one concept of *done*, and one drive to a potentially shippable increment.

Endnotes

[1] L. Koskela and G. Howell, "The Underlying Theory of Project Management Is Obsolete." Proceedings of the PMI Research Conference, 2002, 293–302, available at www.leanconstruction.org/pdf/ObsoleteTheory.pdf.

2 See, for example, the teachings of the Project Management Institute Body of Knowledge, www.pmi.org.

3 Steve McConnell, *Rapid Development* (Redmond, WA: Microsoft Press, 1996), 126.

4 Ken Schwaber and Jeff Sutherland, *Scrum Guide,* February 2010, available at www.scrum.org/scrumguides/.

5 Mike Cohn has popularized a rounding of the series to …13, 20, 40, 100, which has become the more popular form. Ken Schwaber prefers the pure Fibonacci series (http://kenschwaber.wordpress.com/2011/03/11/planning-poker/).

6 Malcom Gladwell, *Blink: The Power of Thinking without Thinking* (Boston: Back Bay Books, 2007).

7 James Surowiecki, *The Wisdom of Crowds: Why the Many Are Smarter Than the Few and How Collective Wisdom Shapes Business, Economies, Societies and Nations* (New York: Doubleday, 2004).

8 Photo by author.

9 Robert D. Austin, *Measuring and* Managing *Performance in Organizations* (New York: Dorset House, 1996), 15.

10 http://dilbert.com/strips/comic/1995-11-13

11 Kent Beck with Cynthia Andres, *Extreme Programming Explained: Embrace Change, Second Edition* (Boston: Addison-Wesley, 2005), 72–3.

12 Cem Kaner, private email. Malcolm Gladwell, *The Tipping Point* (Little Brown & Co., 2000), 141, has popularized the discussion, based on Mayor Giuliani's use in New York City. The statistical evidence supporting the theory is disputable; see Steven D. Levitt and Stephen J. Dubner, *Freakonomics: A Rogue Economist Explores the Hidden Side of Everything* (New York: HarperCollins, 2005). Nonetheless, the psychological argument that communities, including software teams, can become habituated to conditions of disrepair is widely consistent with experience.

13 For a detailed description of OData Access to TFS, see blogs.msdn.com/b/bharry/archive/2011/07/04/odata-access-to-tfs.aspx.

5

Architecture

Simple things should be simple; complex things should be possible.

—Alan Kay

FIGURE 5.1: Every system has an architecture. A beehive is a great example of an emergent architecture.

I N THE PREVIOUS CHAPTERS, you read about how development is done in sprints and how progress is monitored by the team. In the next four chapters, I focus on the activities during a sprint, where product backlog items (PBIs) get transformed to pieces of working software. This chapter covers the specifics of how and when architecture happens and the accompanying tooling provided by Visual Studio (VS).

Architecture in the Agile Consensus

In Scrum, there's no explicit architect role; instead, the team is responsible for the architecture. The first design session happens no later than in the second part of sprint planning, when PBIs are broken down into actionable tasks. This is where the team agrees on *how* to transform a PBI into working software. The team collaboratively chooses one from many possible solutions to each design problem and with its collective wisdom ensures that a best fit emerges.

Therefore, this chapter is not targeted just to architects, but to all developers and the architectural design tasks developers do on a daily basis.

Inspect and Adapt: Emergent Architecture

In the Agile Consensus, success is measured in terms of value delivered per sprint. The ultimate goal is being able to present value, in the form of PBIs that are done, at the end of each sprint. This practice contrasts strongly with the un-Agile notion of a rather long architectural "phase" to get the architecture "in place," before the actual implementation work is started. If teams are used to such phases, the shift can be a challenge.

Scrum prescribes designing "just enough" architecture to fulfill your sprint goals and thus get the PBIs done, according to the team's definition of *done*. There are no sprints dedicated to architecture because every sprint is supposed to deliver value that the customer cares about. By delivering PBIs as well as the required architecture, each sprint proves that the actual architecture works and satisfies all acceptance criteria. This approach has two major benefits:

- First, it ensures that not too much architecture is done up front, based on vague assumptions about future requirements, which leads to waste.

- Second, the risk is minimized because the architectural design is validated by showing PBIs that are built on top of it, at the end of each sprint.

Delivering a "slice"[1] of functionality, each sprint allows the team to inspect and adapt the architecture supporting the features. An experienced Scrum team will not invest too much in architecture up front because the team realizes that trying to make architecture "perfect" creates potential waste (as business requirements might change over time, and architecture will have to adapt to reflect the new needs). The team is aware of the PBIs likely to be implemented in the not-too-distant future and keeps those in mind when planning the implementation of the PBIs in the current sprint.

The term that is used to describe this way of delivering architecture in "slices" is *emergent architecture*. Architectural decisions that do not necessarily have to be done to fulfill the goals of a sprint are deferred to a later sprint, when they become relevant. For example, a team might defer the decision to interface to some external component to a later sprint, when this actually becomes the sprint commitment. In contrast, the team must make some basic decisions in the first sprints about the technology stack to use.

Architecture and Transparency

In Scrum, the primary way to inspect progress and architectural readiness is to inspect the working software. Teams need to have at least one PBI with customer value to demonstrate at the sprint review. (See Chapter 4, "Running the Sprint," for more information about the sprint review meeting.) Because teams are self-organizing in Scrum, they choose what kind of documentation they want to create and maintain within the team, and what can be reduced to eliminate waste.

Teams new to Scrum often complain that the architecture and infrastructure is so complex that it is impossible to get anything done within a single sprint. Imagine the simple scenario where a team wants to prove the architecture is working, but the hardware has not arrived yet and so the team cannot show it on a production-realistic infrastructure.

In this case, the team needs to be aware that its work cannot be fully validated and therefore is not potentially shippable. As a consequence, the team is deferring work to later sprints. Because the exact amount of work left is unknown, risk increases. It is very important to capture the "undone" work on the product backlog to make sure it is transparent for everyone else, and not hidden.

Teams that add undone work to the backlog with every sprint, and fail to resolve those deferred items as quickly as possible, accumulate *technical debt* on the backlog. Just as with bank loans, such teams must "pay interest" as the effort to resolve them increases over time. (You can read more about the unfortunate effects of technical debt in Chapter 1, "The Agile Consensus.")

A similar problem exists if a team has many sprints until a release and the definition of *done* contains too complex qualities of service (QoS), such as performance. Forcing all QoS criteria to be fulfilled after each sprint might actually slow the team down. All QoS need to be understood as early as possible, but in some cases it is acceptable for their fulfillment to be deferred, to be able to deliver customer value in each sprint and keep a steady flow of value to gain feedback.

Consider a team that develops an application that needs to support 5,000 users simultaneously. During each spring, the team might test for 1,000 users as part of its definition of *done* (so as to not slow down development). However, the team must recognize that the goal of 5,000 has to be reached, and some additional performance and scale tuning work will have to be done later, closer to release. Although not all QoS are fulfilled at the end of each sprint, it is important that all QoS are understood and made visible on the backlog through PBIs.

Design for Maintainability

One of the primary values of good architecture is maintainability and supportability. The design intent of good architecture should be that code is maximally maintainable in the future by others. It helps if you imagine yourself in the shoes of a developer who comes in two years from now and has to do something with the code that he has never seen before.

Of course, designing a system for maintainability is not something you do once. Instead, the team should agree to follow design principles and use well-known patterns, wherever possible, so that people other than the original author can easily maintain the code. Many practices that have been around for years allow for this, such as KISS[2] ("Keep it simple, stupid"), YAGNI[3] ("You aren't gonna need it"), and many more. Furthermore, there are not only code-related patterns, but also patterns that apply to Application Lifecycle Management (ALM) and working as a team (for example, branching patterns, as covered in the next chapter).

Exploring Existing Architectures

Understanding the Code

Many developers work on code that belongs to existing systems, referred to as *brownfield projects,* in contrast to freshly started *greenfield projects* that do not contain any existing code. The major challenge for teams on brownfield projects is the inherent complexity inherited from the legacy application.

Besides adding new functionality, the team needs to make sure it does not break any existing features because the sprint result needs to be potentially shippable. Changes to a legacy codebase are a challenge, especially if there are no automated tests available to act as a safety net for future refactoring. As a result, developers responsible for changes to that code need to have a good understanding of the system to see the potential impact in order to safely modify and leverage it.

A key piece of architectural discovery in VS is the ability to generate *dependency graphs* from a snapshot of the current system. Figure 5.2 shows a top-down dependency graph from a Web site and all references between the components represented as namespaces. The relationships are shown as arrows, where a wider arrow indicates more references from/to the same node.

An interesting point to be aware of is that dependency graphs in VS are not scoped or limited to VS solutions and projects. They can be much broader if necessary (for example, to include components from other teams or third parties). Even references to the underlying .NET Framework classes get added (as an Externals node) and can be safely removed from the graph if not required. Note that only static dependencies can be discovered, not dynamic ones.

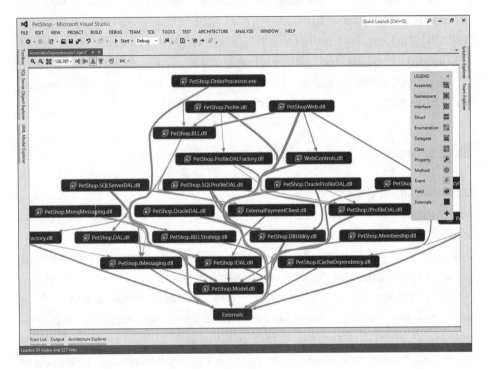

FIGURE 5.2: VS generates dependency graphs that represent all the actual references in code to understand how individual parts of the system fit together. The wider the arrows, the more references exist between two nodes.

To create dependency graphs efficiently, VS indexes the existing codebase on the first creation of a graph and stores this in a SQL Server database for subsequent uses. On large projects, code indexing can be integrated into the daily build, to further reduce load times.

Another way to start exploring dependencies is by creating a graph directly from Solution Explorer. Those bottom-up dependency graphs only show a subset of the available data. (Figure 5.3 shows the CreditCardInfo class and its callers.) While trying to gain a deeper understanding of the code and its relationships, you can follow references by hovering over them and clicking one of the arrows, as shown in Figure 5.4, or you can drill down by opening a node to see its child nodes. (For example, a class node contains the methods as child nodes.) Proposed changes and comments can be directly added to the graph, as shown in Figure 5.5.

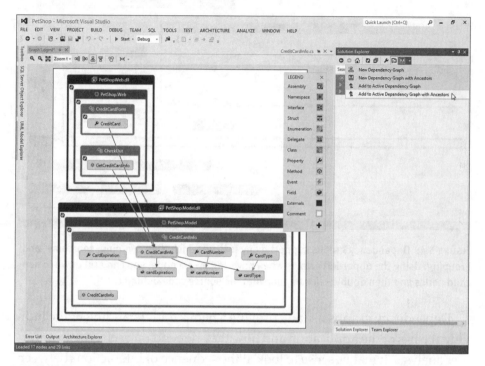

FIGURE 5.3: Dependency graphs can be created right from Solution Explorer, showing assemblies, classes, or methods (with their corresponding relationships and child objects).

Figure 5.6 shows a slightly different layout, the Quick Cluster, which groups nodes with a higher coupling so that classes that are heavily referencing one another are easily spotted. Those should be checked because they might indicate a poorly maintainable architecture. For readability, the Externals node, containing all external references, was manually removed from the graph.

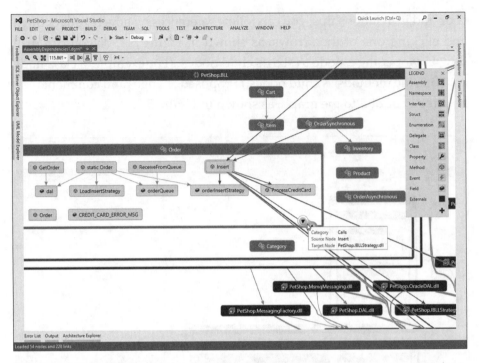

FIGURE 5.4: Dependency graphs support many features, including zooming, searching, and grouping. Using the upper-left arrows when hovering over a node, you can drill down to see child nodes and then double-click to jump into the source code behind them.

Dependency graphs usually provide a better understanding of the individual parts of the application and how they depend on each other. For further analysis, it makes sense to look at the sequence of interactions between them. For this purpose, VS supports generating sequence diagrams, from the actual code, where the depth of the diagram and the references to include/exclude can be configured, as shown in Figure 5.7.

A sequence diagram, generated from code, is a great way to visualize and understand how a particular method is implemented in the actual code.

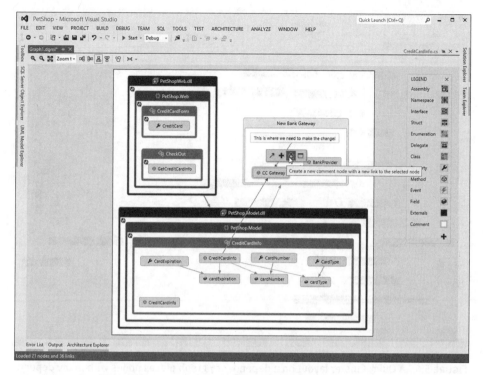

FIGURE 5.5: By adding nodes and links, dependency graphs can be used to communicate proposed changes or to add further clarifications by adding comment nodes.

The MSDN Library describes them as follows:

A sequence diagram describes an interaction between objects as a series of lifelines and messages. Lifelines represent instances of objects, and messages represent method calls between those objects.

Figure 5.8 shows a sequence diagram for the Insert method of the Order class. Conditional statements and loops are framed with a gray border, to indicate that those parts are optional or potentially repeated. For readability, you can group the vertical lifelines of two classes so that they appear as a single line.

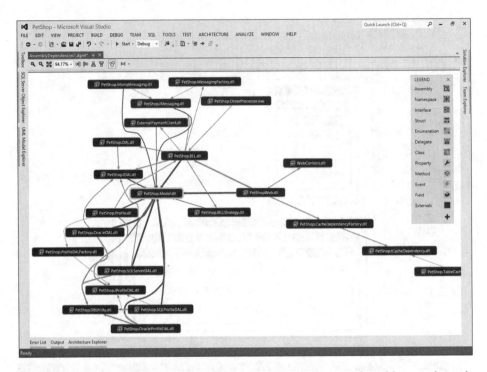

FIGURE 5.6: A Quick Cluster layout on a dependency graph places nodes with many dependencies between each other closer to each other and functions as a cohesion graph.

FIGURE 5.7: VS supports generating UML sequence diagrams directly from code (by right-clicking the method). This dialog shows the options to include or exclude external references.

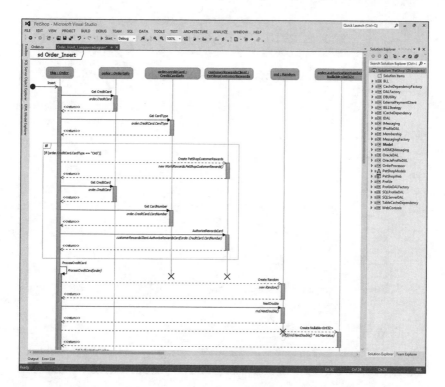

FIGURE 5.8: A UML sequence diagram that was generated from code shows the sequence of interactions between classes. Conditional blocks (such as if statements) and loops are shown in gray boxes.

Besides just "reading" the diagram as it was generated from code, Figure 5.9 shows how the toolbar was used to draw proposed changes right onto the diagram surface, as a basis of discussion with the team, and annotate the diagram with comments.

Maintaining Control

The essential challenge in emerging software architecture is to maintain control of structure, in particular the clean layering of dependencies. As systems continue to evolve over time, and as new developers join the team, both need guardrails. If layering stays clean, the system can be readily refactored and maintained. Otherwise, it risks becoming a "ball of mud."[4]

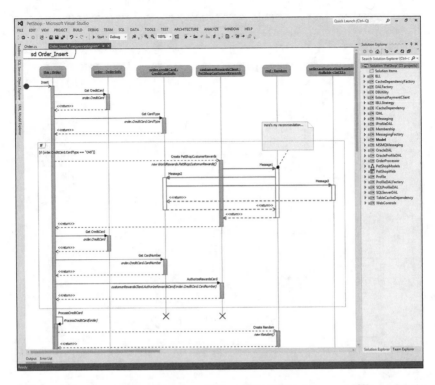

FIGURE 5.9: This UML sequence diagram additionally includes a proposed change to the sequence (highlighted in a different color) as well as a comment with further explanations.

Architecture is often represented on a whiteboard as a couple of boxes and lines. Similarly, VS enables you to draw the intended logical structure on a design surface called a *layer diagram*. On that diagram, you can draw layers that limit the intended dependencies by drawing allowed references between them, as shown in Figure 5.10. This is a purely logical/conceptual view that you need to create manually. (There is no autodiscovery for your intended structure.)

After you define your intended layering and dependencies, you then map your code to the blocks on this graph. VS allows you to drag files, or VS projects, directly from Solution Explorer to the design surface. You can also use the more sophisticated Architecture Explorer, shown in Figure 5.11, to query for all kinds of types, such as assemblies, namespaces, classes, and methods, to drag and drop them onto the layers. As with dependency graphs, you are not limited to a VS solution.

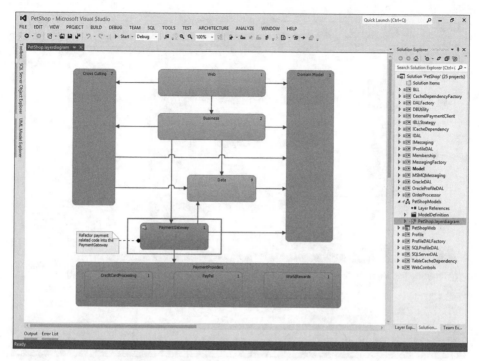

FIGURE 5.10: The layer diagram is the logical intended structure of your system. It can be complicated or simple, as you need it.

You can now use the layer diagram to validate the current structure against your intended one and show all unwanted dependencies, as shown in Figure 5.12. The validation can run locally in the VS Integrated Development Environment (IDE) or as part of the server-side automated build.[5] The result is a list of invalid dependencies that are not allowed according to your intended structure (if there are any). Running layer validation as part of your automated build ensures the build "fails fast" for newly introduced unwanted dependencies. As with all errors in VS, users can use the context menu to quickly create work items out of the validation errors that include all the necessary details to track the progress.

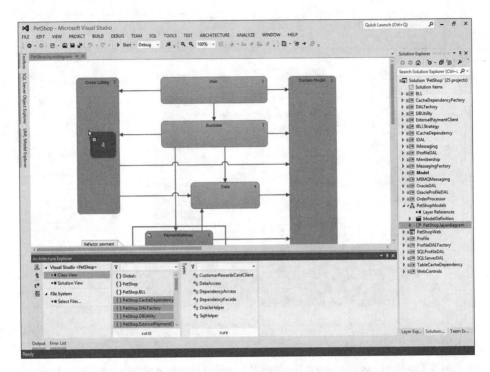

FIGURE 5.11: Architecture Explorer enables you to query, search, and filter for assemblies, namespaces, types, and methods from your system. You can drag and drop these onto the surface to assign them to a logical layer.

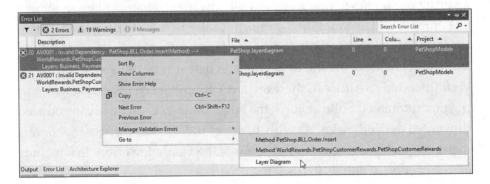

FIGURE 5.12: Layer diagrams validate the actual code against the logical structure and generate errors for unwanted dependencies. The validation happens locally on the client and optionally on the build server and as part of check-in.

Emergence also applies to existing code. For existing codebases, the layer diagram helps to move to an intended architecture and remove unwanted dependencies incrementally over time. After drawing the desired layer diagram, and mapping the system to it, the team selects the top few validation errors in order to tackle them in the same sprint (while suppressing the rest). The team can then reveal all the suppressed errors for the next sprint plan. Based on the increased knowledge of the team, the team then selects the next few top validation errors and includes them in the sprint backlog and suppresses the rest. Effectively, the team iteratively implements more of the intended architecture with each sprint.

Furthermore, the layer diagram itself is extensible with custom commands and validations. For example, you can download the VS extension Application Architecture Guide Layer Diagrams from the Extension Manager in the VS IDE (Tools menu), which includes layer diagram templates for five common application types.

In brief, VS layer diagrams reduce technical debt. On new greenfield projects, a layer diagram ensures that developers adhere to the intended structure. On existing brownfield projects, layer diagrams help to detect the discrepancy between the actual and the intended structure so that the team can improve the structure progressively over time. In both cases, the diagram serves as a documentation of the intended structure and references and enables us to emerge architecture deliberately rather than by accident (even with new developers on the team).

Understanding the Domain

Complex systems are often not only complex in terms of code and the number of modules, classes, and operations they consist of. Today, the problem domain itself and the required knowledge about business processes are also quite complex.

UML[6] emerged as the de facto standard notation used to document models. Those models are then used to collaborate and spread understanding within your team, and especially among external, outsourced teams that by nature have an increased need for more formal documentation.

Diagrams in VS are stored in a separate *modeling project,* which offers the five most frequently used UML diagrams besides the layer diagram, as shown in Figure 5.13.

FIGURE 5.13: VS supports the five most frequently used UML diagram types and stores those diagrams in separate modeling projects that are stored and versioned in the system along with all other artifacts in the system.

The two high-level diagrams, the use case diagram and the activity diagram, can help you to describe requirements in more detail. The use case diagram (shown in Figure 5.14) provides context about actors and use cases available to them. The activity diagram (shown in Figure 5.15) allows for documentation of business workflows using a simple graphical representation rather than plain text to limit potential misunderstanding. The various elements on the diagrams, such as use cases, can then be linked with PBIs and other work items, as shown later.

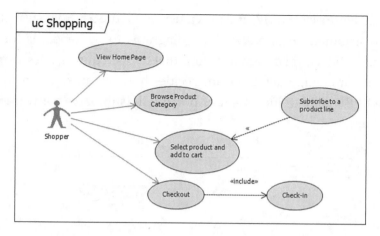

FIGURE 5.14: The UML use case diagram can provide some interesting context about the business domain, the involved actors, and associated use cases that can be performed by the actors.

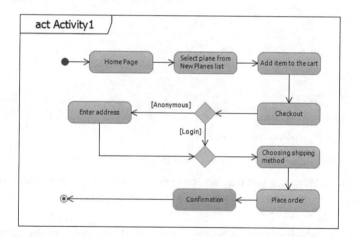

FIGURE 5.15 The UML activity diagram is a great way to document a workflow of activities in a graphical way so that it can be understood by business owners as well as developers.

The three lower-level diagrams (component, class, and sequence) are a way of documenting a proposed architecture or an existing one. The last two can be generated though reverse-engineering from your code, as shown in Figures 5.16, 5.17, and previously in Figure 5.8. Some teams, especially distributed ones, prefer those diagrams to whiteboards for documenting architectural design decisions that happen during the second part of sprint planning, when the team decides how it wants to transform the selected PBIs into an increment of potentially shippable software in that particular sprint.

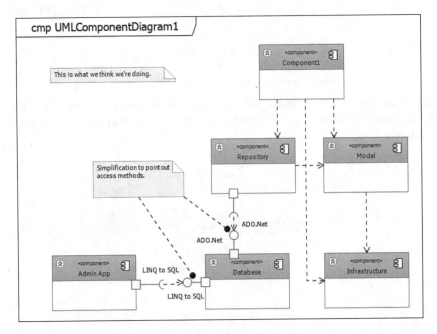

FIGURE 5.16: A UML component diagram is a logical view that represents your component architecture on a higher level than looking at code or VS projects.

In VS, modeling artifacts are version-controlled right along with everything else in your solution, to help minimize the chance they get completely out of date. In addition, all artifacts used on the diagrams can be shared among different diagrams through the UML Model Explorer (see Figure 5.18).

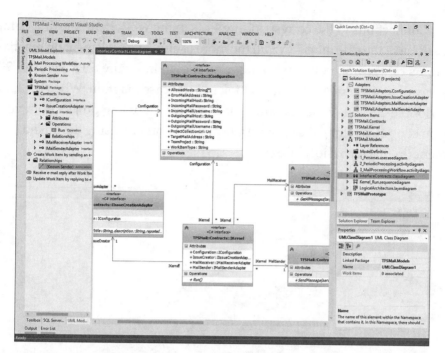

FIGURE 5.17: A UML class diagram can be generated from existing code or used as a logical model to generate template-based code. It is a great basis for a discussion among team members.

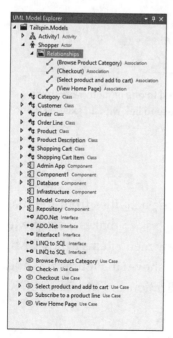

FIGURE 5.18: The UML Model Explorer enables sharing of artifacts across different UML diagrams. To ensure easy maintenance, a change to an artifact impacts its instances on all diagrams where it is used.

Connections to the corresponding PBIs in the work item tracking database make the diagrams in VS all the more useful. Every element on the diagrams can be linked to a work item, as shown in Figure 5.19. Figure 5.20 shows a work item with a Model Link to a use case diagram. When the link is double-clicked, VS takes care of opening the modeling project from version control, opening the appropriate diagram, and focusing the linked element (in this scenario, a use case).

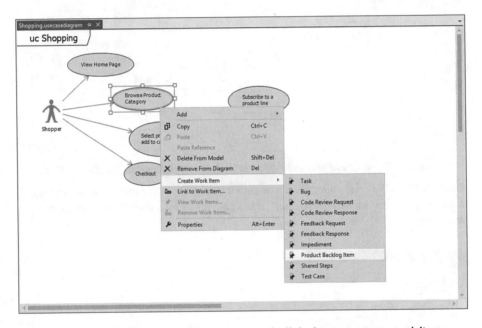

FIGURE 5.19: Every element on a diagram in VS can be linked to one or more work items (PBIs, for example). From the context menu, users can choose to link with an existing work item or create a new one.

Diagram Extensibility

Sometimes it is necessary to do problem-specific activities from the diagram itself. By providing specific project templates, VS makes it simple to extend the diagrams (for example, by adding new menu items to any UML diagram and adding business logic behind it, as shown in Figures 5.21 and 5.22). Those templates are part of the VS Visualization and Modeling SDK, available from the extension manager in VS.

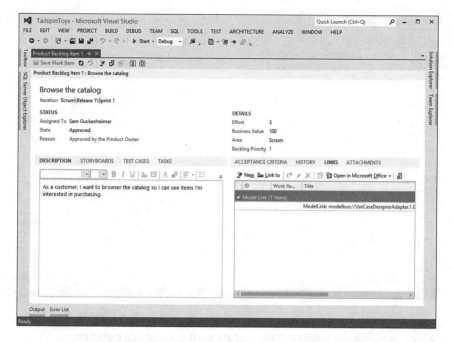

FIGURE 5.20: Model Links appear in work items that are linked to elements on diagrams. When you double-click the link, the diagram is opened from version control and focused on the linked element.

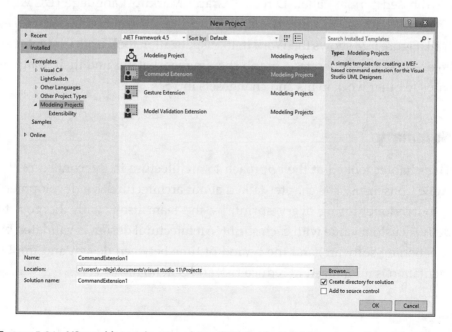

FIGURE 5.21: VS provides project templates that enable developers to easily use the existing UML diagrams as a platform for custom, domain-driven extensions.

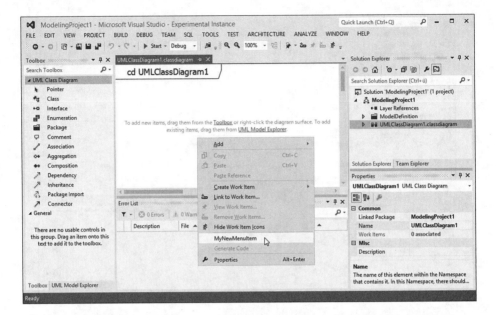

FIGURE 5.22: VS makes it easy to write custom command extensions to hook into the UML diagrams, execute some business logic, and access the underlying metadata.

The underlying file format that all VS dependency graphs share is an XML-based format called Directed Graph Markup Language (DGML).[7] This makes it easy to generate dependency graphs from other sources, as well. Figure 5.23 shows the Work Item Visualization tool[8] from Codeplex as an example that generates a graph showing work items and their relationships to other work items and changesets in VS.

Summary

This chapter looked at the approach to architecture in the context of the Agile Consensus. The chapter talked about architecture as a development activity, done during every sprint, by the team itself, with the goal to deliver custom value with each sprint. Architectural design is validated by functioning software, and the period of time between design and implementation is minimized to reduce risk and potential waste.

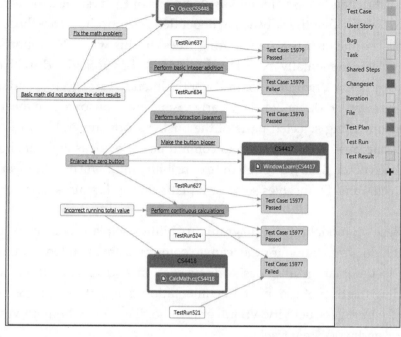

FIGURE 5.23: The VS extension Work Item Visualizer creates DGML files out of the relationships between work items (such as User Stories, Tasks, and Test Cases) and links them with version-control changesets.

In software development, a good architecture is broadly agreed to be one that is maintainable. It does consider the near future but is far from being complete or perfect. Instead, its main goal is to lay the foundations for further development and future architectural changes. This means that the system has cleanly layered dependencies and few or no circular dependencies. In contrast, a "bad" architecture has tangled dependencies and no clear layers, often referred to as *a ball of mud*.

Using VS tools, I showed that you can quickly use dependency graphs and sequence diagrams to shorten the learning curve, even when confronted with unknown code and even with large codebases. When doing bug fixing in existing codebases, this enables you to make the right fix and get to the root cause of the issue, instead of just fixing the symptoms.

The layer diagram represents the logical structure that limits the intended dependencies among large portions of the systems. You can use it to make sure that the only actual dependencies introduced are those that conform to the architectural layering rules. In this way, VS supports the practice of incrementally fixing issues in existing brownfield code with each sprint, by helping maintain control over the intended architecture and making all unwanted dependencies clearly visible and transparent to the team.

Documenting selected parts of the business domain and processes as UML diagrams helps the team to communicate its ideas and collaborate with each other. Lastly, through the extensibility mechanisms, the layer and UML diagrams themselves serve as a platform for domain-specific extensions.

These VS modeling and diagram capabilities help an Agile team create enough documentation for the team to communicate the intent and to use that documentation as a basis for discussion and collaboration, while avoiding the trap of too much documentation that may create waste and actually hurt productivity. VS integrates the diagrams with both version control and work item tracking.

The next chapter covers the daily development activities that happen in the Agile Consensus. These include test-driven development, the red-green-refactor cycle, continuous integration, source management, and the done lists of daily development. Chapter 7, "Build and Lab," takes this a step further with the next layer of done and its automation with continuous integration and continuous deployment into the test lab. At any place along these cycles, architectural validation may apply, relying on the patterns of clean architecture covered here.

Endnotes

[1] Vertically slicing user stories, Simon Baker, www.energizedwork. com/weblog/2005/05/slicing-the-cake

[2] http://c2.com/cgi/wiki?KeepItSimple

[3] http://c2.com/xp/YouArentGonnaNeedIt.html

[4] Brian Foote and Joseph Yoder, "Big Ball of Mud," 1999. http://www.laputan.org/mud/

5 http://blogs.msdn.com/b/camerons/archive/2009/11/25/team-build-and-layer-validation.aspx

6 www.uml.org

7 http://blogs.msdn.com/b/camerons/archive/2009/01/26/directed-graph-markup-language-dgml.aspx

8 Work Item Visualizer by Jeff Levinson, http://visualization.codeplex.com/

■ 6 ■

Development

Working software over comprehensive documentation.

—The Agile Manifesto[1]

FIGURE 6.1: Newton's Cradle is a common desktop toy. When you apply force from one end, the balls swing in a predictable, regular motion. When you add a force from the opposite end, the balls start bouncing chaotically against each other. It is a metaphor for development practice. Simple, directional force encourages predictability, whereas contradictory forces can create chaos.

THIS CHAPTER IS NOT ABOUT PROGRAMMING languages or design patterns. These important topics are well covered in many other books. Instead, this chapter is about getting that code into deliverable software using Visual Studio (VS).

For purposes of this chapter, we assume that you are a skilled developer. Also, we assume that you, like nearly every developer we have ever met, want to do quality work and remove any impediments to delivering that quality.

Development in the Agile Consensus

For 30 years, we've known that ensuring quality early is much cheaper than removing bugs later.[2] Only in the past ten years, however, have practices shifted to the Agile Consensus, where the only deliverables measured are the ones that the customer values. More than anything else, this means working code of quality suitable for customer delivery. Scrum calls this the *potentially shippable increment*, as shown in Figure 6.2.

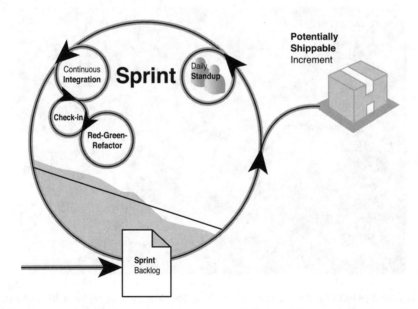

FIGURE 6.2: During a sprint, the team turns product backlog items into a potentially shippable increment. The sprint backlog contains the tasks required to achieve this, and the developers repeat the Red-Green-Refactor cycle multiple times until the code is being checked in to version control.

The Sprint Cycle

During a sprint, the team transforms the selected product backlog items (PBIs) into potentially shippable working software. It's the responsibility of the team to self-organize and choose which practices and technologies should be used to accomplish that goal in an efficient way. Figure 6.2 shows the cycles involved.

In Chapter 3, "Product Ownership," we discussed how to define and manage the product backlog to minimize problems related to requirement misunderstandings. The team has responsibility for ensuring that the conversations happen to clarify the design necessary to implement the requirements stated in the product backlog items.

The team organizes the work by creating tasks on the sprint backlog for each selected PBI, which is typically a user story. The tasks represent all the work that needs to be completed for a user story to be done, according to the team's definition of *done* (as discussed in Chapter 2, "Scrum, Agile Practices, and Visual Studio," and Chapter 7, "Build and Lab"). An initial set of tasks is created during a sprint planning meeting at the beginning of the sprint, and it is normal that the list evolves further as the team gains more knowledge and experience.

In this chapter, we look at the development activities that happen in a typical day. Team members work on the tasks for one PBI and carry it to done before starting another. Done work is checked into version control to feed the build and to be shared with the team. Accordingly, much of this chapter is about the individual developer working in the team context.

The next chapter continues on the same path and covers the automated builds and deployment that are triggered by the check-in. You should think of these two chapters together as describing the development loop of the daily Scrum cycle.

Smells to Avoid in the Daily Cycle

There are four antipatterns that lead (directly or indirectly) to huge annoyance, quality problems, and impediments in a developer's work. They clog the flow in the daily cycle by introducing waste, specifically *Extra Processing*,

Waiting, Correction, Inconsistency, and *Overburden,* in the taxonomy of Table 1.1. They are as follows:

1. **Undetected programming errors.** People write code, and people make mistakes. In particular, it is often very hard to write code that takes all the necessary definitions of *done* into account.
2. **Inability to detect side effects immediately.** Even developers with the best unit tests often discover their software behaves unexpectedly in the wild and they have to respond.
3. **Version skews.** There are a lot of moving files in a software project and they all need to be versioned, tracked to work items, matched to configurations, and usually branched. The complexities of branching can exacerbate the drift over time.
4. **Lack of transparency.** The development infrastructure, project management system, and bug/change request tracking and metrics (if any) are treated as disconnected black boxes. In this situation, there are many surprises at the end of the sprint, or worse, much later.

These four broad categories are the focus of this chapter.

Keeping the Codebase Clean

Benjamin Franklin quipped that an ounce of prevention is worth a pound of cure. Developers who've worked with bad code recognize that it's much harder to isolate the four smells and clean them out than not to let them sneak in at all. To this end, Team Foundation Server (TFS) does everything possible to help the team catch code errors and keep the codebase clean before the smells can be committed. Teams can use TFS' check-in process to maintain cleanliness.

Catching Errors at Check-In

TFS has built-in version control that keeps the full history of changes to the team's source base, all the related files in your VS solution, any others that you include, and all the work items that you associate. When you start to edit a file, it is automatically checked out for you, unless someone else has it locked.

The primary way that you interact with version control is by checking in files. When you check in, you are in effect saying that your files are ready to be used in the team build (see Figures 6.3, 6.4, and 6.5) as well as by other team members.

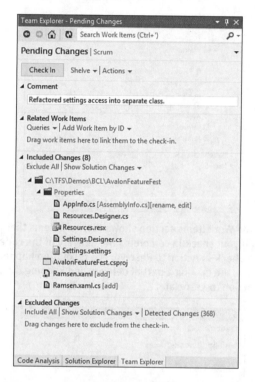

FIGURE 6.3: The Pending Changes pane in Team Explorer shows you an Included Changes section with the files that have been changed so that you can select the ones for the check-in.

When you check in, VS prompts for three things: the list of files, the work items that you are resolving with this check-in, and the check-in notes that you are using to describe the changes. Together, these three items form a *changeset*, which ties together the data of a check-in. The changeset includes the newly added, modified, or deleted lines of code; the work item state changes associated with that code; and the check-in notes.

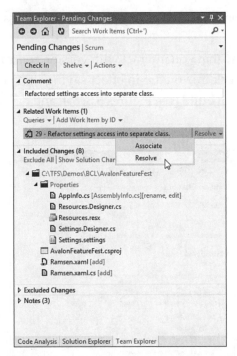

FIGURE 6.4: The Related Work Items section shows the work items that you want to associate with the check-in. If your check-in completes the delivery of the code for a task or other work item, you set the Check-in Action to Resolve. The resolution happens on the next successful team build. If you are making a partial delivery and keeping the work item active, change the Check-in Action to Associate.

FIGURE 6.5: In the Notes section at the bottom, enter notes for this check-in. The fields used for the notes are determined by your settings for the team project on the Team Foundation Server.

Check-In Policies Provide a Local Done List

Most important, VS verifies that you have complied with the team's *check-in policies,* as shown in Figure 6.6. Three standard check-in policies make sure that you have associated work items with your changes, have performed static code analysis, and that the build is not currently broken. The TFS Power Tools[3] add additional policies (for example, to apply policies to specific folders only), as shown in Figure 6.7. Your team may choose to write other policies and have these evaluated at check-in, too. These act as an automated definition of done for the check-in.

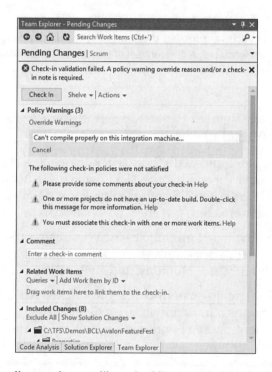

FIGURE 6.6: These policy warnings act like a checklist to remind the developer on each check-in. For special cases, it is possible to override the warnings explicitly.

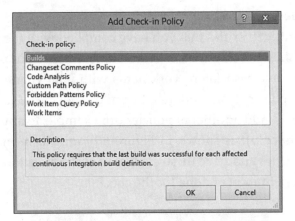

FIGURE 6.7: Check-in policies ensure that check-ins comply with certain rules or that specified actions have been completed. A different set of policies can be applied to different team projects.

■ CHECK-IN POLICIES

Out of the box, TFS comes with three check-in policies. Four additional ones are supplied by installing the TFS Power Tools. More policies are available online from the VS community. For a detailed list, refer to www.teamsystempro.com/go/checkinpolicies.aspx.

For details on how to set up policies for your team projects, I recommend you refer to this book: *Professional Team Foundation Server 2012* by Blankenship, Woodward, Holliday, and Keller (Wrox, 2012).

To learn how to create custom check-in policies, see this blog post: http://blogs.msdn.com/b/jimlamb/archive/2010/03/31/ how-to-implement-package-and-deploy-custom-check-in-policy-for-tfs-2010.aspx.

Gated Check-In Provides Server Enforcement of Done

A stricter way to enforce rules is to start a build on the build server to ensure that the code changes did not break the build or the automated tests. Check-ins in VS optionally can either trigger an automated *continuous integration* (CI) build or a *gated check-in* (GC) build. In the latter case, the code changes are not directly committed to the version control system, but rather packaged as a shelveset and submitted to the build server for validation, as shown in Figure 6.8. The validation build, upon success, creates a changeset in the name of the originator. If any errors are encountered, the changes are not committed and are returned to the originator as a shelveset for inspection and correction, as illustrated in Figure 6.9.

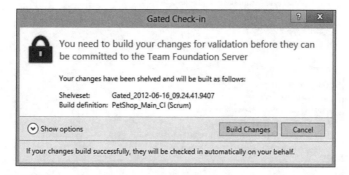

FIGURE 6.8: If gated check-in is enabled, check-ins are stored in shelvesets and validated by the build server, running all the usual build steps, before being committed to the version control repository. If the build fails, the check-in is not committed.

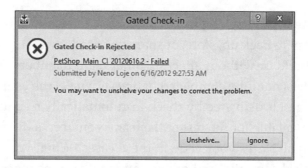

FIGURE 6.9: When a check-in is rejected by the verification build, it is easy to open the "broken" change by unshelving it from version control to fix and then revalidate and submit the change again.

In addition, a *build check-in policy* can be set up to prevent other developers from checking in code until your gated check-in succeeds. In this case, the project alerts system notifies subscribers about the broken build, as shown in Figure 6.10.

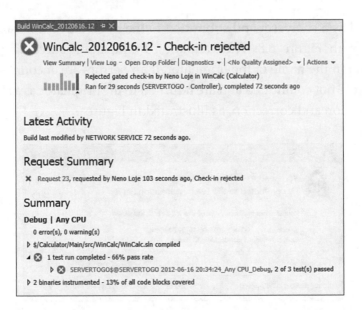

FIGURE 6.10: The Build report shows the detailed compilation and test results from a verification build triggered by a gated check-in. If errors are encountered, the changes are not committed. At the same time, the production build never broke and remained stable.

Shelving Instead of Checking In

Often you want to back up, store, or share your code without submitting it for the next build or without affecting other team members, for instance, when the code is not fully completed or does not meet the team's done list. Because changesets delivered by check-in automatically feed the build system and are available for the rest of the team, you need a different mechanism. In VS, you *shelve* your code in these cases. When you shelve your code, it is stored centrally, and others can view your changes (as long as they have permission), but nothing is submitted for the next build. When you subsequently unshelve your code, there is no record of the shelveset and correspondingly no history to clean up in the source database.

Shelving is very useful in a number of situations. If you need to leave the office before your code is ready for the build, you can back it up. If you need to share your code with someone else prior to check-in for a code review or buddy test, you can shelve your code. When you want to experiment with two solutions to a problem, you can try one, shelve it, try the second, and switch between the shelvesets for local testing. Additionally, some team members might not be permitted to check in code directly and will shelve their changes instead. Those shelvesets can then be reviewed by a dev lead before check-in.

In many cases, VS automatically uses shelvesets to enable richer team collaboration. These scenarios are described next.

Staying "in the Groove"

One of the greatest sources of waste, error, and frustration is the difficulty of restoring your concentration after switching tasks. The *My Work* pane of Team Explorer is a new feature of VS 2012 designed to help you, as a developer, minimize the impact of interruptions on your work. The My Work pane organizes your personal task backlog, as shown in Figure 6.11.

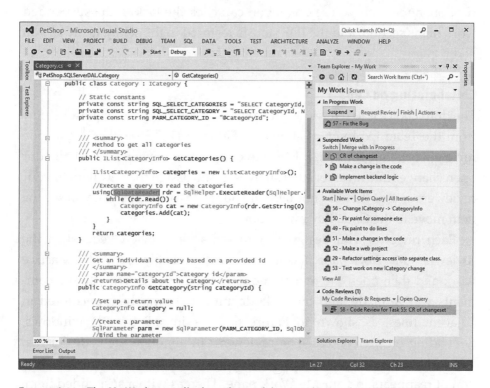

FIGURE 6.11: The My Work pane displays the work item at the top that is currently in progress (in this case Task 57). The sections below list other active work items. The Available Work Items do not yet have code, while Suspended Work items already have associated shelvesets and Code Reviews have shelvesets and workflow for collecting the comments.

The My Work pane displays the currently active task at the top. You can apply any of three commands to this work item and all of the currently open code and tests together: *Check In, Suspend,* and *Request Review.* When you choose to check in, TFS turns your current changes into a changeset and resolves this work item (as shown in Figures 6.3 to 6.5), and then lets you pick the next item off the Available Work Items list in the My Work pane. When you choose to suspend, TFS automatically creates a shelveset of all the open changes, attaches it to the in-progress work item, and moves the unfinished work item to the Suspended Work section of the My Work pane.

In this way, you can switch to a different task (for example, a live-site issue or high-priority bug) and preserve all the context of the previous work item, with its code, tests, and IDE settings. You can handle the interruption, and when you're done, you can click the task in the suspended work items section, and the IDE state is restored to the state exactly as you had it before.

Collaborating on Code

The third choice is to request a code review. When you pick Request Review from the Team Explorer, as shown in Figure 6.11, TFS will create a code review work time for you, ask you to designate reviewers, collect all your open changes into an associated shelveset, and assign the new item to your reviewers so that they are notified. In your My Work pane, you will see the item move to the Code Review section.

Each reviewer you designate will see a new review request in the reviewer's My Work pane. The reviewer will probably suspend any active work and then open the review request. The reviewer will see the comments you've made, and the code document shows changes colored in adjacent lines, as shown in Figure 6.12, or in side-by-side windows, depending on preferences. The reviewer can annotate the code further. When the reviewer resolves the code review work item and reassigns it to you, it reappears in your My Work pane. Then as with a suspended item, when you open the review, all the appropriate shelveset files open within the right solution automatically.

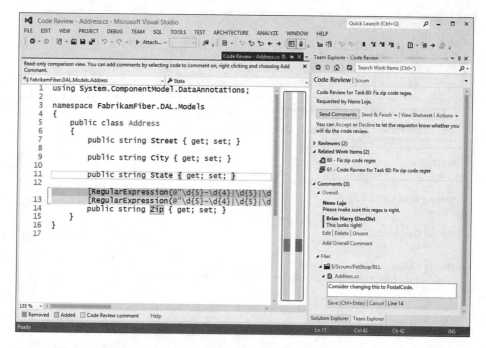

FIGURE 6.12: A designated reviewer sees the shelveset with the colored code changes and review comments. The reviewer can edit or annotate the shelveset further, and when done, the changes and comments are automatically returned to the requestor and the corresponding work item is updated.

When you request a code review, your reviewers receive an email of the pending code review request from TFS and they can open the VS IDE with the right shelveset from a link in the email or view the changes through browser using the Team Web Access, as shown in Figure 6.13. If the IDE is open, the request will appear in the reviewer's My Work pane.

Code review can be as informal or rigorous as you like, up to the standards of formal pair programming,[4] and can be backed by check-in policy if you want. Whatever the degree of flexibility or enforcement, all the workflow and bookkeeping are automatic, so that you as a developer can stay in the groove.

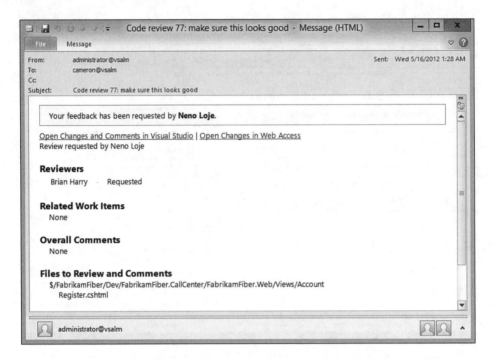

FIGURE 6.13: When requesting a code review, the reviewers are notified by the Project Alerts system that their feedback is requested. From the links in the email, the reviewers can directly jump into VS or Web Access to look at the changes under review.

■ SUSPENDING WORK AND SHELVESETS

In VS, unfinished work can be stored in a shelveset on the server using Suspend. This gives you the advantages of a server (backup, for example) while not affecting the work of other team members.

Shelving supports multiple everyday life scenarios, such as switching between multiple tasks, handing over code for review by other team members, and creating a checkpoint of your work that is a backup of the current state of the code in the local workspace.

To learn how to shelve and unshelve changes, see this MSDN topic: "Suspend Your Work and Manage Your Shelvesets" (http://msdn. microsoft.com/en-us/library/ms181403(v=vs.110)).

Detecting Programming Errors Early

Unit testing is probably the single most important quality practice for a developer. As a practice, unit testing has been advocated for at least 30 years.[5] VS 2012 now supports a broad array of unit test frameworks from Microsoft and Open Source communities for .NET, C++, and HTML/ JavaScript. You can find the current list of plug-ins at www.teamsystempro. com/go/unittestingplugins.aspx.

Test-Driven Development Provides Clarity

In the past decade, test-driven development (TDD) has gained widespread visibility through the work of Erich Gamma and Kent Beck. It is now one of the practices of the Agile Consensus, although a slightly controversial one. TDD requires discipline and the unlearning of old habits of coding. In exchange, it supports clean, maintainable code.

With TDD, you do not write a single line of code until you have written a corresponding failing test. Next, you write just enough code to pass the test, and refactor the code, if needed, to keep the codebase clean and maintainable. This loop is then repeated. This loop is commonly known as Red-Green-Refactor (see Figure 6.14) and can be repeated multiple times before a check-in to version control (see Figure 6.15). Coding with TDD leads to demonstrably higher-quality code and better designed application architectures than coding without the safety harness that this practice provides. Advocates of TDD document repeatedly that the practice forces clear requirements, catches mistakes, enables refactoring, and removes stress.[6]

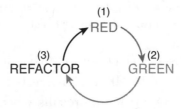

FIGURE 6.14: TDD is a practice in which you do not write a single line of code until you have written a test that fails in the absence of that code (red). Next, you write just enough code to pass the test (green), then you refactor the code to clean it up and eliminate duplications (refactor), and then write a new test that fails, and keep repeating the tight loop.

The strongest argument in favor of TDD is that it uses tests as technical product requirements. Because you must write a test before writing the code under test, you are forced to understand the design and wring out any ambiguity as you define the test. This process, in turn, makes you think in small increments and in terms of reuse, so that you do not write any unnecessary code. In other words, TDD imposes a clear and modular design, which is easy to grow and maintain. To facilitate TDD, VS supports direct test creation and execution, with code coverage, inside the IDE, as shown in Figure 6.15.

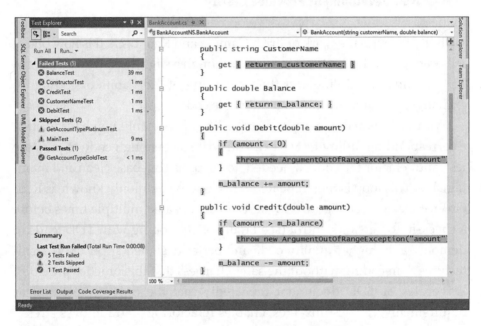

FIGURE 6.15: VS supports unit testing directly in the IDE. This is a view of test run results from the last run, with the source code under test in the right window. The dark shading (red on a color screen) indicates an uncovered exception handler.

The next argument is that TDD helps with continual refactoring to keep the code lean (see Figure 6.16). If you have tests that cover 100% of your code, and immediately report failing results when any side effects from refactoring occur, you have the safety net to refactor with confidence. Indeed, the experience of TDD is that you do much less debugging of your code because your unit tests pinpoint the source of errors that you would

otherwise isolate only by laboriously stepping through the execution with
the debugger.

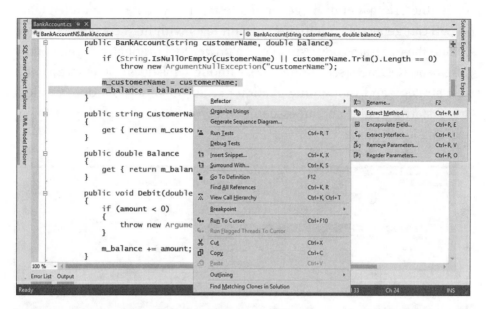

FIGURE 6.16: Refactoring is also supported directly, making VS a powerful IDE for TDD.

The result is that you do not check in code that does not have unit tests
that run and pass with it, and if someone else (or the build system) gets
your code and runs your tests, those tests should pass. In that way, your
unit tests become a safety net not just for yourself but also for the whole
team.

Cleaning Up the Campground

Bob Martin famously advised developers to follow the Boy Scout rule of
"Leave the campground cleaner than you found it" when handling code.[7]
Martin was observing that, much of the time, developers have to maintain
code that they did not create. When you do, you should exercise the same
pride of craftsmanship that you exercise with your own code.

When You Have Code without Tests

Frequently when you have to work on existing code you did not write, it
comes without unit tests. VS can help you build up those unit tests by

generating them programmatically. This has the benefit of creating lots of tests automatically and the drawback that you now have twice as much code (the original and the generated tests) that you have to understand.

VS can generate an initial set of unit tests with high coverage by analyzing the program code using Pex,[8] a power tool originally developed by Microsoft Research (see Figure 6.17). Although this does not replace a good test strategy and thoughtful creation of additional tests, it does create a good starting point and an essential safety net before changing or fixing existing legacy code.

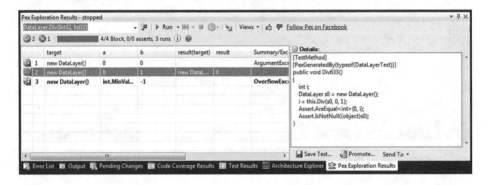

FIGURE 6.17: The Pex power tool automatically generates test suites with high code coverage. (This figure shows Pex in VS 2010. An updated version for VS 2012 will be available subsequently.)

A related framework, Microsoft Fakes, enables you to isolate parts of the code that you want to test from other layers by creating *stubs* or *shims* for other types of methods, including the .NET Framework.

■ PEX AND MICROSOFT FAKES

Pex is a VS power tool that helps to create an initial set of unit tests for existing .NET applications. It is available for MSDN subscribers at http://msdn.microsoft.com/subscriptions.

An introduction to isolating test methods with the Fakes framework can be found at http://msdn.microsoft.com/en-us/library/hh549175.aspx.

Use Code Coverage to Pinpoint Gaps in Unit Tests

When you run tests, VS provides code coverage reporting with the test run results. In the Test Explorer, you can select and right-click any set of tests or use the Run menu at the top to show the coverage in the source that you just exercised. This lets you pinpoint any code that your tests failed to exercise; skipped code is painted red, as shown in Figure 6.18. You can then right-click this code to generate a new test for it, or you can extend an existing test to cover it.

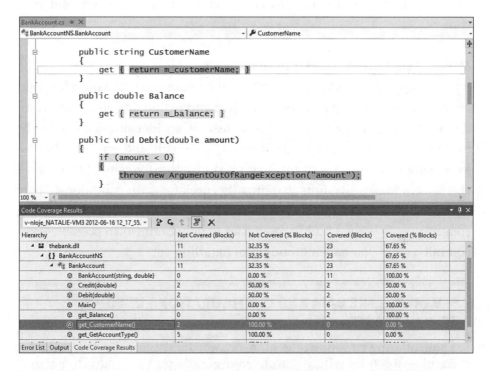

FIGURE 6.18: At the completion of a test run, you can see the source code under test painted to show code coverage. This lets you identify at a glance blocks of code that are not being tested. In a monochrome rendering, they are darker; in color, they appear red. You can then create a new test to exercise the uncovered code areas.

Code coverage is a valuable tool for showing you which blocks of code have not been exercised by your tests. Use code coverage to identify gaps where you need more unit tests. Do not let good code coverage make you too confident, however. Code coverage tells you neither that your tests are good, nor that your code is good, nor that you have written sufficient code to catch error conditions that need to be handled.

Do not be seduced by the question, *How much code coverage is enough?* The ideal is obviously 100%, but this is rarely obtainable. Frequently, there is some error handling, generated code, integration code, or something else for which it is impractically expensive to write unit tests. Focus on writing unit tests first for the code you write and making sure you have an adequate safety net for the refactoring you need to do. Do not focus on coverage for its own sake. You can always use check-in notes to document your choices.

Making Tests Better by Varying the Data

Both security and the cloud have raised our awareness of the need for good error handling and negative testing. When you're thinking about unit tests, it's key that you start with a good list of tests.[9] Consider simultaneously the four variables: output, methods invoked, code path, and error conditions. Make sure that you have inputs that maximize the diversity of those variables. Include negative tests that broadly check for error conditions. There may be a way of using test data to uncover gaps in your error-handling code. You may want a buddy or a tester to help brainstorm possible error conditions that you haven't thought of handling yet.[10]

■ VARYING THE DATA AND CONFIGURATIONS USED BY YOUR TESTS

Think of using your unit tests more broadly by varying the data and by running the tests with multiple configurations. VS makes doing so straightforward.

See the MSDN topic: "How To: Create a Data-Driven Unit Test" (http://msdn.microsoft.com/en-us/library/ms182527.aspx).

VS makes this easy, as shown in Figure 6.19. You can bind unit tests to many different sources, such as simple CSV files or Excel spreadsheets, which make it easy to invite domain experts to provide valid test data.

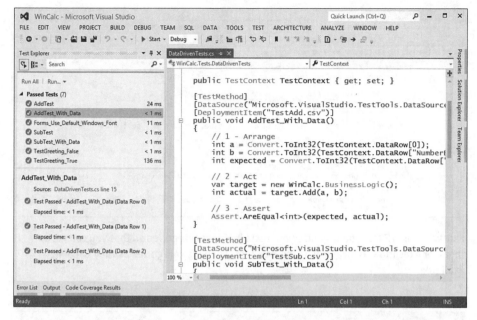

FIGURE 6.19: You can drive your unit tests with variable sets of data. Datasets can be maintained in OLEDB providers and specified as properties on the test.

Reusing Unit Tests as Build Verification Tests

Build verification tests (BVTs) are tests that run as part of the automated build. The purpose of BVTs is to look for unforeseen side effects and errors due to changes in the new code. See Chapter 7 for more information on automated builds and deployment.

Your unit tests should be reusable as BVTs, along with component integration tests and the majority of scenario tests (see Chapter 8, "Test"). To set up BVTs for an automated build in VS, you identify which tests to use by assigning them to the appropriate *test category* (see Figure 6.20) and then refer to the category within the Build Definition Wizard, as shown in Figure 6.21.

```
ConvertExTest.cs*  ⊡ ✕  ConsoleExTest.cs
⁜ ConsoleFramework.Tests.ConvertExTest                    ▾ ⊙ ChangeType_can_convert_from_string_to_int()
        [TestClass()]
        public class ConvertExTest
        {
            [TestMethod(), TestCategory("BVTs")]
            public void ChangeType_can_convert_from_string_to_int()
            {
                string value = "123";
                Type conversionType = typeof(Int32);
                int expected = 123;

                object result = ConvertEx.ChangeType(value, conversionType);

                Assert.AreEqual(expected, result);
            }

            [TestMethod(), TestCategory("BVTs")]
            public void ChangeType_can_convert_from_string_to_nullable_int()
            {
                string value = "123";
                Type conversionType = typeof(Nullable<Int32>);
                int expected = 123;
```

FIGURE 6.20: VS lets you organize your tests into test categories so that you can group them for execution. Typically, you add new tests to these categories as they become available.

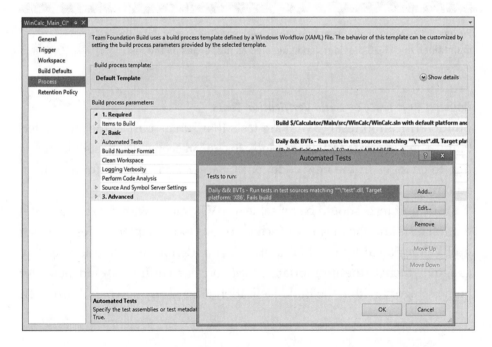

FIGURE 6.21: The build definition includes the designation of the test categories that you want to run as the build verification tests.

> **▪ SPECIFYING TESTS FOR BVTS**
>
> In VS, BVTs are ordinary tests that have been marked with an appropriate test category. You need to group tests into test categories for your BVTs.
>
> See these MSDN topics:
>
> - "How To: Group and Run Automated Tests Using Test Categories" (http://msdn.microsoft.com/en-us/library/dd286683.aspx)
>
> - "How To: Configure and Run Scheduled Tests After Building Your Application" (http://msdn.microsoft.com/en-us/library/ms182465.aspx)

When You Have Redundant Code

When you maintain existing code, it is also often hard to understand what side effects you might cause, as discussed in Chapter 5, "Architecture." Indeed, one of the nastiest characteristics of working with old code is not knowing whether you have fixed a problem everywhere you need to.

This happens because old code is often highly redundant. Your predecessors may not have refactored diligently, but instead resorted to copy and paste. In other words, often they just repeated lines of source code, instead of neatly extracting every duplicate method. (Remember the fallacy of rewarding developers for lines of code discussed in Chapter 4, "Running the Sprint"?)

VS helps you with this problem. It has a new command to find *clones* of selected code, as shown in Figure 6.22. Clones are either exact matches or semantically equivalent patterns (for example, with renamed methods and renamed parameters). In this way, if you plan to fix code in one spot, you can instantly search for all similar occurrences. By finding the clones, you can extract duplicates to a single method, fix the code once, and keep it fixed.

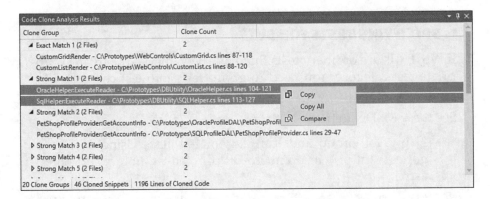

FIGURE 6.22: The output window from Code Clone Analysis shows all the locations of matches for a selected piece of code.

Removing clones is an obvious case where you apply the Red-Green-Refactor cycle although with a slight twist. Because you have the code, you want to write the unit tests that validate the current behavior, and using coverage, ensure that they do cover the existing code well. Then you have a better safety net for extracting the duplicate code into a unique method that can be called from the repeat occurrences. After each refactor, you can run the unit tests. In fact, to help keep you in the groove, VS automatically runs the unit tests *in the background* for you after each code change.

Catching Programming Errors with Automated Code Analysis

Manual code reviews were covered in Figures 6.12 and 6.13. Automated code analysis, or static analysis, is a technology that scans code for detectable classes of errors. Microsoft developed code analysis tools for its own product teams (FXCop for managed code and PreFAST for unmanaged code) that are included as part of VS. They cover coding practices in the areas of design, globalization, interoperability, maintainability, mobility, naming conventions, performance, portability, reliability, and security. You can decide which rulesets to include globally and when to apply specific rules to specific instances of code.

VS enables code analysis on the local build (F5) and presents the code analysis warnings and errors in the same window as the rest of the build output (see Figure 6.23). To encourage consistent practices across the team, VS enables you to set a check-in policy that ensures that code analysis has been run before every check-in (see Figure 6.6 earlier in this chapter). In addition, code analysis can be performed as part of the server-side build process, which can optionally be enforced to run prior to the check-in being committed on the server through a gated check-in. Code analysis does have the disadvantage that it can be noisy, generating false positives, so use it judiciously.

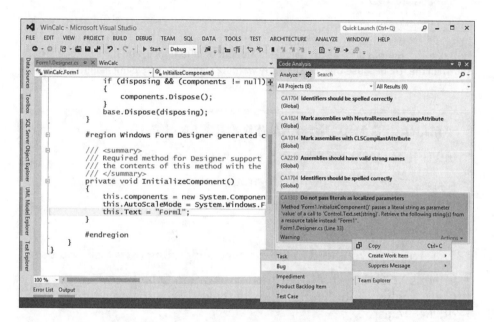

FIGURE 6.23: The warnings from code analysis appear in the IDE in a separate window. You can click each warning and jump to the source for viewing and editing, and directly create work items from a warning.

In addition to code analysis, VS enables you to look for early warning signals in your code, by calculating code metrics of your VS solution (see Figure 6.24). Those metrics include the cyclomatic complexity (the number of logical paths in your code), depth of inheritance, class coupling, and lines of code. Based on those values, VS calculates a maintainability index, which ranges between 0 and 100, where higher values mean that the code is easier to maintain, and lower numbers indicate that the code might be a good candidate for a future refactoring.

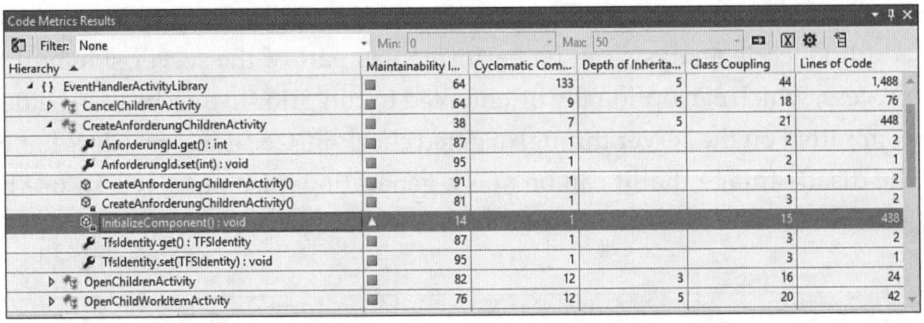
Code Metrics Results

Filter: None · Min: 0 · Max: 50

Hierarchy	Maintainability I...	Cyclomatic Com...	Depth of Inherita...	Class Coupling	Lines of Code
{ } EventHandlerActivityLibrary	64	133	5	44	1,488
CancelChildrenActivity	64	9	5	18	76
CreateAnforderungChildrenActivity	38	7	5	21	448
AnforderungId.get() : int	87	1		2	2
AnforderungId.set(int) : void	95	1		2	1
CreateAnforderungChildrenActivity()	91	1		1	2
CreateAnforderungChildrenActivity()	81	1		3	2
InitializeComponent() : void	14	1		15	438
TfsIdentity.get() : TFSIdentity	87	1		3	2
TfsIdentity.set(TFSIdentity) : void	95	1		3	1
OpenChildrenActivity	82	12	3	16	24
OpenChildWorkItemActivity	76	12	5	20	42

FIGURE 6.24: Metrics such as the complexity, depth of inheritance, and lines of code are shown in the IDE because they can be early warning signs for decreasing maintainability.

MANAGED AND UNMANAGED CODE ANALYSIS

In VS, there are three different code analysis mechanisms:

1. One for C/C++ that works from the source
2. One for managed code that works from the managed assemblies
3. One for T-SQL code

The steps that you need to follow vary depending on which you use.

See this MSDN topic: "Analyzing Application Quality by Using Code Analysis Tools" (http://msdn.microsoft.com/en-us/library/dd264897.aspx).

Catching Side Effects

Despite developers' best efforts to catch programming errors as early as possible, applications will still behave in unexpected ways. Sometimes developers will see them, and unfortunately sometimes they will first be reported by testers and customers.

Isolating Unexpected Behavior

Traditionally, isolating unexpected errors requires debugging. You as a developer have to create an experiment, imagining the initial conditions that led to the error and then manually forcing the steps to re-create the observed conditions. This experiment often requires lengthy trial and error, repeating the almost-same steps while trying to reproduce and locate the problem, while setting breakpoints, stepping through code, and writing log files to understand the command flow during the application's execution, even in production.

During each debugging pass, you look for any value that differs from what you expect. To investigate when and where the value was set, you typically set a few breakpoints, maybe improve your log files, and then restart the debugger and try to reproduce the behavior again (with the hope that it will recur).

VS reverses this manual and tedious approach with a feature called *IntelliTrace*, which is similar to a flight recorder in an airplane. IntelliTrace allows offline debugging, separating by time and space the investigation of a fault from the place of its occurrence.

During capture, IntelliTrace records two kinds of diagnostic information: a log with events and optionally the full call stack of the program's execution. You can control the amount of data collected and the categories of events to record via the Options dialog.

So, instead of setting breakpoints and restarting the debugger, you can break into the debugger at the very moment where the unexpected behavior is observed and be presented with the logged events and the executed calls. Then you can step both backward and forward.

Those IntelliTrace events are triggered by predefined actions in the .NET Framework, mostly raised by classes that access resources (such as file, Registry, or database access) or interaction with the UI (such as a message box or a control that was clicked or an exception that was thrown or caught), as shown in Figure 6.25. Often, just by looking at the events, you can get a sense of what has actually happened or even understand what caused it. Double-clicking an event jumps to the relevant line of code.

When configured to collect call information also, IntelliTrace records a list of all executed methods, including the arguments and return values, and shows them in the Locals window of the IDE. So that you can find out what happened during execution, IntelliTrace enables you to navigate through the method calls to an earlier point in time, by stepping back and forth, and updates the Locals window accordingly, as shown in Figure 6.26.

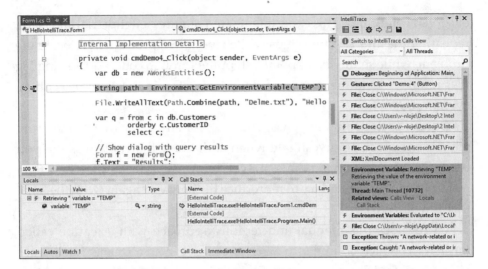

FIGURE 6.25: VS automatically creates an event log by logging certain events from the .NET class library, such as access to resources (files, Registry, database, Web requests).

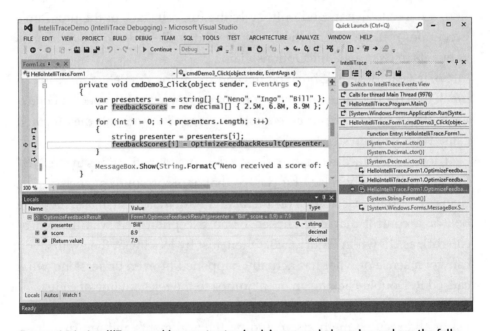

FIGURE 6.26: IntelliTrace enables you to step back in a recorded session and see the full stack trace beginning, from the start of the application, including relevant function parameters and return values.

▪ ENABLING INTELLITRACE DATA COLLECTION

In VS Ultimate, by default, only the IntelliTrace events are collected for every debugging session. The collection of call information needs to be explicitly turned on because it might impact the overall debugging performance.

In addition, Microsoft Test Manager supports recording of IntelliTrace information and attaches the logs to any bugs created during manual testing. (See Chapter 8 for a more detailed description of the tester/developer workflow.) Furthermore, IntelliTrace can be collected on additional test machines through a test agent.

To diagnose issues on production machines, the IntelliTrace Collector (available from the MS Download Center) contains a command-line version as well as PowerShell scripts to allow lightweight collection of IntelliTrace logs.

Isolating the Root Cause in Production

Similar to IntelliTrace, but specifically for production issues, you can integrate TFS with operations. System Center Operations Manager forwards *operational issues* (a new work item type) to TFS, as shown in Figure 6.27.

The payload of an operational issue is similar to an IntelliTrace log. When you open an operational issue, you can see the precise circumstances under which the event occurred, repeat occurrences, similar and related events, performance counters, exceptions, parameters, a stack trace, and the lines of code involved, as shown in Figure 6.28. You can further click to navigate from the execution context of the code to the source view, so that you can correct the error in the right branch and produce a new build for operations.

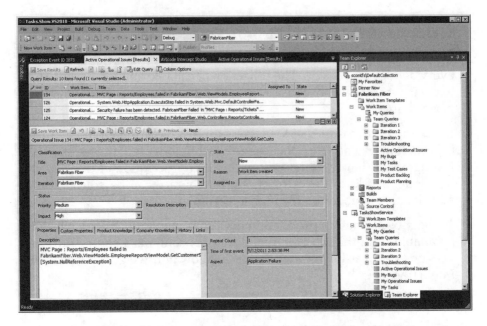

FIGURE 6.27: Operational Issues now appear in TFS automatically, through the Connector, available for Microsoft System Center Operations Manager 2012 R2 and TFS 2012.

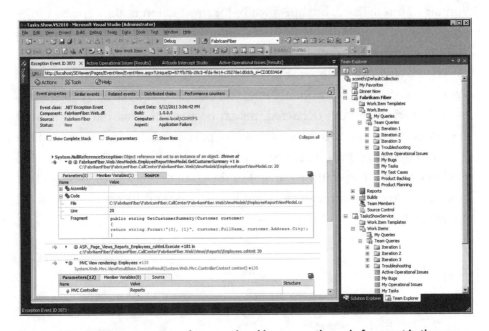

FIGURE 6.28: In VS, you can open the operational issue, see the code fragment in the context of the failure, and then jump to the line of code in the appropriate version of the right branch to make the fix.

Tuning Performance

Unit testing and code analysis are tools that you should apply before every check-in, to make sure that your code does the right thing in the right way. Performance profiling is different. When you have performance problems, it might be a small portion of your code that is culpable, or it might be an external call, so you should focus your tuning efforts there. Frequently, the problems appear under load tests (discussed in Chapter 8); sometimes, though, you can discover them through routine functional testing or exploratory walk-throughs. Usually the first step is to find the parts of your application that are underperforming.

To diagnose performance errors, you launch a profiling session and select from the current solution the code projects on which you want to collect data (see Figure 6.29). Enabling the *Multi-Tier Analysis* feature on Web or database applications includes executed SQL statements as well as ASP.NET Web requests in the resulting performance report. This gives you an end-to-end view on the performance behavior and possible bottlenecks in your multitier application.

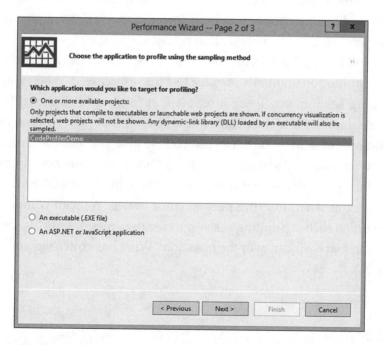

FIGURE 6.29: VS provides a wizard that instruments the code under test for profiling.

■ USING TESTS TO DRIVE PERFORMANCE PROFILING

You can use your unit tests in VS to drive performance profiling sessions. See this MSDN topic: "How To: Create a Performance Session for a Test" (http://msdn.microsoft.com/en-us/library/ms184783.aspx).

You need to choose between four profiling techniques. Sampling enables you to collect data without perceivable overhead, indicating how often a method appears in the call stack, as shown in Figure 6.30. Typically, you start with sampling. Instrumented profiling, on the other hand, lets you walk traced call sequences with much more data, at the cost of some overhead and expanded binary size. Use instrumented profiling to drill into the hot spots that sampling reveals. The .NET Memory Allocation mode helps you identify methods that allocate too much memory. Use this if you suspect parts of your application take up more memory than you expected. Finally, use Concurrency mode to drill down into your multi-threaded application to see how it is performing and to determine whether it is experiencing any synchronization issues.

After you have selected your target and the technique, you can either drive the application manually or run a test that exercises it. When you stop the profiling session, you'll see a report that lets you drill down from a high-level summary into the details of the calls. A "hot path" button marks the most time-consuming parts of your code to give you a starting point for further investigation. As there is always a "hot path," this doesn't necessarily indicate a problem that needs to be fixed, but it would be the first place to look at when hunting performance issues. You can compare the results with an earlier profiling session to see the areas of improvement or degradation and easily answer the question "What has gotten slower?" (see Figure 6.31).

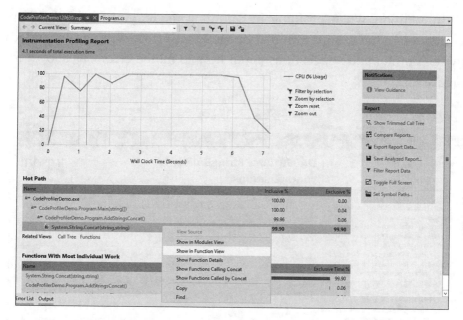

FIGURE 6.30: Profiling data appears in a pyramid of information, with the most important data on the Summary page, as shown here. This might be all you need. From here, you can either drill down into further detail or jump to the source of method shown.

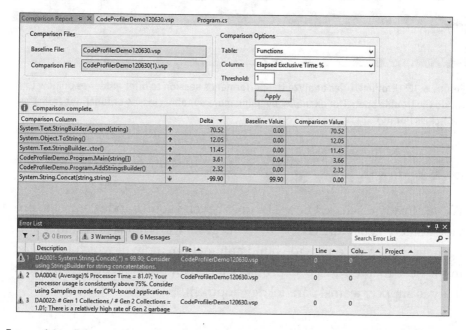

FIGURE 6.31: By comparing two performance sessions, you can see the progress and relative changes in performance between the two points of analysis.

In addition, when profiling in Sampling mode, you can click **View Guidance** on the Results Summary page to see error warnings generated by the profiler and suggestions about how to fix the errors, as shown in Figure 6.32.

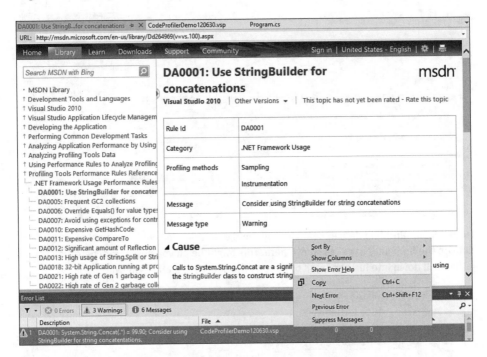

FIGURE 6.32: Profiling rules analyze the performance session to offer guidance on how to tackle the trouble spots (for example, by using more suitable classes or functions from the .NET class library).

Preventing Version Skew

We've already discussed how TFS goes beyond source code control to provide a safety net before check-in, to integrate work items and source code in changesets, and to provide build automation, more of which is covered in the next chapter. TFS also provides a rich and flexible branching capability to support teams' parallel development.

What to Version

Versioning is not just for source code. You should version all files associated with compiling, configuring, deploying, testing, and running your system (see Figure 6.33). By default, the tests and most of the configuration files are part of your VS solution and appear as files to check in when you look at the Source Control Explorer.

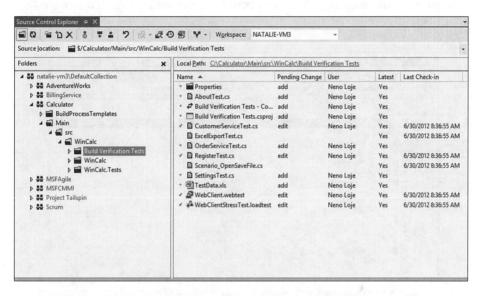

FIGURE 6.33: TFS "Source control" tracks all the files in your workspace, including tests, XML files, icons, and so on. Check in your tests with your source.

Remember that your database is also part of your application. Database schema is checked in and versioned the same way as source code, and stored as a set of SQL scripts. *Schema Compare* analyzes the versioned schema against another version or a physical SQL Server instance and optionally applies those updates directly or saves them as a SQL script, as shown in Figure 6.34.

If you expect to maintain your solution for a long time, it is worth creating a "tools" team project in which you keep the versions of the compiler and support programs (for example, *msbuild* and *mstest*) that you use to re-create and retest the solution. For example, commercial software companies may have contracts to support products for ten years, and in many government situations, contracts are longer. In a world where tool updates are available quarterly, having a definitive record of the build and test environment may be necessary to support your customer. Similarly simple dependencies (such as DLLs) should be kept in version control, making it easy to re-create a complete development environment with a simple GET operation.

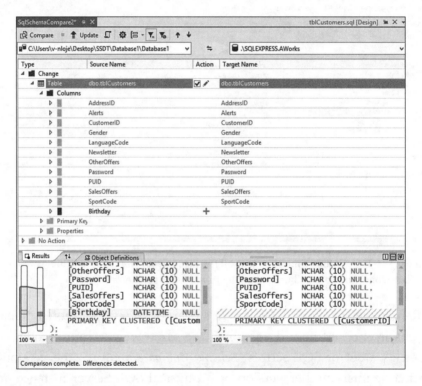

FIGURE 6.34: Database schema gets checked in to version control as a set of SQL scripts. That versioned schema can be compared and synchronized with "live" SQL Server instances.

Branching

If you've used other source control systems, you're probably familiar with the concept of branching. The good news is that having branches lets you keep parallel versions of files that evolve separately. The bad news is that, *whenever you branch, you may be creating a future need to merge.* The bugs you fix for version 1 probably need to be fixed in version 2 as well. If you have multiple branches, you will have multiple merges to consider.

Therefore, *use branches sparingly and intentionally.* If you need to do something temporary, use a shelveset instead. They don't require the maintenance, and when you're done with your shelveset, it goes away. Branches are for separations of code that you intend to maintain separately for extended periods.

Working on Different Versions in Parallel

Branches give you multiple, isolated versions of the same codebase. The main two reasons to branch are as follows:

- To isolate work by team, feature, or purpose (branch by feature)
- To separate released versions for maintenance and hot-fixing (branch by release)

Examples for work isolation include branching to support large teams efficiently or creating experimental branches, which are used to try out new things without interfering with any other ongoing work. An example of a branch plan that uses two branches is shown in Figure 6.35, where development takes place on the development branch and completed PBIs are reverse integrated into a main line that is always kept in a stable and releasable state to minimize risk.

The second frequent use of branches is to track multiple released versions of a solution. When releasing version 1, you can branch before you start work on version 2. If you subsequently need to fix bugs or issue a service release (perhaps for new environments) for version 1, you can do so in its branch without having to pull in any version 2 code. This is often called *branching by release.* Figure 6.36 shows a sample branching plan.

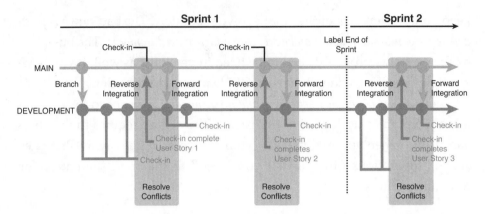

FIGURE 6.35: Branching by feature allows teams to work in parallel work streams and integrate changes once they meet a defined set of done criteria.

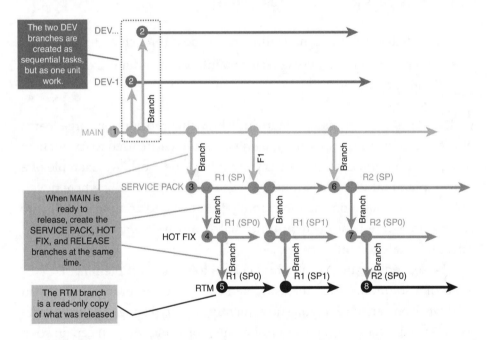

FIGURE 6.36: This is a mature branching scheme with a development line branched by feature and a main line branched by release, as described in http://tfsbranchingguideiii.codeplex.com/.

In VS, branches are a special form of folder and indicated by a special icon (see Figure 6.37). In addition to regular folders, they have an assigned owner and description, and their branch relationships can be shown as a hierarchy (see Figure 6.38).

FIGURE 6.37: In the TFS Source Code Explorer, branches are a special type of folder and, therefore, use different icons to help find the relevant branch folders to work in.

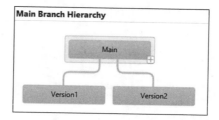

FIGURE 6.38: A visual representation of the full branch hierarchy helps in understanding branch relationships, which do not have to correlate with the source control folder structures.

Merging and Tracking Changes across Branches

TFS tracks changes by changeset. The operation to copy changes from one branch to another is called *merging*. As changes are merged using VS, those changesets can be tracked using a view that shows the branch hierarchy, or in a timeline view as shown in Figures 6.39 and 6.40. Best of all, if a work item such as a user story or task has associated changesets, the work item itself can be tracked using the same view and the merge performed by work item.

In some special situations, it might be necessary to merge changes between branches that do not have a direct branch relationship, as shown in the branch hierarchy. VS enables those *baseless merges* and tracks them accordingly as if they were regular merges (see Figure 6.41).

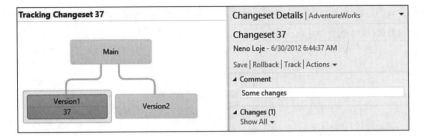

FIGURE 6.39: Tracking a changeset: A change, specifically changeset 37, has been checked into the "Version 1" branch, but has not been merged into the two other branches yet.

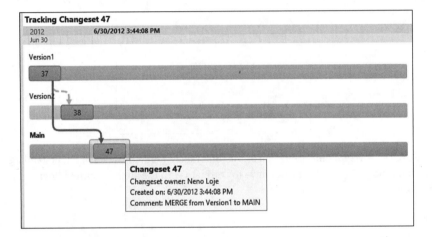

FIGURE 6.40: The merge of changeset 37 to the MAIN branch, committed as changeset, 47, shown in timeline view.

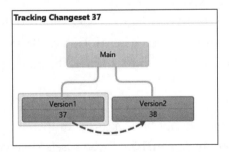

FIGURE 6.41: Changeset 37 has been merged to a branch that does not have a direct branch relationship using a "baseless merge."

■ DEFINING A BRANCHING STRATEGY

For details on how to use branches to structure your development, see the following MSDN topic as well as the Branching Guide on CodePlex:

MSDN topic: "Branch Strategically"

http://msdn.microsoft.com/en-us/library/ee782536.aspx

Visual Studio TFS Branching and Merging Guide on CodePlex:

http://vsarbranchingguide.codeplex.com/

Working with Eclipse or the Windows Shell Directly

Most of the tooling presented so far (check-in policies, shelvesets, branching, and gated check-ins) is not only available within the VS IDE, but also in Eclipse, through the Team Explorer Everywhere (TEE) plug-in, or through Windows Explorer, using the TFS Power Tools (see Figures 6.42 and 6.43).

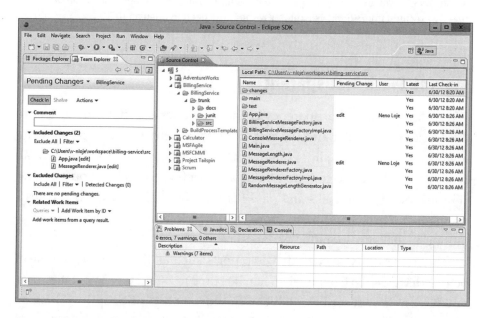

FIGURE 6.42: Team Explorer Everywhere integrates all the TFS capabilities (such as work items, team builds, and version control) right into the Eclipse IDE.

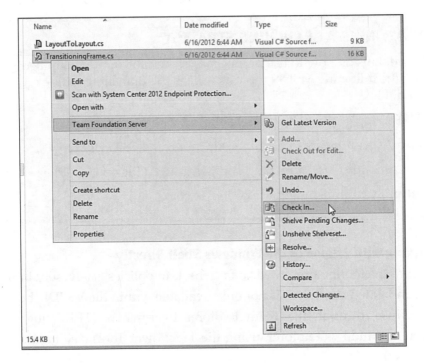

FIGURE 6.43: If you use a Windows shell extension version, control operations can be directly executed from Windows Explorer without the need to open an IDE.

Making Work Transparent

VS applies the same transparency to the developer activities that it does to the work item backlog and the rest of the team activities. It treats all team members as part of one integrated workflow. Because all work items of all types are stored in the common database, when you check in you can (and should) identify the tasks *and the PBIs* that the delivered code and tests implement. This creates a link from those work items that traces their resolution to the corresponding changesets.

This traceability in turn drives reports such as the ones on the dashboards discussed in Chapter 4. When it is time to estimate the next iteration, you have a daily record available of the current and prior sprints' history. These metrics are collected for you, and they take the guesswork (and grunt work) out of determining the actual baseline trends.

Consider, for example, Figure 6.44, the Build Quality Indicators report. Trends have been automatically captured for the team, and the trends show correlations. In this example, rising code churn, falling code coverage, and falling test pass rates are an early warning that tests—in particular, BVTs—are getting stale and that the team should probably update the BVTs now. Typically, this kind of pattern might not show up until the end of the sprint, but with TFS, it shows up every day.

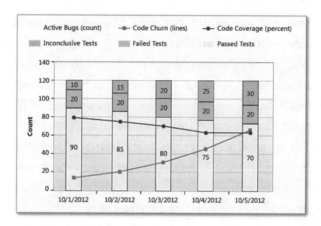

FIGURE 6.44: The Build Quality Indicators report pulls together test results, active bug count, code churn, and coverage in one view so that you can spot unhealthy relationships and warning signs of growing technical debt before it becomes a problem. This report shows a decrease in code being checked in without corresponding unit tests to cover it.

Similarly, this traceability drives the Build report, shown in the next chapter in Figure 7.6, so that the whole team (notably testers) can automatically see what work is available in which build with what quality. There's no mystery of "Did feature X make it in?" or "Did it pass BVTs?" The Build report provides a reliable, friction-free view to trigger the testing cycle based on builds. (See Chapter 7 for details.)

Summary

The Agile Consensus is all about delivering working code of customer-ready quality in a continual flow. This chapter described how to achieve the flow in the daily cycle of development. The first issue is to use TFS not merely as source control, but as an early warning system and gatekeeper to catch problems before they enter the codebase. If you keep the code clean, you don't need to worry about the rework of fixing it later.

Next, the chapter covered the four project smells that you are trying to detect early: errors, side effects, version skew, and lack of transparency. First, test-driven development is your best guard against programming errors. The practice forces clarification of requirements before you begin implementation. The testing support directly inside VS makes it easy to create and run unit tests, to apply test data, and to promote these tests for reuse with every build. You can also use code analysis and reviews to check for programming errors that might not be caught in unit testing.

Second, unforeseen side effects in behavior or environment can be diagnosed with IntelliTrace, an offline type of debugging available from an application log. A similar capability from System Center Operations Manager lets you isolate production errors to the line of code in the right version of source maintained by TFS. Further, VS lets you extend unit testing with test data and configurations and supports direct performance profiling from the test runs to isolate performance hot spots.

Third is the complexity of version control and the tracking of as-built software to the source code. Not only does VS integrate version control and work item and build automation, but it also supports a full branching strategy for the team to maintain parallel versions over time. Branching strategies are discussed so that your team can settle on the right approach for your context.

The fourth and last issue is the difficulty of transparently keeping track of all the information sources. VS does the bookkeeping for you automatically. TFS provides an audit trail of source and work item changes going into every build. Check-in policies work as reminders to support a done list for the team. It supports transparency of the process with its common work item database, metrics warehouse, and integration of code and test changes with work items and the build system. In this way, VS lets you, as a developer, focus on the substance of your work without overhead.

The next chapter looks at the automated build and deployment process and how automating the definition of *done* further accelerates the flow of value.

Endnotes

1 www.agilemanifesto.org

2 Barry W. Boehm, *Software Engineering Economics* (Englewood Cliffs, NJ: Prentice Hall, 1981).

3 TFS Power Tools, http://msdn.microsoft.com/en-us/vstudio/ bb980963.aspx, available from the VS Gallery.

4 www.extremeprogramming.org/rules/pair.html and http://c2.com/cgi/wiki?PairProgramming.

5 Glenford J. Myers, *The Art of Software Testing* (New York: John Wiley & Sons, 1979).

6 For example, K. Beck and E. Gamma, "Test infected: Programmers love writing tests," *Java Report* 3:7, 51–56, 1998.

7 Robert C. Martin, *Clean Code: A Handbook of Agile Software Craftsman-ship* (Upper Saddle River, NJ: Prentice Hall, 2008), 14.

8 Pex and Moles - Isolation and White box Unit Testing for .NET, http://research.microsoft.com/projects/pex/.

9 For example, www.testing.com/writings/short-catalog.pdf

10 Brian Marick, "Faults of Omission," first published in *Software Testing and Quality Engineering Magazine*, January 2000, available from www.testing.com/writings/omissions.html.

7

Build and Lab

Continuous deployment is continuous flow applied to software. The goal of both is to eliminate waste. The biggest waste in manufacturing is created from having to transport products from one place to another. The biggest waste in software is created from waiting for software as it moves from one state to another: Waiting to code, waiting to test, waiting to deploy. Reducing or eliminating these waits leads to faster iterations which is the key to success.

—Eric Ries[1]

Source: Andrejs Segorovs/Shutterstock.com

FIGURE 7.1: If the flow of value is kept constant, like the wheel rotates at a constant speed, and the individual team members focus on the work at their normal pace, a highly productive yet unstressful environment may be created.

AN AGILE SOFTWARE DEVELOPMENT TEAM strives to increase *customer value* delivered through *working* software. The *cycle time* required to deliver the smallest product backlog item (PBI), say a one-line change, to production, so that the customer can use it and benefit, is a good measure of the team's mastery of flow. The shorter the cycle time, the more effectively the team can embrace new PBIs from the customer.

Cycle Time

Of course, cycle time for PBIs is a much more involved concept than it is for the flow of a stream on a waterwheel. First a PBI is broken into tasks in the sprint backlog. Then the team does the tasks, mostly in code and tests driven by related tooling through the intermediate cycles shown in Figure 7.2. For each task, each intermediate cycle, including check-in, integration with other changes, verification, acceptance testing, and deployment, can happen one to many times.

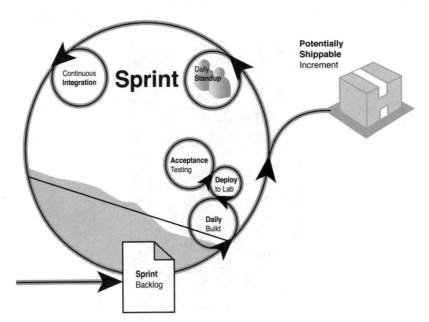

FIGURE 7.2: The developer's check-in triggers a continuous integration build, and the daily build feeds the deployment of a potentially shippable increment into a test lab, including build verification tests (BVTs).

In order to achieve continuous flow through the whole cycle, the smaller cycles need to flow too. It's a circulatory system, where a blockage in one area will quickly create negative feedback that saps resources and flow from the others, causing delivery to become unpredictable or stop altogether. This chapter is about the supporting processes and tools that enable your team to establish continuous delivery of value, by ensuring that intermediate flows are continuous, and thereby enable the continuous deployment of working software.

Defining *Done*

Delivering software continuously is only useful if the software works. The goal is to deliver every piece of functionality in a potentially shippable form with the same defined quality. One of the most important aspects to achieve a constant quality is to have a clear definition of *done* in place. Without the consistent, measurable definition of done, technical debt will grow inevitably.

Although this seems obvious, many teams do not take the time to reflect during release planning and make their definition of *done* for a given project explicit. We urge every team to do that first. During such a discussion, many different perspectives are usually presented about what quality is and what the relevant done criteria are. As discussed in Chapter 3, "Product Ownership," the definition of *done* belongs to the whole team.

When creating your team's definition of *done,* consider the following:

- **Explicit definition of done:** The resulting definition of *done* should be made transparent to everyone (for example, putting it on the wall so that everybody on the team can see it).

- **Constant quality:** All criteria defined as part of the definition of *done* must be fulfilled for every PBI, in addition to any acceptance criteria defined in the PBI itself.

- **Important for estimates:** A clear understanding of what *done* means and what activities are included is a prerequisite for estimation and sprint planning. In addition, if the definition of *done* changes between sprints, the measured velocity (number of story points delivered within a sprint) may not be true and might therefore be worthless.

- **Enterprise standards:** The definition of *done* is owned by the team, but organizational requirements might also influence it.
- **Measurable:** Done criteria should be measurable. This means that every developer on the team should have the same understanding about what it takes to fulfill specific done criteria.
- **Automated:** Because a sprint usually lasts 2 to 4 weeks (which comes down to 10 to 20 working days, minus time for meetings), it makes sense to automate as much of the done as possible.

The definition of done sets the *minimum* quality bar the team has to reach for each PBI. If the team does not reach it, the PBI is not complete and therefore not potentially shippable. If a team is serious about its definition of *done,* that will prevent accumulation of technical debt and the customer can expect a defined and constant level of quality, without regard to whether a feature was implemented at the beginning of a project or shortly before release. Remember that the definition of *done* defined only the *minimum* set. You can still do more if it makes sense or doing so is defined in the PBI itself.

A typical antipattern in many teams is a squishy done criterion, where developers can get away with doing less when pressured for time. An example of that would be "write maintainable code" without a way of determining what makes code maintainable. In contrast, a good done definition might include a goal that the changes do not increase the measured complexity of the codebase, a code review process (manual and automated), and a set of conventions and patterns to apply. Layer diagrams that validate dependencies against the intended structure, as shown in Chapter 5, "Architecture," are a great example of the automated review.

The rest of this chapter focuses on automated checking against the definition of *done* so that individual team members have more time to concentrate on their core activities. Manual activities should be kept to a minimum. For instance, new builds should be available for testing without any manual intervention. The first assessment that happens right after the developers check in is the continuous integration cycle, shown in Figure 7.2. It can occur many times a day, after the developer finishes working on a task.

Continuous Integration

Continuous integration[2] (CI) refers to the practice of automatically triggering a build after every check-in to verify the changes made to the system. This is an essential Agile practice to automate the definition of *done* by validating the checked-in changes against a set of defined criteria.

CI has been proven very successful in eXtreme Programming and the Agile Consensus in that it delivers immediate feedback about integration errors to a developer who has just checked in. It is much easier for developers to investigate and fix bugs they just checked in a few minutes ago than three weeks later when they are probably working on something else.

Ideally, if the build breaks, the developer who broke the build can fix it right away without losing context. During that time, no other developer should check in.

The larger a team is, or more specifically the larger the number of developers checking in to a folder or branch, the more likely it is that the build will break. Without a build, there is no "heartbeat" to the project (because the testers depend on a working build to validate against the requirements). In this way, CI also warns the rest of the team about "patient health."

Visual Studio (VS) has two different CI modes: (classic) continuous integration (CI) and gated check-in (GC). You can set up any build definition for CI and trigger the build from check-in events (see Figure 7.3).

A less-permissive form of CI is the *gated check-in*. The GC acts as the "gatekeeper" of the source code repository. In contrast to the classic CI approach, which is optimistic (after all, the build is validated *after* it has already been committed to version control), a GC turns this process the other way around. When a developer checks in code, it is not automatically committed. Rather, the GC triggers the build definition first, including all validation steps (such as test runs, code analysis, and architectural validation) and checks in the code on behalf of the developer only after the build completes successfully. Figure 7.4 shows a team project that is guarded by a build definition with GC.

```
┌────────────────────────────────────────────────────────────────────────────┐
│ General        │ Select one of the following check-in triggers:            │
│ Trigger        │                                                            │
│ Workspace      │  ○ Manual - Check-ins do not trigger a new build          │
│ Build Defaults │                                                            │
│ Process        │  ● Continuous Integration - Build each check-in           │
│ Retention Policy│                                                           │
│                │  ○ Rolling builds - accumulate check-ins until the prior build finishes │
│                │     ☐ Build no more often than every [        ] minutes.  │
│                │                                                            │
│                │  ○ Gated Check-in - accept check-ins only if the submitted changes merge and build successfully │
│                │     ☐ Merge and build up to [        ] submissions.       │
│                │                                                            │
│                │  ○ Schedule - build every week on the following days      │
│                │     ☑ Monday  ☑ Tuesday  ☑ Wednesday  ☑ Thursday  ☑ Friday│
│                │     ☐ Saturday  ☐ Sunday                                  │
│                │     Queue the build on the build controller at:           │
│                │     [3:00 AM              ▼] | Pacific Daylight Time (UTC -07:00) │
│                │     ☐ Build even if nothing has changed since the previous build │
└────────────────────────────────────────────────────────────────────────────┘
```

FIGURE 7.3: Create a separate build definition to perform CI. Keeping the daily build as a separate build definition will keep trend metrics tracked to the daily build.

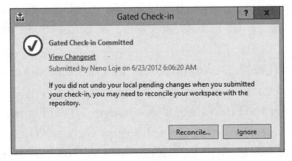

FIGURE 7.4: Gated check-ins ensure that checked-in changes are validated through an automated build definition before being committed to the repository. The Reconcile option syncs the local workspaces with the server by removing the committed pending changes.

With GCs, bad check-ins affecting the work of other team members are kept to a minimum.

The next step of validating the definition of *done* occurs at the daily build cycle. This cycle gathers important metrics and produces the official binaries for testing and later release.

Automating the Build

CI is only part of an automated build system, as shown in Figure 7.2. The build system needs to automate not only compilation but also the tracking and testing of the binaries against the source versions. The build needs to provide as many quality checks as possible so that any errors can be corrected before investment of further testing. This approach ensures that testing time (especially human time) is used appropriately.

In VS, automated builds can be configured from Team Explorer (see Figure 7.5). You can have differently named build definitions, such as a daily build, a CI or GC build, and a branch build, each running separate scripts and tests. The team should designate which build definition produces the official binaries that are going to be deployed for further testing and released afterward.

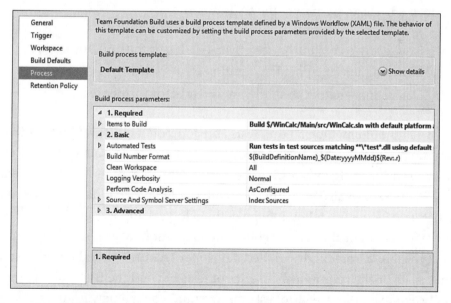

FIGURE 7.5: In this dialog, you can create a build definition (that is, the daily build and other regular builds that you automate for the full team project).

> ### ▪ CONFIGURING BUILD DEFINITIONS
>
> For more information about build definition options in VS, see this MSDN topic: "Creating and Working with Build Definitions" (http://msdn.microsoft.com/en-us/library/ms181715.aspx).

Daily Build

Using separate build definitions for CI and daily builds ensures that daily metrics are gathered through the daily builds.[3] At a minimum, you should have a build configuration for daily builds that not only creates the binaries that you install but also runs all the code analysis and BVTs and generates the metrics that track the health of your project. This allows appropriate trends to be gathered in the metrics warehouse and shown in reports and dashboards, like the ones used in Chapter 4, "Running the Sprint."

BVTs

Every build should go through a consistent series of BVTs to automate the definition of *done*. On many projects, these are the primary regression tests performed. The objectives of the BVTs are to

- Isolate any errors introduced by check-ins or the build process, including unanticipated integration errors
- Determine whether the software is ready for further testing

BVTs should include all unit tests and component integration tests that are run prior to check-in, plus any other tests that are needed to ensure that it is worth spending time testing the software further. BVTs are automated. In VS, builds can also perform an architectural layer validation, to detect whether changes are following the defined logical application design. (For more information about the architecture validation toolset, see Chapter 5.)

Typically, a tester or designated developer "scouts" a build for the team; that is, he or she runs a further series of tests beyond the BVTs, often manually. For example, scenario tests may require using a new graphical user interface (GUI) that is still rapidly evolving, and automation may not be cost-effective yet. For this reason, the report contains a Build Quality field that you can set manually. After build completion, the field is empty. You can set it after that to Rejected, Under Investigation, Ready for Initial Test, Lab Test Passed, Initial Test Passed, UAT Passed, Ready for Deployment, Released, or other values that you have customized.

Build Report

Upon completion of the daily build, you get a Build report (see Figure 7.6). This shows you the results of build completion, code analysis, and BVT runs. In the case of a failed build, it gives you a link to the Bug work item that was created so that you can notify the appropriate team member to fix and restart the build.

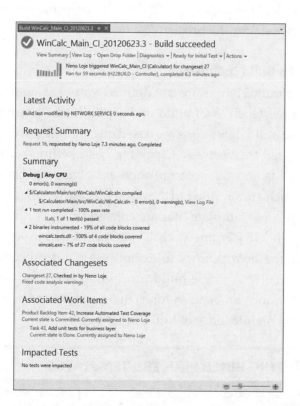

FIGURE 7.6: The Build report both monitors the real-time execution of a build and aggregates the details of a build upon completion.

Use the Build report to monitor the execution of a build and view the details of a completed build and the work item changes documenting what went into the build. The test result details show you the BVT results and the code coverage from BVTs. Build warnings include the results from static code analysis. From this report, you can publish the build quality status.

The list of associated changesets and work items is calculated between the current and the last successful build of the same build definition. Therefore, a daily build shows all code changes and work items incorporated since the last daily build, whereas a release build shows a list of all changes checked in since the last release.

Note that you can navigate directly from the Build report to the changesets that are included, the code-analysis warnings, and the test results. The data shown on the Build report is fed directly to the metrics warehouse to create historical data for the project.

Maintaining the Build Definitions

In VS, multiple build definitions are defined for the same project to serve different purposes (such as CI build or daily build) or to support different branches. Those build definitions are based on *build process templates* (which can be customized themselves). Changing basic settings of what a build definition does is mostly accomplished by changing build definition parameters, which are supplied to the build process template file upon execution. Build process template files are created using Windows Workflow Foundation from .NET Framework 4.5 and are stored in XAML files. You can customize these workflows to extend the build process beyond the built-in functionality. A single build process template can serve multiple build definitions and can be used for as many projects as necessary, which eases the central maintenance of build processes.

■ CUSTOMIZING BUILD PROCESS TEMPLATES

For information about how to customize build process template files in VS, refer to *Inside the Microsoft Build Engine: Using MSBuild and Team Foundation Build*, by Sayed Ibrahim Hashimi and William Bartholomew (Microsoft Press, 2011).

Maintaining the Build Agents

Build definitions execute on build agents. A controller manages those agents. At minimum, you need one build controller and one build agent. You can have as many agents as necessary to support different needs. Build agents are categorized using tags, and the required tags can be defined as part of the build definition (see Figures 7.7 and 7.8).

Using automated builds and BVTs ensures that a build is ready to be considered for further testing. BVTs are executed on the build server, and should contain tests that check whether the code actually does what it is supposed to, but they do not answer whether the application works in a production environment. The next step is to validate the application in a test lab environment. Ideally, the test environment matches the later production environment, so that automated and manual testing can be conducted against that environment with confidence.

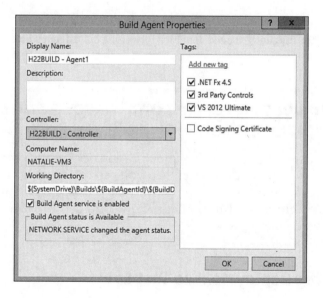

Figure 7.7: Different build agents can be used for different projects and purposes. Each build agent can be categorized using tags.

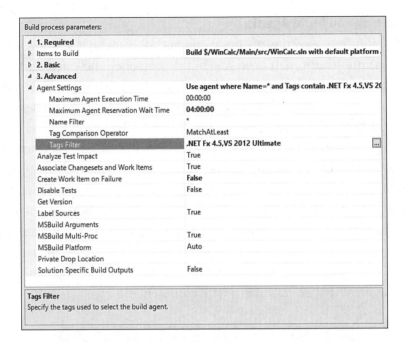

Figure 7.8: When triggering, a build definition looks for a build agent with a matching set of tags.

> ■ **CONTINUOUS DEPLOYMENT INTO WINDOWS AZURE FROM TEAM FOUNDATION SERVICE**
>
> If you are using the hosted Team Foundation *Service* and creating an Azure Web site or cloud service, then you can set up your build automation to deploy continuously into the public cloud. For a step-by-step guide, see http://tfspreview.com/en-us/learn/build/continuous-delivery-in-vs/.

Automating Deployment to Test Lab

VS optimizes the way you work with virtual machines (VMs) for labs,[4] by supporting the following scenarios:

- Speeding up the creation and maintenance of virtual machines with different configurations that are as equal as possible to the production environment in use

- Automating deployment to the VMs right from the build process (a potentially long, vastly manual, error-prone, and recurring process)
- Running automated tests on the VMs before handover to manual testers (and saves time by making sure the current build actually works)
- Enabling snapshots of complete test environments (to aid later bug reproduction)

Setting Up a Test Lab

When you have combinations to test, cycling physical test lab machines among them can be a huge drain on time. Normally, you must clean each machine after a previous installation by restoring it to the base operating system, installing the components, and then configuring them. If you are rotating many configurations, this preparation time can dwarf the actual time available for testing.

A great amount of time is wasted in manually setting up test environments and verifying that current builds actually work (which can be complex for multitier applications, as shown in Figure 7.9). In the worst case, you might spend time deploying the application only to discover that it actually does not even start as expected. Because this is often a manual process, testers tend to work with a build for quite a while (sometimes even weeks) before (manually) deploying the next one. This leads to unnecessarily long cycle times (because testers usually prefer to test what they have than to wait with nothing to test while a new build, even if fresher, is being deployed).

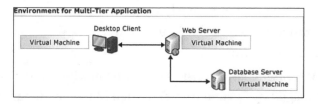

FIGURE 7.9: A Web application might require a complex test environment (because it consists of a client, a Web server, and a database server).

An alternative is to set up the different configurations on virtual machines using Microsoft Hyper-V Server, System Center Virtual Machine Manager, and the Lab Management feature included in Team Foundation Server (TFS; see Figure 7.10). Instead of installing and configuring physical machines, you install and configure virtual machines and store them in the VM library. When the virtual machine is running, it appears to the software and network to be identical to a physical machine, but you can save the entire machine image as a disk file and reload it on command.

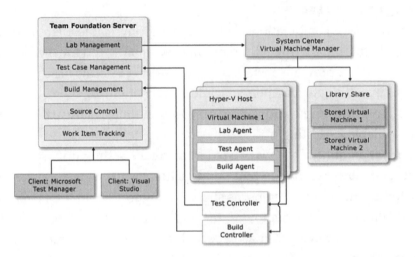

FIGURE 7.10: TFS includes System Center Virtual Machine Manager and Hyper-V to enable the creation of complex, virtualized lab environments, in which applications get automatically deployed and tested.

VS offers two ways to set up test environments:

- A *Standard environment* is a machine that already exists. This can be a physical machine or any virtual machine instance created with any virtualization technology. VS can deploy the application and run tests on those environments.

- A *SCVMM environment* consists of virtual machines on a Hyper-V host managed by System Center Virtual Machine Manager (SCVMM). In addition, these test environments support deployment, automated starting/stopping, and snapshots via MTM.

For the following examples in this chapter, we assume the second case of VMs running on Hyper-V and with SCVMM.

Does It Work in Production as Well as in the Lab?

Have you ever filed a bug and heard the response, "But it works on my machine"? Or have you ever heard the datacenter complain about the cost of staging because the software as tested never works without reconfiguration for the production environment?

These are symptoms of inadequate configuration testing. Configuration testing is critical in three cases:

1. Datacenters lock down their servers with very specific settings and often have a defined number of managed configurations. It is essential that the settings of the test environment match the datacenter environment in all applicable ways.
2. Software vendors and other organizations that cannot precisely control customers' configurations need to be able to validate their software across the breadth of configurations that will actually be used.
3. Software that is used internationally will encounter different operating system settings in different countries, including different character sets, hardware, and input methods, which will require specific testing.

Fortunately, VS supports explicit configuration testing both by enabling you to set up test labs with virtual as well as physical machines and by explicitly tracking test configurations and recording all test results against which all test results are reported. That means that you have to install and prepare virtual machines just once, store them as templates in the library, and then you can create as many test environments from them as necessary. Figures 7.11 to 7.14 show the creation of new test environments. Test machines are installed like regular machines, with the exception that an agent that supports automated deployment and testing is installed on them.

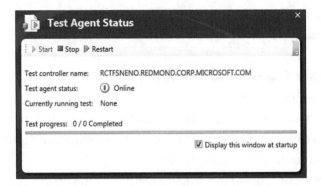

FIGURE 7.11: Agents are installed on the test machines to enable automated deployment, running of tests, and extensive data collection for bug reporting.

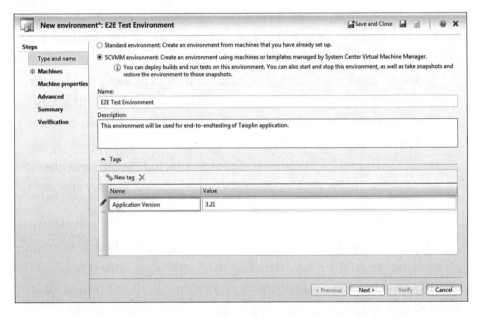

FIGURE 7.12: Test environments consist of one or more virtual or physical machines that are required to adequately represent the production environment.

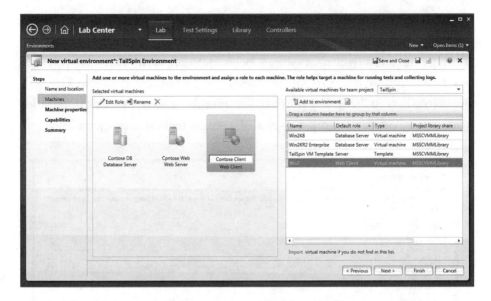

FIGURE 7.13: Your solution might need to run in different target environments. These might be different localized versions of the operating system, different versions of supporting components (such as databases and Web servers), or different configurations of your solution. Virtual machines are a low-overhead way of capturing the environments in software so that you can run tests in a self-contained image for the specific configuration.

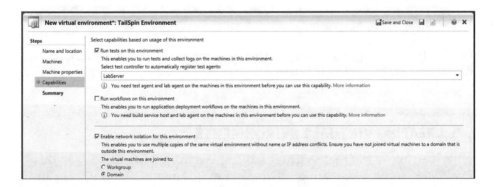

FIGURE 7.14: VS supports running automated tests through agents on the test machines. In addition, you can spin up multiple environments without worrying about name or IP address conflicts.

Setting up a library of virtual machines means that you will go through the setup and configuration once, not with every test cycle.

After test environments have been defined, you can use physical machines right away; virtual machines can be deployed to real Hyper-V hosts (see Figure 7.15). If different team members have to work in parallel, you usually deploy multiple copies of a single test environment.

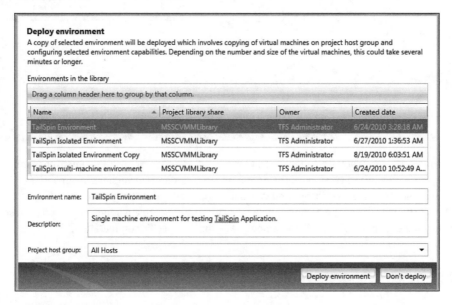

FIGURE 7.15: Deploying an environment deploys the contained virtual machines to a Hyper-V host and leaves them in a state ready to be used for testing.

▪ CREATING VIRTUAL ENVIRONMENTS

To learn how to create virtual lab test environments in VS, see this MSDN topic: "Creating Virtual Environments" (http://msdn. microsoft. com/en-us/library/dd380688.aspx).

Automating Deployment and Test

Your process goal, as suggested in Figure 7.2, should be to have every daily build deployed into the test lab automatically for a full testing cycle.

Anything else slows down the cycle and flow of PBIs to completion. Accordingly, part of your daily build definition should be the deployment.

In VS, a section of the build definition is responsible for the deployment of the build to the appropriate test machines in the lab environment (as shown in Figures 7.16 to 7.19). Optionally, you can revert to a clean state using virtual machine snapshots, if desired, and you can run a set of automated tests, including UI tests that exercise the user interface. (See Figures 7.20 and 7.21 and Chapter 8, "Test," for more information about UI testing.) Manual testing does not begin to verify the changes in the test environments until automated tests certify a defined level of quality.

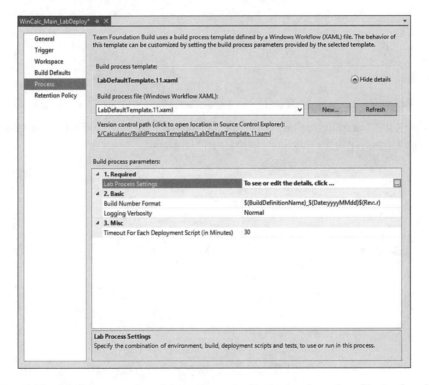

FIGURE 7.16: A build process template manages deployment and running of tests of applications through a build definition.

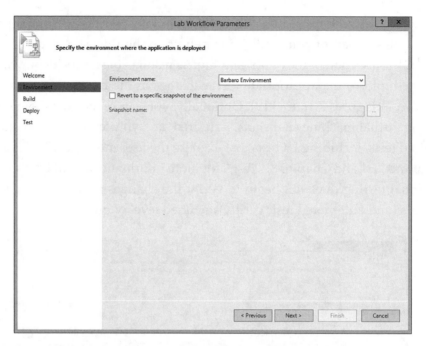

FIGURE 7.17: Snapshots can be used to revert to a clean state each time before the application gets deployed to the actual test environment for testing.

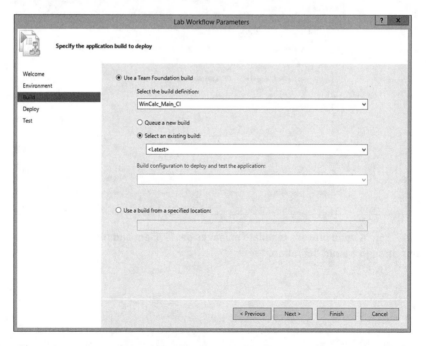

FIGURE 7.18: The version of the application that gets deployed can either be the output of the current build (the normal case) or a pointer to the output of another build.

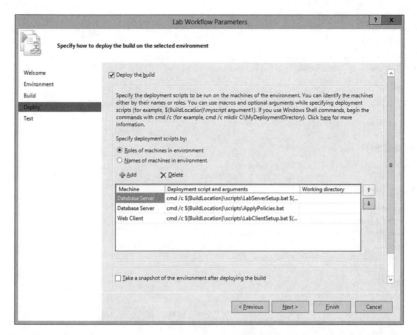

FIGURE 7.19: For each machine in a test environment, you can specify the deployment scripts that will do the actual deployment steps, such as copy files, install applications, or attach databases.

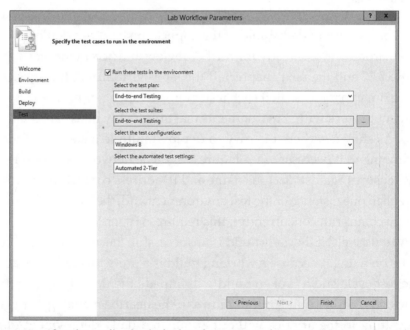

FIGURE 7.20: After the application is deployed to a test environment, VS supports running a defined set of automated tests to ensure no regressions are found before manual testing happens.

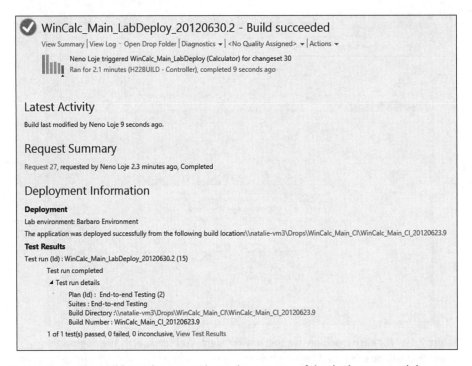

FIGURE 7.21: The Build Results report shows the outcome of the deployment and the associated test results.

After the current daily build of the application has been deployed to the test environment, it is ready for further review and acceptance testing (see Figure 7.22 and the next chapter). If the lab is virtualized, the application can be run in parallel so that each tester or developer gets his own test environment to work with. Environments that are already in use are marked as busy. As shown earlier, it is easy to deploy multiple instances of the test environment, if necessary (see Figure 7.23). The network-isolation feature in VS ensures against machine name and IP address conflicts (even though more than one instance of the test environment and, therefore, the same virtual machines run concurrently); this requires Hyper-V.

Alternatively, if the daily build is unsuccessful, the team should focus its efforts on fixing it because a working build is a prerequisite for the acceptance test cycle and a broken build will impede the flow. Testing can continue on an earlier build, but to return to the heartbeat analogy, oxygen is not getting to the arteries without automated daily deployment of new builds flowing smoothly.

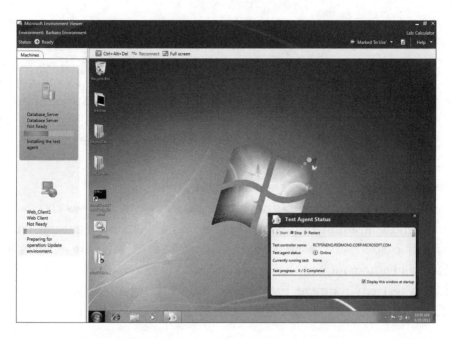

FIGURE 7.22: After a test environment has been deployed, it is ready to be used for automated and manual testing. Using Microsoft Test Manager (part of VS), you can connect to the corresponding machines.

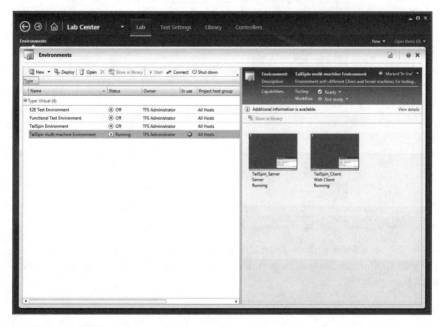

FIGURE 7.23: Multiple instances of a test environment can exist. Environments that are in use are marked with a red icon in the In-use column.

■ RUNNING AUTOMATED TESTS IN VIRTUAL ENVIRONMENTS

To learn how to configure automated tests to run in a virtual lab test environments in VS, see this MSDN topic: "How to Configure and Run Scheduled Tests After Building and Deploying Your Application" (http://msdn.microsoft.com/en-us/library/ee702477.aspx).

Creating Virtual Test Environments in the Cloud

A partner company, CloudShare, provides a service that allows you to easily extend your build automation to stand up test environments hosted in its public cloud service, as shown in Figure 7.24. CloudShare extends the TFS build automation so that your new build is automatically deployed as a new test environment that can be launched from MTM. See www.cloudshare.com/ for details.

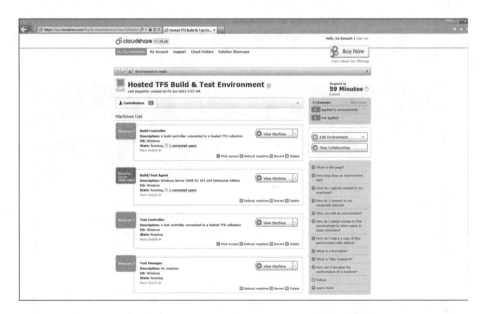

FIGURE 7.24: CloudShare offers direct integration into the TFS Build integration workflow to allow your continuous integration to create hosted dev/test environments that you can launch through MTM.

Elimination of Waste

Get PBIs Done

It is important for a team to understand that only PBIs that are *done* at the end of the sprint provide value. Undone or "almost done" items are counterproductive. They are not potentially shippable and cannot be evaluated by the product owner. Therefore, the team should concentrate its effort on finishing the top PBI (in the order of importance). When it is complete, the team should move on to the next one. This reduces risk; for whatever unforeseen things happen, the team can present those completed PBIs at the sprint review.

An example of a dysfunction is the team that commits to a handful of PBIs and at the end of the sprint has many of those PBIs all "almost done," with at least one done criterion unfulfilled. In most cases, this would be either integration work or testing. This creates insidious technical debt. The product owner cannot tell how much work remains before the PBIs really are potentially shippable—usually the team can't either. Unpredictability ensues. If you see this, stop. Put the undone work back on the backlog, review your done criteria, review your dashboard, and improve your transparency.

Integrate as Frequently as Possible

In Scrum, every sprint ends with a sprint review, during which the newly implemented user stories are presented to the stakeholders. Only stories that have been tested and integrated are potentially shippable and may be shown.

A potential dysfunction is that integration fails. Integration issues, such as merging,[5] are a common source of unhappiness and waste in teams. Integration work, where changes from multiple sources are merged into the main version, can be difficult, error-prone, and long lasting. These issues arise when developers work in isolation and do not integrate their code and tests on a regular basis. A long integration "phase" at the end of a sprint is a typical indication of an unsteady flow of value, technical debt, and waste.

The more frequently teams integrate code and tests, the less difficult it becomes. Regular integration ensures appropriately loose coupling of code and builds up integration tests that can become BVTs and prevent future problems. And when problems occur, there are only a few of them to fix.

In TFS, each branch, as well as each workspace, is an isolated version of the source code and should be integrated often (or retired if not required anymore). Every branch can add overhead and complexity. Therefore, a team should create just enough branches as necessary to support parallel development and maintenance of released versions, but not more.

Detecting Inefficiencies within the Flow

It is a team responsibility to deliver working, tested, and integrated software during each sprint. If the software isn't passing the BVTs, or if the BVTs and unit tests are inadequate, or if the changes are stuck in testing, the problem should be fixed at its source. VS helps to discover inefficiencies or first signs of those in the following reports.

Remaining Work

One of the several ways to track the continuous flow is to track work as it flows from development, to testing, to a completed state. Besides the very useful Stories Overview report you saw in Figure 1.4, one of the most useful diagrams to do that is a cumulative flow diagram (see Figure 7.25).[6] It gives you an understanding of the flow over time. This proves most useful when looking at days within an iteration or iterations within a project.

Each data series is a colored band (reproduced here as shading) that represents the number of stories that have reached the corresponding state as of the given date. The total height is the total amount of work to be done in the iteration:

- If the top line increases, total work is increasing. Typically, the reason is that unplanned work is adding to the total required. That may be expected if you've scheduled a buffer for unplanned work (such as for fixing newly discovered bugs).
- If the top line decreases, total work is decreasing, probably because work is being rescheduled out of the iteration.

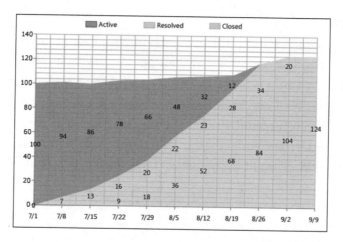

FIGURE 7.25: How much work is left and when will it be done? This cumulative flow diagram shows work remaining measured as PBIs being resolved and closed in the sprint.

Current status is measured by height on a particular date:

- The remaining backlog is measured by the current height of the leftmost area (Active in this case).

- The current completions are shown by the current height of the rightmost area (Closed in this case).

- The height of the band in-between indicates the work in progress (in this case, items Resolved but not Closed).

Watch for variation in the middle bands. An expansion can reveal a bottleneck (for example, if too many items are waiting to be tested and testing resources are inadequate). Alternatively, a significant narrowing of the band could indicate spare capacity.

Visually, it is easy to extrapolate an end completion inventory or end date for the backlog from a cumulative flow diagram like Figure 7.25. A small caution applies, however. Many projects observe an S-curve pattern, where progress is steepest in the middle. The commonsense explanation for the slower starting and ending rates is that start-up is always a little difficult and that unforeseen tough problems need to be handled before the end of a cycle.

Build Failures

Once again, a daily build is the heartbeat of your project. If your builds are not completing successfully or are not passing BVTs, as shown in Figure 7.26, you need to do what is necessary to fix the problem immediately. Otherwise, there's a risk that the flow of new PBIs gets stuck. Usually, the team will self-correct and restore the working build. The Build Success Over Time report, shown in Figure 7.27, helps to determine whether there are only individual build problems or if there are permanent or frequently recurring issues.

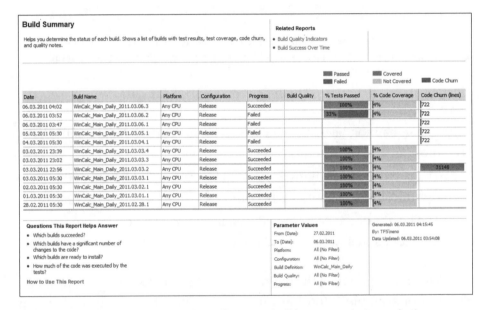

Figure 7.26: This build summary shows that some builds are completing and others are failing BVTs. A growing number of failed builds can be a symptom of dysfunction.

No Build	Build Failed	Build Succeeded, No Tests	Tests Failed	Tests Passed, Low Coverage	Passed

Build Definition	Platform	Configuration	7/8	7/9	7/10	7/11	7/12	7/13	7/14	7/15
Code Coverage	Mixed Platforms	Debug								
Continuous Integration	Mixed Platforms	Debug								
Main Night Build	Mixed Platforms	Debug								
Storefront 12 Nightly	Mixed Platforms	Debug								
Storefront 13 Nightly	Mixed Platforms	Debug								

FIGURE 7.27: This Build Success Over Time report shows the current results of all build definitions over a specified time range using colors for the different results.

Watch Tests and Code Coverage Too

Be on the lookout for the unintended consequences of code churn, often due to refactoring. The Build Quality Indicators report, as shown in Figure 6.44 in the previous chapter, lets you see several trends together, so that you can spot unhealthy trends, such as rising code churn, rising inconclusive tests, and falling code coverage, which together would probably mean that unit tests are not getting delivered with new code during refactoring. This is an example of keeping your eye on tests, coverage, and code churn trends all at once to spot warning signs of technical debt before it becomes a serious problem.

Summary

This chapter covered automating builds and deployment to create a smooth flow and short cycle time, the measurement from concept to potentially shippable increment of working software. In order to achieve the smooth flow, your team needs to agree on a consistent definition of *done,* implement continuous integration (conventional or gated check-in), and automate the *done* criteria with CI. In this way, you will not check in "undone" work and build up technical debt.

The next step is continuous deployment[7] into the test lab. Automatically deploying new builds when they become available (and pass BVTs) and running "smoke" tests in a preproduction lab are the logical next cycles. Automated tooling can significantly help to make continuous deployment a reality, as you have seen in this chapter using VS, and further prevent against unwanted debt.

To reduce cycle time should be a major goal of every software development team. The more quickly a PBI can be turned into working, deployed software, the more satisfied the customer will be and the more the team can respond to new priorities in the product backlog. The less undone work impedes the team's ability to begin new PBIs, the greater the satisfaction the team will have at staying in the groove of delivery. And, of course, Scrum prescribes that teams need to present a fully tested, integrated, and potentially shippable increment of the application at the end of each sprint.

The next chapter looks at the extended testing process under the Agile Consensus and its contribution to delivering the potentially shippable increment. Where this chapter focused on reducing waste through automation, the next one focuses on adding value through human activities where not everything can be automated. It's a piece of the Agile Consensus that's often underappreciated.

Endnotes

[1]   www.startuplessonslearned.com/2010/01/case-study-continuous-deployment-makes.html

[2]   For example, www.martinfowler.com/articles/continuousIntegration.html and http://c2.com/cgi/wiki?ContinuousIntegration

[3]   For example, www.stevemcconnell.com/ieeesoftware/ bp04.htm

[4]   Rational User Conference (RUC) 2002, "Using Rational PurifyPlus and VMware Virtual Machines in the Development of the Quality Engineering Process" by Daniel Kerns and "Automated Configuration Testing with Virtual Machine Technology" by Scott Devine.

5   Continuous Integration, talk by Ray Osherove at TechEd Developers 2006, http://download.microsoft.com/download/2/3/8/238556cb-06dc-4e16-8f81-4874e83ded23/CI%20with%20Team%20System.ppt.

6   Cumulative flow diagrams were introduced to software in Anderson 2004, *op.cit.*, 61.

7   http://continuousdelivery.com/2010/02/continuous-delivery/.

■ 8 ■

Test

---

*The role of professional testing will inevitably change from
"adult supervision" to something more closely resembling an
amplifier for the communication between those who generally
have a feeling for what the system should do and those who will
make it do.[1]*

—Kent Beck

THE LANDING OF THE PILGRIMS,

FIGURE 8.1: Testing is a primary assessment of done for the sprint, the landing of the product backlog items as intended.[2]

THE PREVIOUS CHAPTERS HAVE all been about driving quality upstream, ensuring that we have a clean product backlog, clean code and unit tests, and a reliable build process that cleanly deploys new bits into a test lab (see Figure 8.2). This cleanliness allows acceptance testing to focus on issues related to the completeness of product backlog items (PBIs) that can't be caught earlier.

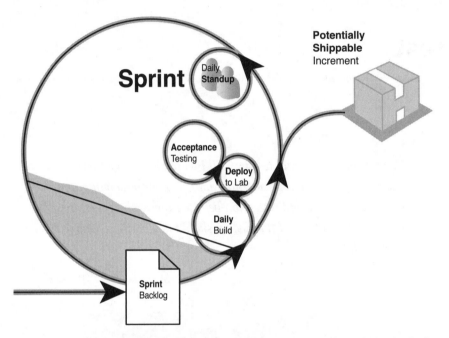

FIGURE 8.2: The daily build is the natural unit to deploy into the test lab automatically for acceptance testing.

Testing in the Agile Consensus

Chapter 1, "The Agile Consensus," discussed the need to focus on flow of value, reduction of waste, and trustworthy transparency as the three mutually supporting tenets of the Agile Consensus. The discrepancy between frequently practiced work rituals and these values hit me vividly recently. We spoke to an industry analyst who shared that his most frequent customer inquiry was, "Can we get rid of our testers?" For all the money that gets spent on software testing, it is amazing how rarely teams and their organizations can clearly answer what the testers do or should be doing.

In this chapter, we try to fix that.

Testing and Flow of Value

The primary unit of customer value is the product backlog item (PBI). The team's goal in terms of flow has to be to move each PBI to done. Testing is usually the primary measure of done, where the testing is done on the software in a production-realistic environment from a deployed installation of the software. Testing like this ought to include the following:

- Acceptance testing for functionality. In other words, does the software meet the requirements of the PBI from the user perspective?

- Acceptance testing for qualities of service (QoS), such as performance, world-readiness, security, and other attributes as may apply from Chapter 3, "Product Ownership."

- Environmental compatibility with anything else deployed in production, to prevent future problems in deployment.

Accordingly, there are often several test cases per PBI. As discussed in Chapter 4, "Running the Sprint," and shown here in Figure 8.3, the User Story Test Status shows, for each PBI taken into the sprint, how many test cases have never been run, are blocked, are failing, or are passing as of their last test run.

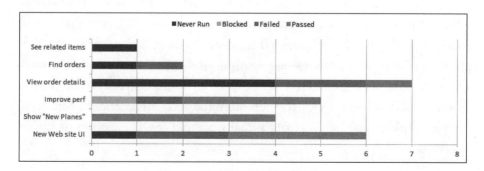

FIGURE 8.3: Throughout the sprint, the User Story Test Status on the Test dashboard shows how many tests for each PBI have been run and have passed.

Inspect and Adapt: Exploratory Testing

Unfortunately, planned test cases cover only what you anticipated *before* you saw the working software. Testing, as much as any discipline, requires inspecting the product and adapting techniques to learn more. As soon as one testing approach fails to yield bugs, consider how you can vary your approach to find more. That's the philosophy of *exploratory testing*.[3] It's about using varying techniques, sometimes called *tours*, to look for blind spots.

Consider the difference in perspective between these two sentences:

1. As an admin, I want to use security groups to prevent unauthorized access to key data.

2. Given that I want to prevent unauthorized access to key data, when there is an attempted intrusion by an unauthorized user, I want immediate notification, tagging of all compromised data, an audit log of the attempt, correlation to other breach attempts, and the intrusion blocked.

They might be describing the same user story. There might be 15 other "given/when/then" phrases that testers discover by exploring this PBI. In fact, good testers will *discover* acceptance criteria in this way as much as they are validating the existing statements of requirements. In this way, testers round out the work of the product owner.

The "given/when/then" approach is also a good way to devise *negative tests* (that is, tests of what should not be possible as part of the user story), which typically correspond to error paths that the software under test should handle gracefully. James Whittaker calls these *back-alley tours*. A simple example is withdrawing a negative amount of money from a back account. Not only should it not be allowed, it should also not be caught just when input (lest it mysteriously increment the account balance). More complex examples might be security attacks, such as SQL injection or buffer overruns.[4]

Testing and Reduction of Waste

In the past, testing happened in its own silo. Under the Agile Consensus, testing is an integral part of the flow from backlog to working software.

Getting software into a testable state under production-realistic conditions is an integral part of the team's responsibility because a PBI cannot be brought to done otherwise.

An additional tenet is to bring PBIs to done in the shortest possible time (a few days) and thereby to keep work in process to a minimum. In other words, the team does not try to start many PBIs at once, but tries to bring active PBIs to done before starting new ones. This means that developers and testers are working in parallel on a very few PBIs on any given day. It also means that testers are not waiting long for working software to test because it is flowing continuously.

Testing and Transparency

Testing is necessary for transparency. While burndown charts show task completion, they show no assessment of the end result, the working software. Testing does that. When the software is failing its tests, the team works to fix the software until the tests run green. That's why the Stories Overview report, shown previously in Figure 1.4, combines both sources of data tasks and tests. Similarly, of the five dashboards in Figures 4.8 through 4.12, only one displays burndowns; the remaining four cover quality, test, bugs, and builds to give you the best insight into real progress of PBIs toward done.

There should be planned test cases for every PBI, and maybe additional test cases for QoS and risks, but you never know for certain whether unforeseen gaps remain in your end product. For this reason, it is important to measure test progress and coverage from as many dimensions as possible and to continue to explore the software for potential bugs or opportunities for improvement. For examples, see the Quality and Test dashboards shown in Chapter 4.

Testing Product Backlog Items

In Visual Studio (VS), a separate user interface (UI) is provided for testing: the Microsoft Test Manager (MTM), as shown in Figure 8.4.[5] With MTM, you can capture and manage test cases, associate them with user stories and other PBIs, run automatic and manual tests, and track test results as well as bugs found during testing. All information in MTM is stored on the server and therefore immediately shared with the team.

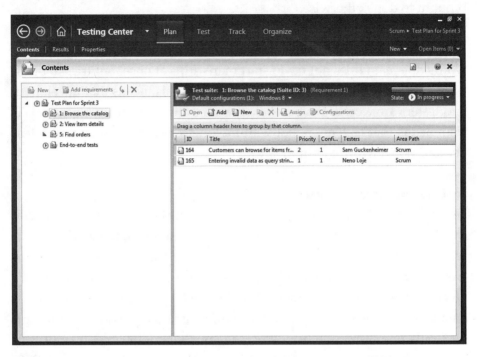

FIGURE 8.4: In Microsoft Test Manager, part of VS, you can describe manual tests as Test Case work items with prescriptive steps and notes to the tester. The test results are captured, tracked, and fed to the warehouse for manual and automated tests.

VS does not require that you explicitly define test cases. If you have them, they will appear in MTM. In addition, MTM infers test cases from the user stories or other requirements (see Figure 8.4). By doing so, MTM creates a test suite for each user story, and test cases are grouped into those suites. Every test case contained in a test suite gets automatically linked to the corresponding user story, which ensures later reporting can identify coverage and gaps by requirement. In addition, you can define other test cases from the bottom up, independent of requirements, and link them explicitly as you want for reporting or group them as you want for execution.

VS uses two types of high-level containers to organize and track test cases: test suites and query-based suites. *Test suites* are conceptual groupings around intent. For example, all the test cases related to one user story might be a test suite. *Query-based suites* allow a dynamic selection of test cases based on a work item query. For example, a test suite could include all test cases with a high priority to make sure all important test cases are rerun in each iteration. Test suites can contain other test suites, too.

Test plans, in contrast, are collections of suites with run settings and test environments grouped to identify what should be tested in a sprint. This allows the doneness of the sprint, from the testing viewpoint, to match the completion of the test plan for the iteration.[6]

The Most Important Tests First

Normally, one of the hardest pieces of test management is knowing what to test next. Especially when testing is heavily manual, the cost of not testing the most important changes first is enormously wasteful because it delays providing critical feedback to the whole team.

A great way to identify what to test next is the list of *Recommended Tests* in MTM. This makes clear what tasks and user stories have actually been delivered and integrated in the recent build, compared with the previously tested build, and which automated and manual tests were impacted, based on a comparison of the last successful test run and the analysis of code changes checked in by the developers (see Figure 8.5).

Moreover, based on an analysis of the existing action recordings from manual and automated tests, MTM recommends which tests to rerun (see Figure 8.6). This helps identify unforeseen side effects (where other, less-expected parts of the application are impacted by those changes) and allows for more focused testing. Furthermore, if you have reasonable build verification tests (BVTs), you can check their results and code coverage.

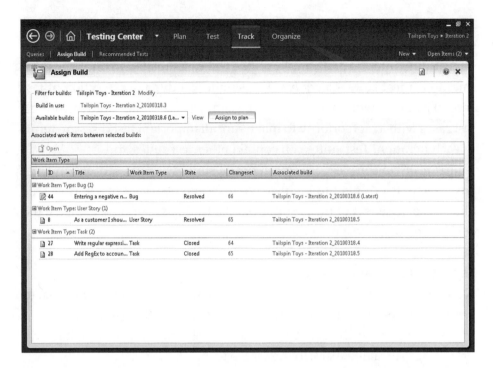

FIGURE 8.5: The Assign Build command of MTM computes differences between two builds based on the work completed from the earlier build to the current one and the changes in the code over that period. Based on these two streams of data, MTM suggests what backlog items are ready to test and which test cases ought to be run first. You can use the Assign Build command to assess build changes before deciding to take the build into the testing cycle.

Test cases include *test steps*, which can either be simple actions or validations where the tester compares the actual with an expected result. Optionally, parameters can be used to reference *test data* that does not have to be part of the steps themselves (see Figure 8.7). In addition, because test cases are regular work items in VS, they can be customized like all other work item types. A special form of a case is a *Shared Steps* work item. It can be used to share common steps that are frequently used and referenced in other test cases. For example, think of a bunch of login steps. If those steps change, only the steps in the referenced shared step need to be updated; upon doing so, all referencing test cases are immediately up to date.

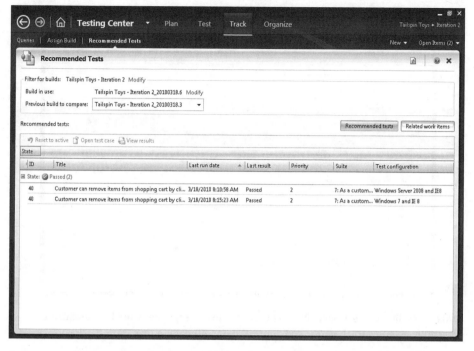

FIGURE 8.6: After you assign a new build for testing, MTM provides a list of recommended tests, whose prior results may have been affected by the changes checked in to the build. These are recommended because of the impact of changes to code, requirements, and bugs on existing test cases. The recommended tests are the ones most likely to find bugs and are, therefore, the ones you should run first.

Actionable Test Results and Bug Reports

Another common source of waste in most testing comes from the difficulty of capturing enough information to reproduce an observed failure. This leads to the all-too-common bug resolution of "no repro" or the standing joke of the developer saying, "But it works on my machine!"

MTM addresses this problem with diagnostic data adapters (DDAs). The DDAs collect valuable information to eliminate the need for subsequent reproduction of the test run. For example, DDAs include full-screen video, system information, an action recording that can be used to automate the test at a later stage, an IntelliTrace log for postmortem server debugging, and, if the test lab is in use, snapshots of the virtual machine images.

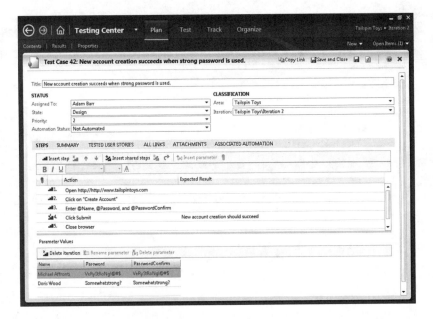

FIGURE 8.7: Test cases are managed and tracked like every other work item and capture prescriptive steps, attachments, and optional parameters for a test.

Test settings (as shown in Figure 8.8) organize which DDAs are turned on and off and therefore what information will be collected. Separate settings can be defined for manual and automated tests. Because most modern applications use multiple tiers, test settings specify which DDAs to enable for the test agents running on each of the machine roles involved in the test.

When you "run" a test, MTM collapses its UI into a narrow panel and docks itself along the edge of the screen, usually placing the application under test to the right, as shown in Figure 8.9. This layout is used whether you are trying exploratory testing, recording a test, or replaying previously recorded steps, as shown in this example.

A manual test often includes a certain sequence of steps that the tester follows each time (for example, to bring the application into a meaningful state before the interesting part of the test begins). If the test was exercised before, MTM can replay those recorded UI actions and fast-forward up to a more meaningful step, where the tester takes over again and validates the result (as shown in Figure 8.9).

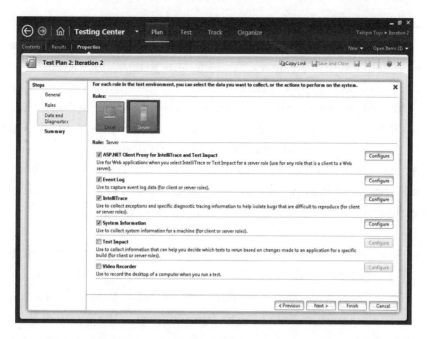

FIGURE 8.8: Test settings define what data is collected during automated and manual testing and from which machine roles to collect that data.

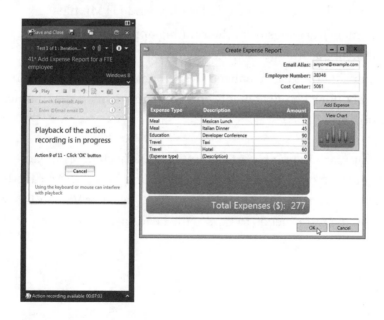

FIGURE 8.9: If a test case has been manually executed in the past, you can click Play to replay the UI actions and fast-forward to a certain step that requires manual verification, to save time.

No More "No Repro"

In the Preface, I claimed that one of the greatest sources of waste in software development today is the developer's inability to reproduce a reported bug and the ensuing ping-pong game to collect the information. VS fundamentally attacks this source of waste. When you click the **Create Bug** button on the MTM test runner panel, all the data specified in the test settings is gathered from the test run and attached to the bug automatically.

Whether using MTM or VS, developers can see within the bug both the actual behavior of the app and its root cause (see Figure 8.10) by looking at the various test result attachments, such as the following:

- The steps followed so far and the results, taken from the test runner.
- A screenshot, if added by the tester using the test runner.
- A full-screen video index so that every step has the corresponding starting time from the video to directly jump to that point of the recording.
- Configuration information of the systems under test.
- A list of all UI actions recorded (as text and HTML files).
- The IntelliTrace logs from the running application. (For more information about IntelliTrace, see Chapter 6, "Development.")
- A snapshot of the (virtualized) test environment. (For more information about test environments and lab management, see Chapter 7, "Build and Lab.")

This approach to bug reporting fundamentally changes the tester's job. Testers get to be experts in testing, not in filing defects. We can stop the debate about "what makes a good bug report?" because VS handles that for us now. All the tester needs to type is the headline.

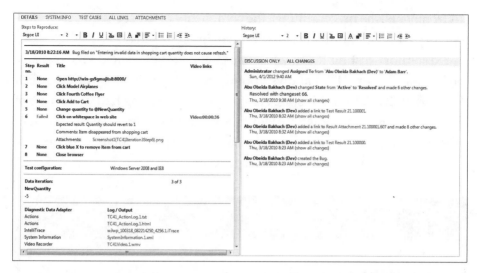

FIGURE 8.10: The details of a bug captured from a test case show all the test steps, the time-stamped video recording, the action log, the IntelliTrace from the server, the system configuration information, and, if applicable, the snapshot of the virtualized test environment.

Use Exploratory Testing to Avoid False Confidence

When you have highly scripted or automated testing, you run the risk of what Boris Beizer calls the *pesticide paradox:*[7]

> Every method you use to prevent or find bugs leaves a residue of subtler bugs against which those methods are ineffectual.

In other words, you can make your software immune to the tests that you already have. This pattern is especially a concern when the only testing being done is regression testing and the test pool is very stable. Exploratory testing is the best antidote to the pesticide paradox. Just like microbes evolve to develop resistance to pesticides, your software evolves to not have bugs where the old tests look for them. Therefore, your tests also need to evolve to find the remaining bugs. Vary the data, the sequences, the environments, the preconditions, the complexity of the scenarios, the error-recovery choices, and so on until you see different behavior.

Exploratory testing helps you guard against the pesticide paradox. In the Testing Center, MTM allows you to select any user story or other PBI and start an Exploratory Testing session, without having had to define test cases in advance, as shown in Figure 8.11. In this way, you can discover behavior of the application through usage and capture notable bugs or test cases that you would otherwise have missed.

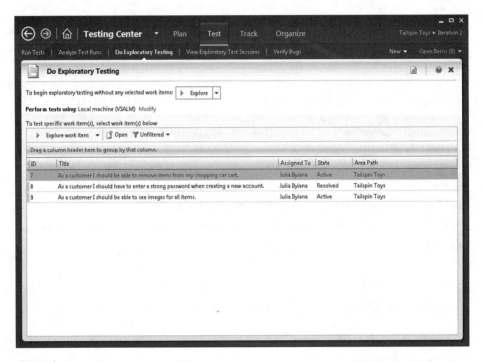

FIGURE 8.11: MTM allows you to select any item from the product backlog and simply start exploring.

During exploratory testing, MTM captures rich bug information, as described earlier for manual test cases. Although you can explore for as long as you like, when you file the bugs you find during an exploratory test session, you can decide how much of the recorded data you want to include, as shown in Figure 8.12. In other words, you can discard the extraneous part of the exploration.

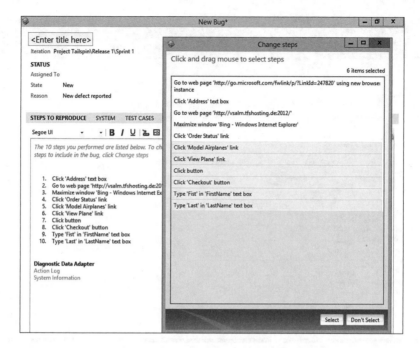

FIGURE 8.12: When running an exploratory test, MTM enables you to snip the data collection to only the last few steps of history so that you focus the bug reader on the right data.

With MTM, you can select a user story or other PBI to start exploratory testing and MTM will optionally create both new bugs that you find and test cases from the exploration (see Figure 8.13). The test cases can then be reused for future regression testing.

Testing Immersive Apps on Windows 8 Devices

When you are testing apps on Windows 8 that consume the full screen, you may want to use the full screen on a Microsoft Surface or tablet device, for example. In this case, you can run MTM on one machine on the desktop and the app under test on a second machine, as shown in Figure 8.14. MTM lets you specify the IP address of the target machine for the testing. (If you want to run the tests locally, specify the local hostname.) For setup details, see the MSDN topic, "Running Manual Tests Using Testing Runner."

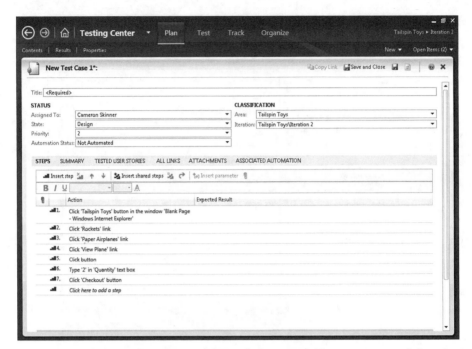

FIGURE 8.13: A test case that was created out of a bug report. The test steps are inferred from the UI interactions that were recording while the bug was filed using MTM.

FIGURE 8.14: When testing on a Microsoft surface or other Windows 8 or mobile device in full screen mode, you can run MTM on a separate computer to collect test results and diagnostic data.

Handling Bugs

There are two different paths for handling bugs on a Scrum team, depending on the content of the bug. When the bug found relates to a PBI that is being implemented *in the current sprint,* the bug is simply the result of undone work and is treated like any task related to the completion of the PBI: It goes on the *sprint backlog.*

However, there are many bugs found (and sometimes inherited) that are not related to the PBIs of the current sprint. These should be treated as part of the *product backlog.* Often, these bugs are much smaller than the other PBIs, and there are too many of them to stack rank individually against each other and the meatier PBIs. Together, however, they might feel like death by a thousand paper cuts.

In this case, it makes sense to create a PBI to the effect of "Remove the top dissatisfiers" and group bugs of suitable priority by making them children of that PBI. Then they can be collectively stack ranked as a group against other PBIs of comparable granularity. In Chapter 3, I discussed how to group these paper cuts into a sufficiently large PBI to be stack ranked into a sprint.

An alternative that I discuss in the next chapter is an approach for handling accumulated technical debt by investing in a debt payoff period in the schedule to remove all accumulated bugs and broken tests. In any event, handling out-of-sprint bugs, like other product backlog decisions, is a question of priority. It belongs to the product owner in consultation with stakeholders and the team, and it should be transparent and consistent.

Which Tests Should Be Automated?

In the past ten years, a lot has been written about the pitfalls and benefits of test automation.[8] I simplify the argument here. Automation is useful when it achieves high coverage and when the tests will be used many times for many configurations across many changes in the software under test (SUT).

However, automation is expensive and hard to maintain, especially if based on the SUT's UI. Moreover, automation often leads to a false sense of security, especially when its results are not balanced against views of coverage and when its test cases are not balanced with harsh exploratory and negative testing.

These considerations lead to some guidelines:

1. Automate tests that support programming, such as unit tests, component/service integration tests, and BVTs, and make sure that they achieve very high code coverage, as discussed in Chapter 6. This category includes negative tests that exercise correct error handling under fault conditions.
2. Automate configuration tests whenever you can.
   If you expect your software to be long-lived, then …
3. Automate scenario tests for the PBIs when possible, but expect that they will need maintenance. Minimize your dependence on user interface changes in your software design and test automation strategy.
4. Automate load tests, but again, expect that they will need maintenance.
   And …
5. Guard against a false sense of confidence with exploratory testing, to keep your testing diverse.

Automating Scenario Tests

The primary way to automate scenario tests in VS is as *coded UI tests* (see Figure 8.15). Coded UI tests interact with applications, both Windows or Web-based, as the user would: by playing back all actions, such as clicks and keystrokes, to simulate a real user. Using VS, a developer can record Coded UI Tests either from scratch or by converting an automation strip of a previous manual test run.

Remember that software test automation is fundamentally software and will need to be maintained like other software. Expect that if the UI changes, your UI tests need to change. Accordingly, if you know the UI is temporary, it is probably too early to automate UI testing.

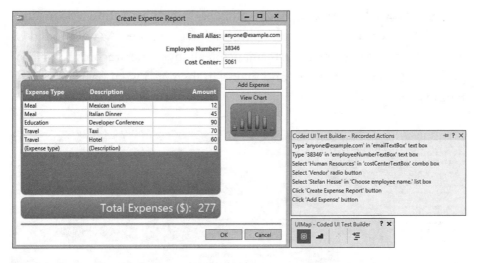

FIGURE 8.15: Coded UI tests record and replay UI actions on different types of applications, such as classic Windows apps and browser-based apps.

However, if you expect the UI not to change and want to be able to test for regression and configurations, coded UI tests are a convenient way to do that. Because UI tests are easy to create, they are also easy to *re*-create when a scenario changes. For maintenance, they are also easy to componentize. MTM lets you record small components called *shared steps* to handle repeated tasks, such as a common login. Use shared steps when you can.

■ SUPPORTED CONFIGURATIONS AND PLATFORMS FOR CODED UI TESTS

Coded UI tests support UI automation of both rich client applications and Web applications running in the browser. You can find a full list of supported configurations on the MSDN Web site, at http:// msdn.microsoft.com/en-us/library/dd380742.aspx.

Testing "Underneath the Browser" Using HTTP

Coded UI tests are designed to exercise the full UI of the application (for example, all the JavaScript running in the browser and all the mouse activity of the user). An alternative way to automate scenario tests with VS, bypassing the UI, is to create *Web performance tests*, which allow you to automate the server interaction happening behind the scenes. As with coded UI tests, you can create Web performance tests by either recording or programming, and still enhance and maintain them in Visual Basic or C# (see Figure 8.16).

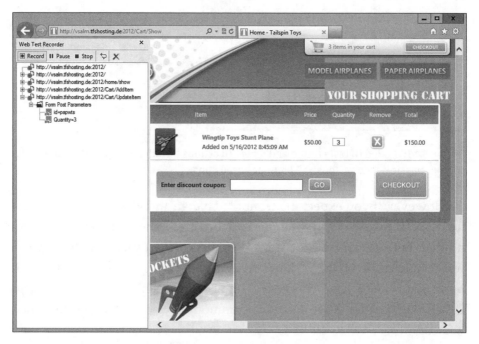

FIGURE 8.16: When you add a Web performance test in VS, you drive the scenario as a user would—but the instrumented Web browser captures the interaction at the HTTP level and produces a parameterized test against the server.

Although Web performance tests are created by recording, they do not depend on the browser UI for running because they exercise the SUT at the server level. During playback, you can see both the browser interaction and the HTTP or HTTPS traffic (see Figure 8.17). Web performance tests are the primary way to do automated performance and load testing.

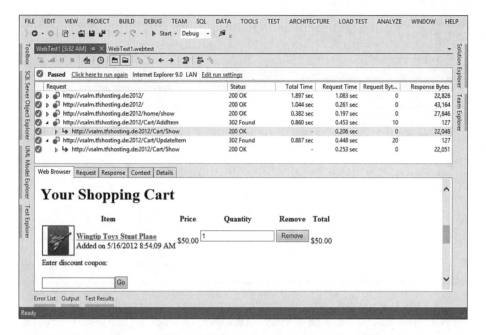

FILE   EDIT   VIEW   PROJECT   BUILD   DEBUG   TEAM   SQL   DATA   TOOLS   TEST   ARCHITECTURE   LOAD TEST   ANALYZE   WINDOW   HELP

WebTest1 [3:32 AM] ⊡ ✕ WebTest1.webtest

✅ **Passed** Click here to run again Internet Explorer 9.0 LAN Edit run settings

Request	Status	Total Time	Request Time	Request Byt...	Response Bytes
▷ http://vsalm.tfshosting.de:2012/	200 OK	1.897 sec	1.083 sec	0	22,826
▷ http://vsalm.tfshosting.de:2012/	200 OK	1.044 sec	0.261 sec	0	43,164
▷ http://vsalm.tfshosting.de:2012/home/show	200 OK	0.382 sec	0.197 sec	0	27,846
▲ http://vsalm.tfshosting.de:2012/Cart/AddItem	302 Found	0.860 sec	0.453 sec	10	127
▷ ↳ http://vsalm.tfshosting.de:2012/Cart/Show	200 OK	-	0.206 sec	0	22,048
▲ http://vsalm.tfshosting.de:2012/Cart/UpdateItem	302 Found	0.887 sec	0.448 sec	20	127
▷ ↳ http://vsalm.tfshosting.de:2012/Cart/Show	200 OK	-	0.253 sec	0	22,051

Web Browser | Request | Response | Context | Details

Your Shopping Cart

	Item	Price	Quantity	Remove	Total
	Wingtip Toys Stunt Plane Added on 5/16/2012 8:54:09 AM	$50.00	1	Remove	$50.00

Enter discount coupon:

[   ] Go

Error List   Output   Test Results

Ready

FIGURE 8.17: The playback of the test shows you both what was rendered in the browser and what happened in the HTTP stream so that you can watch the full server interaction, including the invisible parts of the traffic.

Using Test Data

Varying test data to represent a mix of realistic inputs is an important part of scenario testing, whether you are running UI tests or Web tests (see Figure 8.18). Depending on the domain, the best way to capture requirements from your stakeholder may be as spreadsheets of test data representing similar cases of desired behavior, often called *equivalence classes.*

Accordingly, you can have your automated tests access external test data from any OLEDB data source, including CSV files, Excel, Access, and SQL Server databases.

Web tests are easy to create. When the scenario changes and requires a new execution sequence, it may be easier to *re*-create the test and reuse the data than to try to edit the test. Consider this carefully as part of your test maintenance.

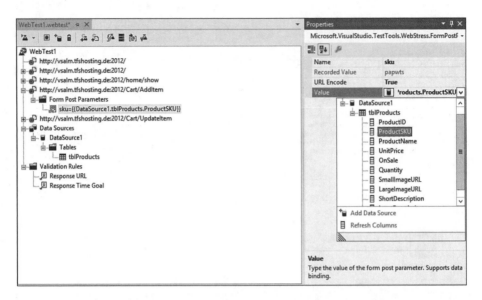

FIGURE 8.18: In almost all cases, you should vary the data used for testing, either to cover different combinations based on different equivalence classes or to apply unique values for each transaction present in a multiuser workload.

■ WALKTHROUGH: ADDING DATA BINDING TO A WEB PERFORMANCE TEST

For a step-by-step example of how to add a dataset to a Web test so that you can vary the data, consult http://msdn.microsoft.com/en-us/library/ms243142.aspx.

Load Tests, as Part of the Sprint

In the past, load testing was considered a specialist activity requiring rare skills with expensive tools and equipment. Although it is true that *sometimes* you need to wait until late in the release cycle to run some of the load tests, in a healthy development process, you shouldn't wait for all of them.

With VS, you can create and run load tests as part of every sprint. The earlier you identify performance problems, the cheaper it is to fix them. When you design a load test, you need to look at two primary questions:

1. **Does the software respond appropriately under expected load conditions?** To answer this, you compose performance tests that combine reasonable scenario tests, data, and workloads.

2. **Under which stress conditions does the software stop responding well?** For this, you take the same scenarios and data and crank up the workload progressively, watching the corresponding effect on performance and system indicators.

All the automated tests managed by VS—Web performance tests, unit tests, coded UI tests, and any additional test types you create—can be used for load testing (see Figures 8.19 through 8.25). With VS, you can model the workload to represent a realistic mix of users, each running different tests. Finally, VS automatically collects diagnostic data from the servers under test to highlight problems for you.

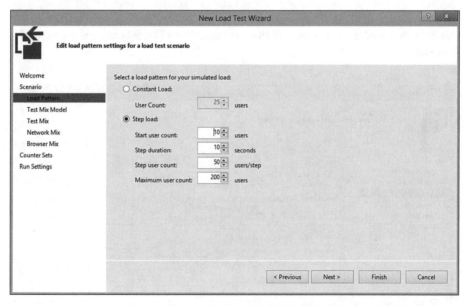

FIGURE 8.19: In VS, a load test is a container for any arbitrary set of tests with workload settings. First, you choose how to ramp the load. Often, you want to observe the system with gradually increasing user load so that you can spot any "hockey stick" effect in the response time as the user load increases.

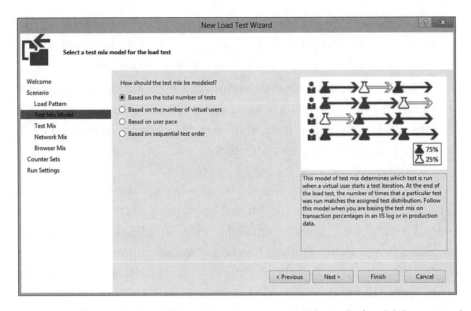

FIGURE 8.20: You use load modeling options to more accurately predict/model the expected real-world usage of a Web site or application that you are load testing. It is important to do this because a load test that is not based on an accurate load model can generate misleading results.

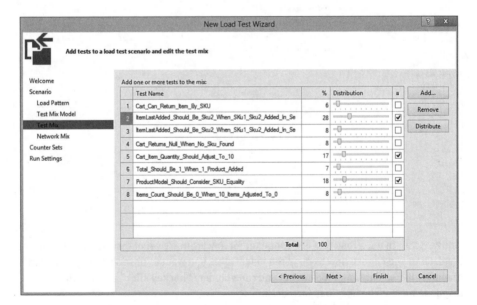

FIGURE 8.21: Next, you choose the tests (unit, Web, or other) and the percentage of load to create from each of the specific tests.

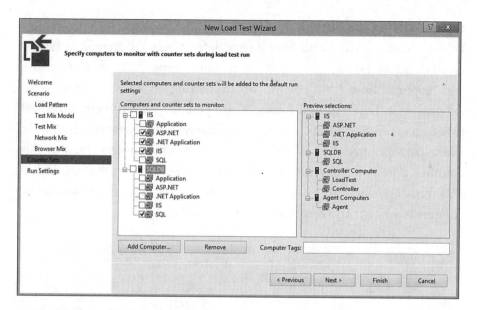

FIGURE 8.22: Load tests can generate huge amounts of data from the SUTs, and it is often hard to know what is relevant. VS simplifies this by asking you to choose only which services to watch on which machines and by automating the rest of the decisions.

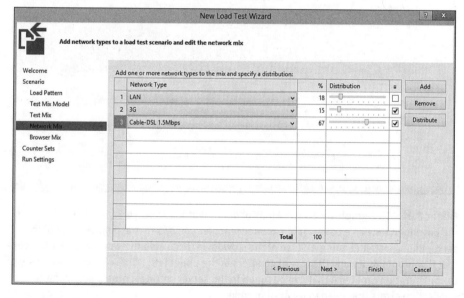

FIGURE 8.23: You then choose the browser and network mixes that best reflect your end-user population.

Understanding the Output

While a load test runs, and after it completes, you need to look at two levels of data (see Figure 8.24). Average response time shows you the end-to-
end response time for a page to finish loading, exactly as a user would
experience it. That's straightforward, and you can assess whether the range
is within acceptable limits. At the same time, while the test runs, all the relevant performance data is collected from the chosen servers, and these
counters give you clues as to where the bottlenecks are in the running system. VS sets thresholds by default according to the type of application and
triggers warnings and errors if any levels are being exceeded.

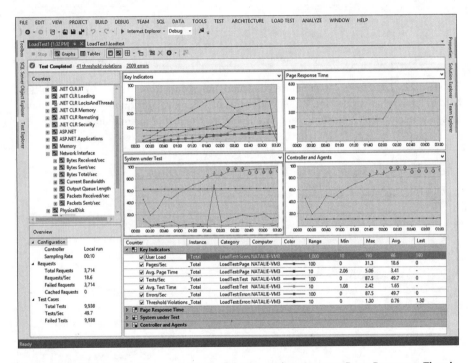

FIGURE 8.24: This graph shows two kinds of data together. Average Page Response Time is
the page load time as a user would experience it. Requests/Sec is a measurement of the
server under test, indicating a cause of the slowdown. Note also the warning and error icons
that flag problems among the tree of counters in the upper left. Some of these may lead you
to configuration problems that can be tuned in the server settings; others may point to
application errors that need to be fixed in code.

Diagnosing the Performance Problem

When a load test points to a likely application performance problem, the developer of the suspect code is usually the best person to diagnose the problem. As a tester, you can attach the test result to a bug directly to forward it to an appropriate teammate, and when your teammate opens the bug, the same graphs will be available for viewing. Your teammate can then use the Performance Wizard to instrument the application and rerun the test that you ran, as shown in Figure 8.25.

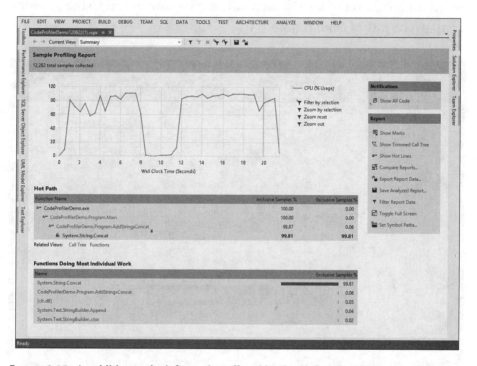

FIGURE 8.25: In addition to the information offered by the perfmon counters, you can rerun the test with profiling (or attach the test result to a bug and have a colleague open it and rerun with profiling). This takes you from the System view to the Code view of the application and lets you drill into the hot path of the specific methods and call sequences that may be involved during the slowdown.

The profiling report can rank the actual suspect functions in a "hot path analysis" that leads you straight to the code that may need optimizing. This sequence of load testing to profiling is an efficient way to determine how to tune an application. You can use it in any iteration as soon as enough of the system is available to drive under load.

Production-Realistic Test Environments

Chapter 7 described how to connect test environments to the build workflow, so that you can always test the latest build in a production-realistic environment. MTM enables you to choose which test environment to use when running a set of tests so that you can be sure to run tests across the appropriate mix of configurations (see Figure 8.26).

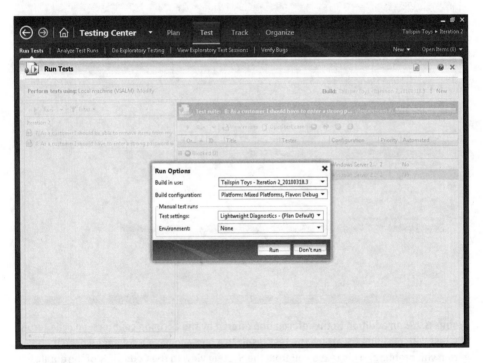

FIGURE 8.26: When you run a set of tests in MTM, one of the choices is the test environment to use. Here, it is <None>, to run tests locally, but it could be any virtualized or physical environment, as shown in Chapter 7.

Reporting

Of course, you need to track test configurations and report what has been tested so that you can identify gaps in configuration coverage and prioritize your next testing appropriately. Fortunately, VS tracks the configuration used on every test. A test configuration in VS consists of one or more variables, such as the OS version, browser version, or similar run (see Figure 8.27). Because the results are stored in the data warehouse, this makes it easy to track the configurations that have been used and those that lack good test coverage.

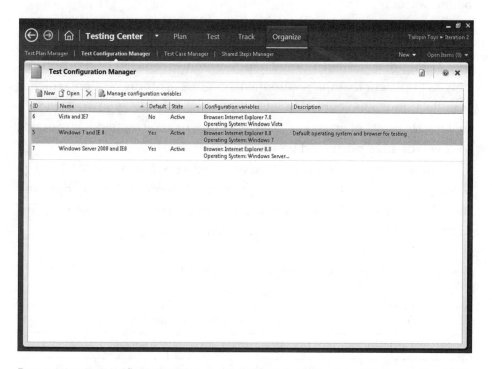

FIGURE 8.27: Test configurations can capture the representative target environments of the SUTs. The metrics warehouse accumulates test results by configuration so that you can build a picture over time of the test coverage against configurations.

It is usually a good idea to vary the configurations with every round of testing so that you cycle through the different configurations as a matter of course. Because the test results are always tracked against the test configuration, you also have the information to reproduce any results, and you improve your coverage of configurations this way.

Risk-Based Testing

Most risk testing is negative testing (that is, "tests aimed at showing that the software does not work"[9]). These tests attempt to do things that should not be possible to do, such as spending money beyond a credit limit, revealing someone else's credit card number, or raising an airplane's landing gear before takeoff.

Risk testing can give you a lens that other approaches do not offer. Note that coverage testing does *not* provide any clue about the amount of negative testing that has been done, and requirements-based coverage helps only to the extent that the requirements capture error prevention, which is usually at much too cursory a level. In testing for risks, you are typically looking for errors of omission, such as an unwritten error handler (no code to cover) or an implicit (and hence untraceable) requirement.

To design effective negative tests, you need a good idea of what could go wrong. This is sometimes called a *fault model.* You can derive your fault model from any number of knowledge sources. Table 8.1 lists sources of a fault model illustrating constituency-based knowledge.

TABLE 8.1: Typical Sources and Examples for a Fault Model

Source	Sample Fault to Test For
Business rules	Customers can't spend over their credit limits.
Technical architecture	The authentication server could be down.
Domain knowledge	This spending pattern, although legal, could indicate a stolen credit card.
User understanding	If there's no rapid confirmation, a user could click the Submit button many times.
Bug databases	Under this pattern of usage, the server times out.

VS lets you capture these potential faults in the work item database as risks. You usually start during early test planning, and you review and update the risk list in planning every iteration (and probably more frequently). The same traceability that tracks Test Cases to User Story work items enables you to trace Tests to Risk work items so that you can report on testing against risks in the same way (see Figures 8.28 and 8.29).

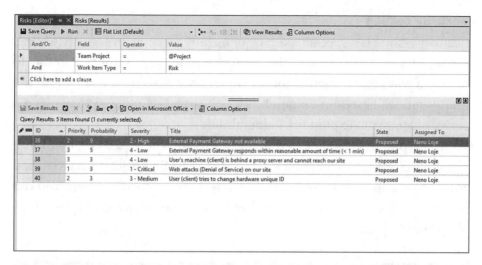

FIGURE 8.28: Risks are captured as work items so that they can be managed in the same backlog, tracked to test cases, and reported in the same way as other work item types.

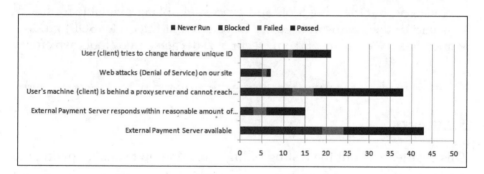

FIGURE 8.29: Because risks are a type of work item, you can measure test coverage against risks in a manner similar to the coverage against user stories.

Capturing Risks as Work Items

By default, a Risk work item type is available in Microsoft Solutions Framework (MSF) for Capability Maturity Model Integration (CMMI) Process Improvement, but not in the other TFS process templates. Of course, you can still capture risks as PBIs or customize your process template to include them.

Security Testing

Security testing is a specialized type of negative testing. In security testing, you are trying to prove that the software under test is not vulnerable to attack in ways that it should not be. The essence of security testing is to use a fault model, based on vulnerabilities observed on other systems, and a series of attacks to exploit the vulnerabilities.

Many published attack patterns can identify the vast majority of vulnerabilities.[10] Many companies provide penetration testing services, and many community tools are available to facilitate security testing. You can drive the tools from VS test suites, but they are not delivered as part of the VS product itself.

> **■ TESTING FOR SECURITY VIOLATIONS**
>
> VS uses the code analysis described in Chapter 6 to check for security violations, but there are tools and process templates available for free as part of the Microsoft Security Development Lifecycle (SDL) guidance. See www.microsoft.com/security/sdl/getstarted/tools.aspx for a current list.

Summary

This chapter is about the testing of high-functioning teams following the Agile Consensus. Far from the misconceptions that agilists only do unit tests, or that testers have no role on Agile teams, tests of PBIs are essential to the definition of *done*. Indeed, work should be sequenced to facilitate getting PBIs through acceptance testing to done as quickly as possible.

VS has a unique approach to supporting Agile teams. It flows from the idea that only the bugs that get fixed add customer value, and all the activity around reporting bugs that don't get fixed is, from the customer viewpoint, waste. MTM is designed to make every bug captured fully actionable, so that a developer does not need to attempt to reproduce the case but can instead work directly from the captured data.

VS also enables early load testing, so that design flaws affecting performance can be caught in early sprints, when there is time to refactor and change the design. Configuration testing with virtualized labs is built in to the build automation workflow, and so testing can happen immediately in production-realistic environments.

This is a fundamentally collaborative approach to testing, where the multidisciplinary team can work as a unit toward a common goal. It breaks down the traditional walls among disciplines, avoids the messy handoffs of work, and focuses instead on a single flow of customer value and reduction of waste.

The next chapter is an experience report of our application inside Microsoft of the principles you've read so far. Not everything was perfect, and we had to repeatedly inspect and adapt. You'll soon understand how that experience shaped the product line described thus far.

Endnotes

1   Kent Beck, *Test-Driven Development* (Addison Wesley, 2002), 86.

2   Sarony and Major, The Landing of the Pilgrims, on Plymouth Rock, Dec. 11th 1620 (lithograph, published 1846).

3   James Bach, "Exploratory Testing Explained," 2002, available from www.satisfice.com/articles.shtml; and James A. Whittaker, *Exploratory Software Testing* (Pearson Education, 2010).

4   James A. Whittaker and Herbert H. Thompson, *How to Break Software Security* (Addison Wesley, 2003); and Michael Howard, David LeBlanc, and John Viega, *24 Deadly Sins of Software Security: Programming Flaws and How to Fix Them* (McGraw-Hill Osborne Media, 2009).

5   This chapter provides a drive-by look at the testing capability in VS 2010. For an in-depth survey, see Jeff Levinson, *Software Testing with Visual Studio 2010* (Addison Wesley Professional, 2011).

6   Anutthara Bharadwaj, "Guidance for Creating Test Plans and Suites," September 22, 2010, http://blogs.msdn.com/b/anutthara/ archive/ 2010/09/22/guidance-for-creating-test-plans-and-test-suites.aspx.

7   Boris Beizer, *Software Testing Techniques* (Boston: International Thomson Computer Press, 1990), 9.

8   For a classic discussion of the risks of bad automation, see James Bach, "Test Automation Snake Oil," originally published in *Windows Tech Journal* (November 1996), available at www.satisfice.com/ articles/test_automation_snake_oil.pdf.

9   Beizer, *op. cit.*, 535.

10 Whittaker and Thompson, *op. cit.* Whittaker and Thompson have identified 19 attack patterns that are standard approaches to hacking systems.

9

Lessons Learned at Microsoft Developer Division

We must, indeed, all hang together or, most assuredly, we shall all hang separately.

—Benjamin Franklin, upon signing the treasonous Declaration of Independence

FIGURE 9.1: At any one time, Developer Division has to balance multiple competing business goals.

JOINED MICROSOFT DEVELOPER DIVISION (DevDiv) in 2003 to participate in the vision of turning the world's most popular *individual* development environment, Visual Studio (VS), into the world's most popular *team* development environment. Of course, that meant embracing modern software engineering practices for our customers.

At the same time, DevDiv faced significant challenges to improve its own agility. I had no idea how long a road lay ahead of our internal teams to change their culture, practices, and tooling. It has been and continues to be a fascinating journey.

In this chapter, we compare three waves of improvement that we undertook, each of approximately two years. The first big change in our practices was the transition from the release of VS 2005 with .NET 3.0 and VS 2008 with .NET 3.5,[1] where we focused on the reduction of waste and trustworthy transparency. Second came VS 2008 to VS 2010, where we emphasized flow of value. And most recently, from VS 2010 to VS 2012, where we shortened cycle time.

Scale

For context, let me review the scale of work. DevDiv is responsible for shipping the VS product line and .NET Framework. These major releases are used by millions of customers around the world. They have ten-year support contracts. They are localized into nine languages. More than 3,500 engineers contribute to a release of the stack. Our divisional Team Foundation Server (TFS) instance manages more than 20,000,000 source files, 700,000 work items, 2,000 monthly builds, and 15 terabytes of data.[2]

We are also continually "dogfooding" our own products and processes. This means that we experiment internally on ourselves before releasing functionality to customers. For example, we implemented the hierarchical product backlog I describe on TFS 2005 although TFS didn't really support hierarchy until its 2010 release, and our internal experience drove the TFS product changes. In the next chapter, we describe a breadth of practices we pioneered internally and will be releasing in vNext.

Like many customers at our scale, we had to customize our TFS process template, both to allow the innovations and to deal with specific constraints, notably interoperation with our own legacy systems. As we have been developing TFS, we have had to interoperate with five separate internal predecessors for source control, bug tracking, build automation, test case management, and test labs. These predecessor systems were all home-grown and designed over decades in isolation of each other, not to mention of TFS.[3]

Business Background

As with any organization, it's important to start with the business context. DevDiv provides tools and frameworks that support many different Microsoft product lines. Many of DevDiv's products, such as the .NET Framework, Internet Explorer's F12 tools, and Visual Studio Express, are free. They exist not to make money, but to make it easier for the community and customers to develop software to target Windows, Windows Azure, Office, SQL Server, and other Microsoft technologies. Other products, such as the rest of the VS product line and MSDN, are commercial, typically licensed by subscription.

An obvious tension exists among the business goals. Different internal and external stakeholders have very different priorities. And very frequently the number one top item for one constituency is invisible to other groups.

As I've explained this situation to customers over the years, I've realized that these sorts of tensions among conflicting business priorities are quite common. Every business has different specifics, but the idea that you cannot simply optimize for one goal over the rest is common. As a result, divergent business goals create conflicting priorities among stakeholders.

Scrum teaches us that the right way to reconcile these priorities is through a single product owner and common product backlog, and at this scale, we have to aggregate to coarser-grained portfolio items. When I started in 2003, prior to the availability of TFS, the division had no way to look at its investments as a single backlog or portfolio. No one (literally) had the ability to comprehend a list of more than a thousand features. Accordingly, the primary portfolio management technique when I joined was head-count allocation. Head count, in turn, had become the cherished currency of status.

Culture

Microsoft has three very healthy HR practices:

1. Hiring the best, brightest, and most passionate candidates, usually straight from university
2. Delegating as much responsibility as far down the organization as possible
3. Encouraging career development and promotion through rotation into new roles and challenges

These practices make Microsoft a great place to work. In 2003 DevDiv, however, they were creating an unexpected consequence of reinforcing Conway's law, that *organizations which design systems … are constrained to produce designs which are copies of the communication structures of these organizations.*[4]

USC Professor Dave Logan and his colleagues have probably studied company culture as much as anyone. In their book *Tribal Leadership*, Logan et al. identify five stages of organizational maturity. Stage Three covers 48% of the professionals that they have studied.

> The essence of Stage Three is "I'm great." Unstated and lurking in the background is "and you're not." …The key words are "I," "me," and "my."[5]

This dysfunctional tribalism was widely visible in the DevDiv I saw in 2003. At the time, the main organizational tribe was a "product unit" (PU), averaging roughly 60 people. The dysfunction was characterized by five behaviors, which I stereotype here:

- **Don't ask, don't tell.** There was an implicit convention that no manager would push on another's assertions, in order not to be questioned on his own.

- **Schedule chicken.** Scheduling was a game of who blinked first. Each PU self-fulfillingly knew that the schedule would slip because someone else would be late. Therefore, each PU kept an invisible assumption that it would be able to catch up during the other team's slippage.

- **Metrics are for others.** No PU particularly saw the need for itself to be accountable to any metrics, although accountability was clearly a good idea for the other guys because they were slipping the schedule first.

- **Our customers are different.** Because DevDiv has such a broad product line, with many millions of users of VS and hundreds of millions of users of .NET, it was very easy for any PU to claim different sources of customer evidence from another and to argue for its own agenda.

- **Our tribe is better.** Individuals took great pride in their individual PUs, and their PUMs (product unit managers) went to great lengths to reinforce PU morale. Rarely did that allegiance align to a greater whole.

Waste

In 2003, DevDiv experienced every kind of waste listed in Table 1.1 in Chapter 1, "The Agile Consensus." One illustration of this is shown in Figure 9.2. This chart shows the bug trends to Beta 1 of what became VS 2005. Different colors show different teams, and the red downward-sloped line shows the desired active bug "step-down" for Beta 1. This is a prescriptive metric with all the negative behavioral implications listed in Chapter 4, "Running the Sprint."

More important than the "successful" tracking of the step-down is the roughly flat line on top. This represents the 30,000 bugs whose handling was *deferred* to the next milestone, Beta 2. Imagine a huge transfer station of nondegradable waste, all of which has to be manually sorted for further disposal. This multiple handling is one waste from bug deferral.

This line is the consequence of the prescription: a growing invisible backlog of deferred bug debt.

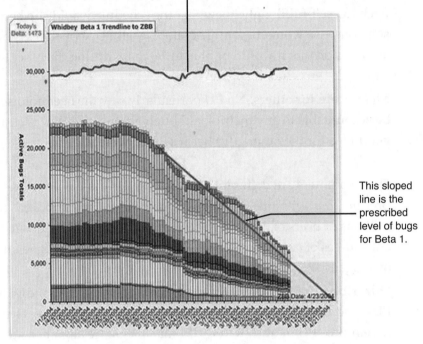

This sloped
line is the
prescribed
level of bugs
for Beta 1.

FIGURE 9.2: This chart shows the actual VS 2005 bug step-down, as of two weeks before Beta 1.

Debt Crisis

In everyday life, debt incurs interest, and the less creditworthy the borrower, the higher the interest rate. When the subprime lending bubble of 2003–8 burst, it clearly showed the "moral hazard" of not following such basic economic principles. Similarly, the uneven product quality implied by this high bug count creates its own moral hazards:

- It makes the beta ineffective as a feedback mechanism. Customers see too many broken windows to comment on the positive qualities.
- Internal teams see others' bug backlogs and play schedule chicken.
- Teams are encouraged to overproduce (that is, put in pet features) rather than fix the fundamentals.

- The endgame is very hard to predict. No one knows how much of the iceberg still lies below the water and, therefore, how much real work remains in the release.

Not surprisingly, we experienced significant schedule slippage in the 2005 release cycle and, by the time we shipped, had very uneven morale.

Improvements after 2005

So what did we do differently the next time? Broadly speaking, we put seven changes in place for the next release cycle. I cover each in turn:

- Get clean, stay clean
- Tighter timeboxes
- Feature crews
- Defining done
- Product backlog
- Iteration backlog
- Engineering principles

Get Clean, Stay Clean

Prior to the start of any product work, we instituted a milestone for quality (MQ for short). The purpose of MQ was to eliminate our technical debt and to put in place an engineering system that would prevent its future accumulation. The two main areas of technical debt we addressed were bugs and tests. Both of these were large sources of multiple handling.

The goal was to have zero known bugs at the end of MQ. This meant that any bug that had been previously deferred needed to be fixed (and validated with an automated regression test) or closed permanently. As a result, we would no longer waste time reconsidering bugs from earlier releases. This idea runs contrary to a common practice of seeding a release by looking at previously deferred work. It is enormously healthy; you start the new release plan from zero inventory.

The goal with tests was to have all tests run green reliably. Unreliable tests would be purged and not used again. In other words, we wanted to eliminate the need for manual analysis of test runs, especially build verification tests (BVTs). In the past, we had found that test results were plagued by false negatives (that is, reported test failures that were not due to product failures but to flaky test runs). This then led to a long manual analysis of test runs before the "true" results could be acted on. (Have you ever seen that?) Eliminating the test debt required both refactoring tests to be more resilient and making improvements to test tooling and infrastructure. (You can see the partial productization of these capabilities in the build and lab management capabilities of VS 2010.)

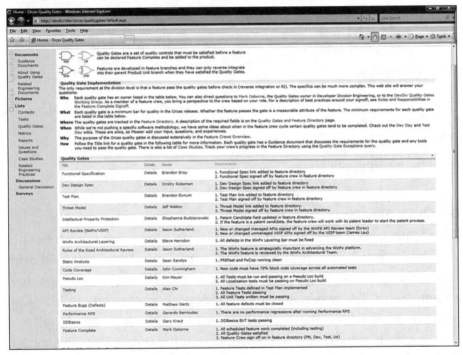

FIGURE 9.3: Divisional quality gates were the definition of done for the feature crew.

Different quality gates applied to different components of the product line. For example, redistributable platform components, such as the .NET Framework, required architectural reviews around compatibility and layering that were not necessary for the VS IDE. These rules were visible to the whole division.

Integration and Isolation

When developing a complex product like VS, a constant tension exists between the need of feature crews to be isolated from other teams' changes and the need to have the full source base integrated so that all teams can work on the latest code. To solve this, we allowed feature crews to work in isolated branches, and then to integrate with closely related crews, and then to integrate into Main. Figure 9.4 shows the branching structure to support the feature crews.

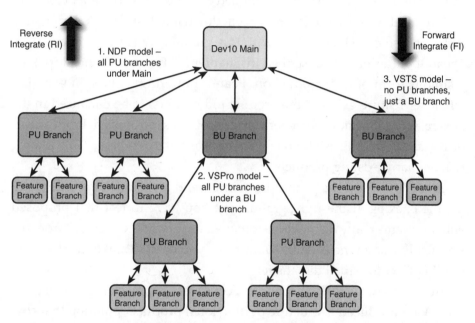

FIGURE 9.4: The branching structure balances isolated workspaces for the feature crews during the sprint with easy integration of related features by value propositions in a PU.

The third level of done was the integration tests to support the promotion of code across branches. When the feature passed the quality gates, the source code, and the tests, the feature crew promoted it to the "product unit branch," where the integration tests would run. Upon satisfying these, the crew then promoted the feature into Main and it became part of the divisional build. The fourth level of done criteria was applied to Main. Both nightly and weekly test cycles were run here.

It's worth noting that both the *branch visualization* and *gated check-in* of VS 2010, as described in Chapter 6, "Development," and Chapter 7, "Build and Lab," were designed based largely on our internal experience of enforcing quality gates for feature promotion. The core idea is to automate the definition of *done* and ensure that code and test quality live up to the social contract.

Product Backlog

DevDiv was an organization conditioned over a decade to think in terms of features. Define the features, break them down into tasks, work through the tasks, and so on. The problem with this granularity is that it encourages "peanut buttering" (as described in Chapter 3, "Product Ownership"), an insidious form of overproduction. Peanut buttering is the mind-set that whatever feature exists in the product today needs to be enhanced in the next release, alongside whatever new capability is introduced. From a business standpoint, this is obviously an endless path into bloat. This is a big risk on many existing products.

A key to reverse the peanut-buttering trend is the need to conceptualize the backlog at the right granularity. You have to test that proposed enhancements really do move customer value forward, when seen from the product line as a whole. At the same time, you need to make sure that you don't neglect the small dissatisfiers.

Accordingly, we took a holistic and consistent approach to product planning. We introduced a structure of functional product definition that covered value propositions, experiences, and features. For each level, we used a canonical question to frame the granularity. We rolled out training for all the teams.

Conceptually, the taxonomy is shown in Figure 9.5. To manage this data, we set up a team project in our TFS with separate work item types for each of the value proposition, experience, and feature.

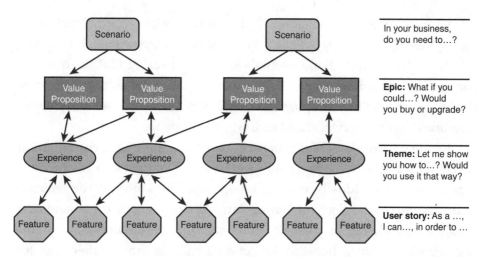

FIGURE 9.5: To keep the backlog at the right level of granularity for a product line of this scope, we used scenarios, experiences, and features, each at the appropriate level of concern.

Scenarios

In Agile terms, scenarios are epics. In a scenario, we start by considering the value propositions that motivate customers (teams or individuals) to purchase or upgrade to the new version of our platform and tools. We consider the complete customer experience during development, and we follow through to examine what it will take to make customers satisfied enough to want to buy more, renew, upgrade, and recommend our software to others.

A scenario is a way of defining tangible customer value with our products. It addresses a problem that customers face, stated in terms that a customer will relate to. In defining a scenario, we ask teams to capture its value proposition with the question: *What if you could..., would that influence you to buy or upgrade?* This question helps keep the scenario sufficiently large to matter and its customer value sufficiently obvious.

We also created two categories that didn't really belong to scenarios, but were managed similarly. These were called *Fundamentals* and *Remove Customer Dissatisfiers.* Fundamentals speak to ensuring that the qualities of service are suitably met. In the case of the VS product line, these include compatibility, compliance, reliability, performance, security, world-readiness, user experience, and ecosystem experience.

Remove Customer Dissatisfiers, in turn, was there to ensure that our users didn't "die from a thousand paper cuts." Plenty of small complaints can show up individually as either low-priority bugs or small convenience features, but can collectively create large distractions. If these items are triaged individually, they usually don't get fixed. This is an example of the aggregation of small items in the product backlog into meatier ones for stack ranking that I described in Chapter 3. Accordingly, we suggested a discretionary level of investment by teams in this area.

Experiences

Scenarios translate into one or more experiences. Experiences are stories that describe *how we envision users doing work with our product:* What user tasks are required to deliver on a value proposition? The test question here is to imagine the demo to a customer: *Let me show you how….*

Features

Experiences, in turn, drive features. As we flesh out what experiences look like, we define the features that we need to support the experience. A feature can support more than one experience. (In fact, this is common.) Most features are defined as user stories.

Figure 9.6 shows a top-down report of the product backlog. It is opened to drill down from a scenario (called *value propositions* here) into the experiences and features.

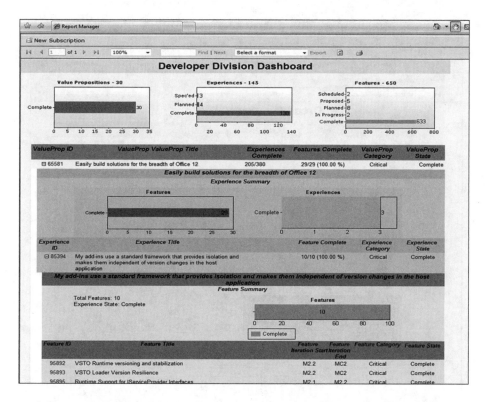

FIGURE 9.6: An internal custom TFS report showed the status of features, rolling up to experiences, rolling up to scenarios (value propositions). This has been superseded in TFS 2010 by hierarchical queries.

Iteration Backlog

Features were the connection between the product backlog and iteration backlog (see Figure 9.7). As we moved into a sprint, feature crews committed to delivering one or more features according to the quality gates. This affected how we had to define features when grooming the product backlog.

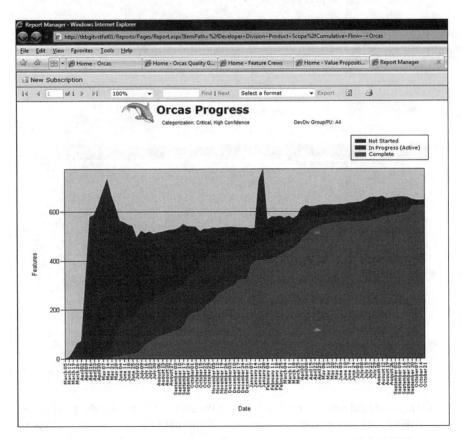

FIGURE 9.7: Because features were the deliverable units of the product backlog, overall progress could be tracked as a cumulative flow of features. Again, this was a custom report, now superseded by the TFS dashboards.

Because features turned into units of delivery, we tried to define them to optimize productivity. Well-defined features were *coarse-grained enough to be visible to a customer* or consumed by another feature, and *fine-grained enough to be delivered in a sprint*. To pass the quality gates, they needed to be independently testable. Dependencies among features needed to be clearly defined. Figure 9.8 shows a track of remaining work for a single feature, and Figure 9.9 illustrates an intermediate organizational view of features in flight.

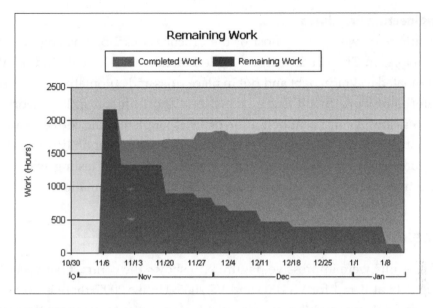

FIGURE 9.8: This simple burndown chart measures the progress of a single feature.

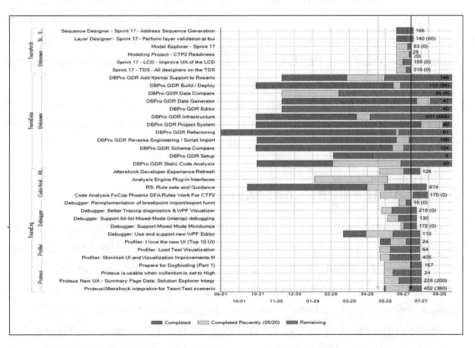

FIGURE 9.9: Features in progress can be viewed by organizational structure. The black vertical line shows today's date. There are three status colors on this chart: dark green for completed more than seven days ago, light green for completed in the last seven days, and red
for remaining.

Engineering Principles

In summary, we applied most of the practices described as engineering principles in Chapter 2, "Scrum, Agile Practices, and Visual Studio." We eliminated technical debt and put in place rules and automation to prevent deferral of work. Small feature crews and short timeboxes kept work in process low. A consistent definition of *done,* coupled to the correct branching strategy and automation, kept the codebase potentially shippable. Automated testing was used widely, and exploratory testing was used selectively where new scenarios were not ready for automation.

Results

The results were impressive. Figure 9.10 shows the contrast between the bug debt at Beta 1 for VS 2005 and VS 2008. Unlike 2005, there is no overhang of deferral, and *the reduction in debt was greater than 15x.* At the same time, the schedule from beginning of the release work to general availability was *half* as long. And the transparency of process allowed reasonable engagement of stakeholders all along the way. Post release, we saw the results, as well. There has been a huge (and ongoing) rise in customer satisfaction with the VS product line.

In addition to improving our product delivery, this experience improved the VS product line. Many of the practices that we applied internally became product scenarios, especially for TFS.

Acting on the Agile Consensus

Having significantly reduced waste and improved transparency in the VS 2008 product line allowed us to act on the third principle of the Agile Consensus: We could improve the flow of value to our customers. As we entered the VS 2010 product cycle, we laid out several ambitious scenarios, based on the combination of customer requirements and what we discovered through our own usage. As you can see from the names in Figure 9.11, these were informed by the journey so far and have been described through the previous chapters.

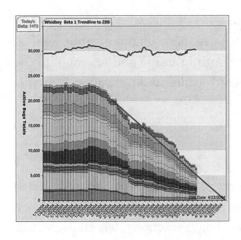

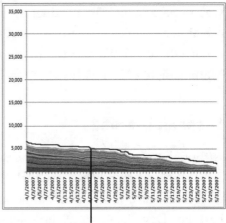

Total bug debt at Beta 1 of VS 2008.

FIGURE 9.10: Comparison of bug debt at Beta 1 between VS 2005 and VS 2008. The left chart is identical to Figure 9.2, and the right shows the total bug debt leading to Beta 1 of VS 2008. The improvement is a reduction from 30,000 to 2,000 at comparable points in the product cycle.

Aspirational Lean Scenarios

What if you could experience No More...

No repro	Late surprises
Production mismatches	Build breaks
Waiting for build setup	Parallel development pain
UI regressions	Bewildering admin
Performance regressions	Butterfly effects or legacy fear
Planning black box	Code & fix
Missed requirements or changes	

FIGURE 9.11: The scenarios planned for VS 2010 show how the team embraced reducing waste and increasing transparency through the development life cycle.

We succeeded. VS 2010 achieved a level of customer recognition that was unparalleled. The product line won readers' choice awards, analyst acclaim, and market share, measured both in usage and revenue, to the point where it is largely the undisputed leader in Application Lifecycle Management (ALM) software.[6]

Lessons Learned

Although the improvements we achieved from the 2005 to 2008 and 2008 to 2010 releases of VS were very real, there were some subsequent surprises. Newton's third law states that actions beget reactions, whether good or bad. For DevDiv, some of these were due to "soft" issues around people and culture; others resulted from unforeseen effects of the engineering practices.

When we ship a release at Microsoft, people often change jobs. For employees, this rotation is an opportunity both to develop a career and improve personal satisfaction in trying new challenges. Indeed, several of Microsoft's divisions build a reorganization period into the beginning of their release planning. Although this is a healthy pattern for the company and its employees overall, in the short term it can create a sort of amnesia.

Social Contracts Need Renewal

Unfortunately, one success is not enough to create long-term habits. In 2008, DevDiv experienced excessive optimism after a successfully executed release. As many new managers took their jobs, they confidently plowed ahead without an MQ and without planning and grooming the backlog. Accordingly, the road to the 2010 release suffered from some considerable backslides.

It was reminiscent of a scene in 1981, when an assassination attempt incapacitated President Ronald Reagan, the vice president was abroad, and Secretary of State Al Haig convened the White House press corps to announce, "I am in charge here." Haig prompted wide and immediate ridicule because he demonstrated his own ignorance of the line of succession specified by a constitutional amendment two decades earlier. During the reorganization after we shipped VS 2008, some positions were vacant longer than usual, and in the interim, several folks declared themselves in control of release planning. Of course, this self-declared authority did not work here either.

Lessons (Re)Learned

DevDiv recovered, and in the end, VS 2010 has been the best release of the VS product line ever. The progress was not linear, however. We learned several engineering lessons from the sloppy start in 2008 and skipping MQ in particular.

Product Ownership Needs Explicit Agreement

With ambiguous product ownership, there was no clear prioritization of the backlog and no way to resolve conflicting viewpoints. We did not yet have a consistent organizational process, and we needed to renegotiate the social contract.

Planning and Grooming the Product Backlog Cannot Be Skipped

If you don't have a backlog that provides a clear line of sight to customer value, all prioritization decisions seem arbitrary. As a result, individuals revert to the local tribes that they know best.

The Backlog Needs to Ensure Qualities of Service

A particular oversight was the lack of suitable requirements in the backlog around the fundamentals, such as performance and reliability, and lack of clear product ownership for these. With both betas of VS 2010, we earned significant negative feedback regarding product performance. Figure 9.12 shows sample results of the performance instrumentation that we introduced after Beta 1 to make performance visible for common customer experiences.

Fortunately, we recovered by the time of release to manufacturing (RTM), but at considerable cost (including some schedule delay). Had we set the fundamentals early, established the ownership, and put in place the instrumentation and transparent reporting at the beginning of the release cycle, we would not have had to pay for the recovery.

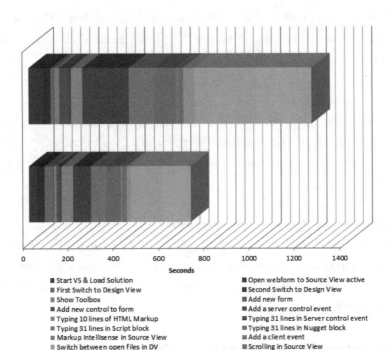

0	200	400	600	800	1000	1200	1400	

Seconds

- Start VS & Load Solution
- First Switch to Design View
- Show Toolbox
- Add new control to form
- Typing 10 lines of HTML Markup
- Typing 31 lines in Script block
- Markup Intellisense in Source View
- Switch between open files in DV

- Open webform to Source View active
- Second Switch to Design View
- Add new form
- Add a server control event
- Typing 31 lines in Server control event
- Typing 31 lines in Nugget block
- Add a client event
- Scrolling in Source View

FIGURE 9.12: The chart compares an early build of VS 2010 and VS 2008 SP1 through a common scenario from starting the IDE to producing a simple application and closing the IDE. This is an example of transparent measurement raising awareness and focusing action.

One Team's Enhancement Is Another's Breaking Change

In a product line this complex, it is easy for one team's great enhancements to be crippling changes for another team. We had put a clear definition of *done* in place for the previous release, and automated much of it, but we didn't maintain the practices or the automation cleanly. Most visibly, our integration tests were not acting as a suitable safety net. As a result, we had significant friction around code integration.

Test Automation Needs Maintenance

We had invested heavily in test automation to validate configurations and prevent regressions, but we let the tests get stale. They effectively tested 2005 functionality, but not the new technologies from 2008. Without an MQ to update the integration tests in particular, we discovered we could not predict the effects of integration. As a result, a team promoting changes had no way of determining the effects on other teams until the recipients complained.

Complicating the problem was the false sense of security given by automated test runs. If the tests are not finding important problems fast, and catching quality gaps *prior* to integration, they are the wrong tests.

Broken Quality Gates Create Change Impedance

There is a side effect to having the engineering infrastructure in this broken state. There were still quality gates, but they weren't ensuring the intended quality because we hadn't maintained them. As a result, they became impediments to change rather than enablers. As we realized this, we cleaned up the problem, but again much later than we should have. This pointed out clearly not only why it was important to *get clean* at a point in time, but also why we then needed to *stay clean.*

Celebrate Successes, but Don't Declare Victory

The overriding management lesson for me is to celebrate successes but not declare victory. In our case, we forgot the pain of the VS 2005 release, and after the success of VS 2008, we decided to skip MQ, neglect our backlog, and underinvest in our engineering processes. We have since recovered, but with the reminder that we have to stay vigilant and self-critical.

It takes strong leadership, a strong social contract, and consistent language among the tribe to counteract this tendency. Part of this is the move from dysfunctional to functional tribalism, or in Dave Logan's terminology, from Stage Three to Four. People in a Stage Four organization do the following:

> Build values-based relationships between others. At the same time, the words of Stage Four people are centered on "we're great" … When people at Stage Four cluster together, they radiate tribal pride.[7]

The Path to Visual Studio 2012

The Visual Studio 2012 wave represents the third major phase of improvement for DevDiv. We had worked on reducing waste, increasing trustworthy transparency, and expanding flow of value. Once you have mastered the three principles of the Agile Consensus, the next challenge you face is to get better at expanding continuous flow. We believe that there are two key actionable metrics here: cycle time, how long it takes to turn an idea from the product backlog into working software in customer's hands, and mean time to repair (MTTR), the interval from an unwanted event in production to the root cause being fixed and the service redeployed and in use by the customer. These metrics are shown in Figure 9.13.

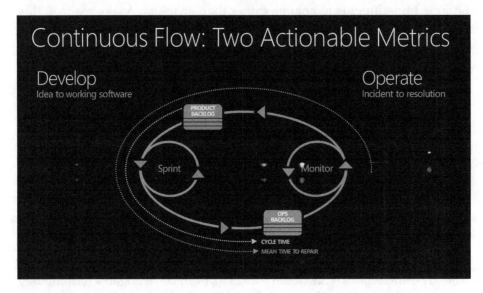

FIGURE 9.13: The two key metrics for improvement of continuous flow are cycle time and MTTR.

During the development of Visual Studio 2012, teams worked in synchronous sprints of three weeks. At the end of each sprint, we would update our "pioneer" server of TFS, and new builds of the client IDE were available daily intrasprint. Because of the earlier practice improvements, builds were just expected to work.

We coordinated across geographies by recording the sprint review demos as videos, individually accessible by PBI. That way, colleagues in

Hyderabad, India, could see progress in Redmond, Washington, without the entire cohort having to stay up late into the night. (One representative from each site would be present at the other site's review.)

We would also extend our sprint reviews to include customers. Through a regular cadence of Web calls with our customer advisory councils, we would use the video demos and extend the sprint review into a broader panel to drill into areas where the team needed more feedback.

The Visual Studio 2012 wave coincided with a shift in the industry from on-premises deployment of software to the early use of the public cloud. Microsoft's public cloud, Windows Azure, is one of the major "Platforms as a Service" (PaaS), and we used that to pioneer a new form of TFS, Team Foundation Service, which became available as a developer preview in September 2011.

Team Foundation Service raised the bar on our expectations once again. In the past, at the end of every three-week sprint, code was ready for internal "dogfooding." On the Service, every three weeks it is deployed live for customer use. And because we are connected to our users, we monitor Twitter and email continually as a support channel. Although we have extensive monitoring through instrumentation, synthetic transactions, and points of presence, an individual customer may still be the first to experience a problem. As soon as the customer notifies us, we can ask for permission to attach to the customer's instance and remediate, and we can measure our ability in minutes.

Endnotes

[1] For simplicity, I refer to these as VS 2005 and 2008, without differentiating the .NET platform components, the VS IDE, TFS, or the ALM components formerly known as Team System. I also skip the dozens of power tools and releases of Internet Information Services (IIS), ASP.NET, Silverlight, and so on that shipped in between the major releases.

[2] There are approximately 30 other instances in Microsoft, but I'm writing here about DevDiv, where I have firsthand experience.

3 You can download the process template we used internally from http://mpt.codeplex.com/. However, the process templates that we ship are much leaner, take advantage of the 2010 features, and aren't tinged by the internal constraints.

4 Melvin E. Conway, "How Do Committees Invent?" *Datamation* 14:5 (April, 1968): 28–31, available at www.melconway.com/research/committees.html. Amazingly, Conway's law was completely anecdotal for 40 years, until empirical validation by Microsoft Research in Nachiappan Nagappan, Brendan Murphy, and Victor Basili, "The Influence of Organizational Structure On Software Quality: An Empirical Case Study," January 2008, available at http://research.microsoft.com/apps/pubs/default.aspx?id=70535.

5 Dave Logan, John King, and Halee Fischer-Wright, *Tribal Leadership: Leveraging Natural Groups to Build a Thriving Organization* (New York: HarperCollins, 2008), 77.

6 For example, see Gartner ALM Magic Quadrant, published May 2012, available from www.gartner.com.

7 Logan, *op. cit.*, 255.

■ 10 ■

Continuous Feedback

The best way to predict the future is to invent it.[1]

—Alan C. Kay

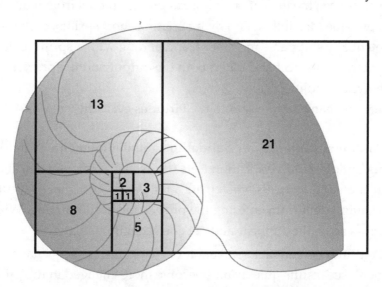

FIGURE 10.1: Fibonacci described his numeric sequence in his *Liber Abaci* (Book of Calculation) in 1202. It is now one of the most widely discovered sequences in nature. Its reuse for estimation (Chapter 3, "Product Ownership") nearly a millennium later is hardly a coincidence.[2]

B Y NOW, WE HOPE WE'VE convinced you of three things:

1. The Agile Consensus is empirically sound, practical, and here to stay.
2. Visual Studio (VS) 2012 provides broad tooling to help you follow the Agile Consensus practices.
3. And if you do, you can practically improve the flow of value to your customers, reduce waste, and improve transparency in your software development.

This chapter summarizes these points and builds on them, showing you where VS is going in its next release and how it will help you even further.

Agile Consensus in Action

You've now seen the idea of an empirical process model from many lenses. Scrum puts the idea into action by mandating short sprints, each resulting in a potentially shippable increment, and ending with a sprint review and retrospective to inspect and adapt both the output and the process. Figure 10.2 shows a simplified view.

There are many advantages to the virtuous cycle this creates:

1. **Continuous integration, validation, and deployment.** By automating builds, build verification tests (BVTs), lab deployments, and production deployments, you create a regular process that prevents technical debt from entering the project and accumulating. When errors arise, they appear and get corrected immediately.
2. **Continuous feedback.** Stakeholders (customers, users, management) see results quickly and become more engaged in the project, offering more time, insight, and funding. The most energizing phenomenon on a software team is seeing early releases perform (or be demoed) in action. No amount of spec review can substitute for the value of working bits.

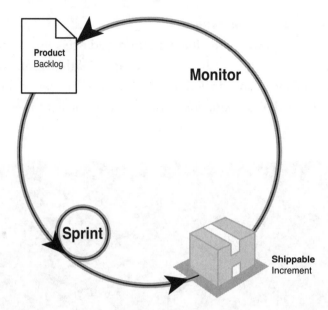

FIGURE 10.2: The simplest view of the continuous feedback cycle

3. **Continuous learning.** People can retain only so much in their heads. By batching work into product backlog items (PBIs) and PBIs into small sprints, all the team players focus more closely on the work at hand. The entire team learns from each iteration, improving the accuracy, quality, and suitability of the finished product.

As cycles get faster, the opportunity to expand this continuous flow of value grows ever greater.

Continuous Feedback Allows Build/Measure/Learn

Along with the acceptance of the Agile Consensus in the last decade, the Lean Startup movement has emerged, based on the teachings of Steve Blank and Eric Ries.[3] They call the three steps we just described *Build/ Measure/Learn.* For Lean start-ups, the key to success is to capture the business hypothesis in the product backlog, build and deploy the minimum increment necessary to test the hypothesis, measure results against that increment, and accumulate validated learning against the hypothesis. This allows you to persevere or pivot in the next cycle.

Continuous Feedback Everywhere

In many ways, continuous feedback flattens and accelerates the software life cycle, as shown in Figure 10.3. Every chapter of this book has taken an aspect of the life cycle and drilled into its practice. In every chapter, we've introduced the notion of feedback appropriate to the activities in that part of the cycle.

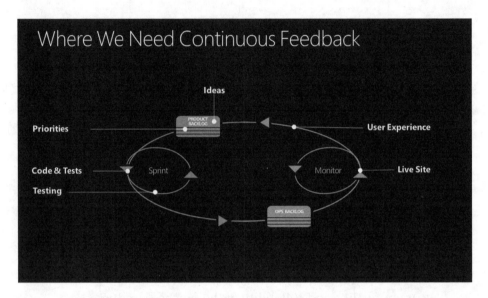

FIGURE 10.3: Continuous feedback applies to all aspects of software, in all the components of the life cycle.

Chapter 3 discussed product ownership and the need for grooming the ideas in the product backlog. At a minimum, you should gather feedback after every sprint cycle with sprint reviews. VS 2012 takes this further. VS now provides storyboards, Feedback Requests, and Feedback Responses specifically to allow you to bring the stakeholder and customer perspective into the team continuously, as frequently as with the initiation and completion of the individual PBI.

Chapter 4, "Running the Sprint," covered just that, which requires the balancing of priorities and execution. The Team Web Access task board provides a real-time view of progress and its backlog view lets you see capacity. The portal gives you a multidimensional view of project health so that you can spot "smells" that would require any change in priority.

Feedback is not just for the team; it is also for the individual developer and tester. Chapter 5, "Architecture," showed how architectural layer validation can prevent drift from entering a codebase and creating future technical debt. Especially when used with gated check-in, this becomes a powerful source of immediate feedback from the code itself.

Unit tests are, of course, a key source of feedback to you, as a developer, and were discussed in Chapter 6, "Development." They allow the safety of red-green-refactor and reliable continuous integration and deployment. Code analysis allows your code to be checked against rules for correctness. Code reviews allow you to have a fellow team member give you feedback on your changes. Gated check-in will catch any mistakes you make by running a full build workflow before accepting your changes into the source codebase.

Because Team Foundation Server (TFS) tracks all of the changes with work item associations made at check-in—whether from the VS or Eclipse IDEs—you or your reviewer has the full context from the time you start work. And with the My Work pane of VS 2012, which allows you to suspend and resume work, you can stay in the groove even when you have to switch tasks to handle a live site issue or a code review for a buddy.

Chapter 7, "Build and Lab," covered the automation to make these workflows frictionless. If they require manual bookkeeping, they're simply too cumbersome and prone to error. Fortunately, continuous integration and deployment give you the freedom of automated builds, test labs, and deployment, without the overhead.

Testing from the users' perspective is also key feedback, and this was covered in Chapter 8, "Testing." Some of this is planned from the product backlog, some is based on qualities of service, and some emerges through exploration.

There's No Place Like Production

The best feedback is production use. In Chapter 9, "Lessons Learned at Microsoft Developer Division," we covered how the functionality that we ship in VS has grown through productizing what we use at Microsoft, and how we use our own versions internally well before releasing to customers. That has been our practice for years.

Actually, the cloud is accelerating that considerably.

Cycle Time and Feedback in the Cloud

The largest transformation of computing since the Internet explosion is the *cloud*. Microsoft's cloud offering is Windows Azure, and we have been moving TFS to Windows Azure to make it available as a Software as a Service (SaaS) offering. Figure 10.4 shows the home page as of June 2012.

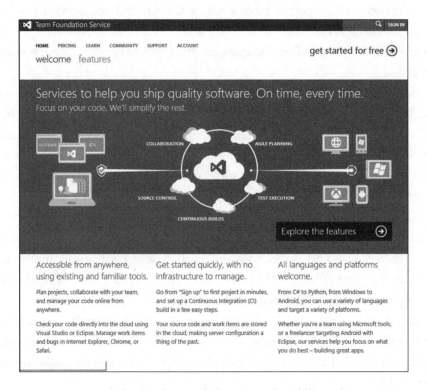

FIGURE 10.4: Team Foundation Service on Windows Azure in public preview

With Team Foundation *Service*, we deploy functionality to *customers* every three weeks. We collect feedback in real time. This would not be possible without great monitoring. It's worth noting that we watch not only internal metrics from our servers and synthetic transactions from points of presence, but also consider the Twitter stream a key source of information, as shown in Figure 10.5.

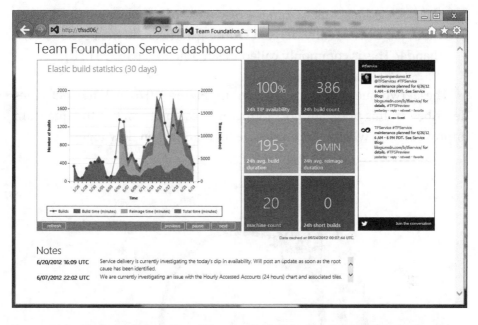

FIGURE 10.5: The internal Team Foundation Service monitoring dashboard cycles through service-generated metrics on the left and in the tiles, shows a log of operator notes at the bottom, and displays the Twitter stream on the right.

With Twitter, any user can report an issue in production. We can respond by requesting permission to attach to the user's instance. Once we have permission, we can start the clock and track our ability to fix the user's problem in minutes. This helps us mature beyond the measure of Service Level Agreements (SLAs),[4] which average out the user experience, mask the diagnosis to root cause, and hide the core improvement in service availability.

Summary

We've just offered a whirlwind tour of many of the capabilities of VS 2012. Not surprisingly, VS 2012 extends our vision of enabling a continuous flow of value. You can think of the flow in terms of two measures:

1. How long does it take from an idea entering the product backlog to the availability of working software in the user's hands? In standard Lean terminology, this is cycle time.

2. How long does it take from the discovery of a problem in production to the availability of fixed working software in the user's
hands? This is commonly called mean time to repair (MTTR).[5]

These two measures are shown in Figure 10.6. All the activities
described in this book support reducing these metrics, but the quantum
improvement is when you can see the total impact on flow together.

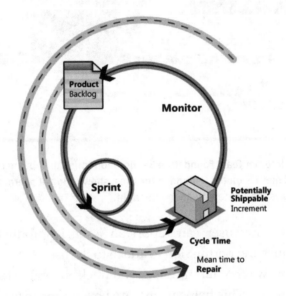

FIGURE 10.6: Cycle time and MTTR are the two key end-to-end measures of the flow
of value.

These are the ultimate measures of continuous flow. The transformation
of computing to cloud platforms, such as Windows Azure, is going to accelerate these flows and make the end-to-end measures evermore important.
The pressure to increase transparency, reduce waste, and improve flow of

value shown in Figure 1.2 will be more intense than ever. Not only will the most sophisticated Web sites practice continuous delivery, but the cloud will also help democratize the practice broadly and demand that we all practice *continuous feedback,* as described previously.

Living on the Edge of Chaos

The Great Recession changed many perspectives. At the beginning of this book, we cited the 2009 bankruptcies of Detroit manufacturers who had failed to catch up to Lean. Toyota, however, had its own surprises. It had mastered Lean, but not Agile. In the terminology of the Stacey Matrix of Figure 1.1, it adapted to a *complicated* world, but not a *complex* one. When safety problems became apparent with cars in use, Toyota stumbled in a massive recall and PR blunder. Here's what the *New York Times* reported:

> "The very culture that works so well for [Toyota] when things are stable and predictable really doesn't work when you're dealing with a fast-paced crisis," Jeremy Anwyl, the chief executive of the vehicle information Web site Edmunds.com, said.[6]

The Great Recession changed how many of us look at software practices, too. This period of economic crisis flipped the perspective on Agile practices from *let's wait and see* to *we can't afford not to.* Everything wasteful, everything contextual not core, everything not central to the customer's definition of value suddenly became superfluous.

Welcome to the edge of chaos. For the foreseeable future, we will be applying new technology as fast as we can. We will try to stay ahead of ambiguous customer desires as insightfully as we can. We will use continuous feedback loops to adjust as frequently as we can. The shorter our sprints, the more opportunities we have to inspect and adapt.

FIGURE 10.7: In chaos theory, the butterfly effect is the phenomenon of extreme sensitivity in a system to initial conditions, such as weather, leading to unpredictability. The only practical approach is to frequently inspect and adapt.[7]

Endnotes

[1] Alan C. Kay, "Predicting the Future," *Stanford Engineering* 1:1 (Autumn 1989), 1–6, www.ecotopia.com/webpress/futures.htm.

[2] www.aishdas.org/gallery/fibonac_8.gif and www.mathacademy.com/pr/prime/articles/fibonac/index.asp

[3] http://steveblank.com/ and http://theleanstartup.com/

[4] 0.999 translates to 40 minutes downtime for maintenance per month.

[5] There is an equally important use of MTTR as mean time to recovery, which is strictly in operations, keeping the site up so that the user does not experience the failure again. This may be done by masking the root cause (for example, by rebooting after a period of time, rather than by fixing the underlying problem).

[6] Nick Bunkley, "Recall Study Finds Flaws at Toyota," *New York Times*, May 23, 2011, B1.

[7] http://en.wikipedia.org/wiki/File:Lorenz_attractor_yb.svg

Index

7-Day Bug Trend Rates chart, 95
7-Day Issue Trend Rates chart, 93

A

acceptance tests, 27
Active Bugs by Assignment chart, 95
Active Bugs by Priority chart, 95
activity diagrams, 118
Agile Alliance, 2
Agile Consensus
  back to basics, 15
  flow of value
    defined, 5
    Scrum, 8-9
  principles, 5-6
  transparency
    defined, 5
    Scrum, 8
    self-managing teams, 11
  waste reduction
    defined, 5
    Taiichi Ohno's Taxonomy of Waste,
      9-11
Agile Manifesto, 2
ALM (Application Lifecycle
  Management), 258
analysis
  automated code, 152
  paralysis, 31

Anderson, David J., 38
application performance problems,
  diagnosing, 233-234
architecture
  ball of mud, 113
  dependency graphs, creating, 107
    broad coverage, 107
    code indexing, 108
    Quick Cluster layout, 109
    sequence of interactions between,
      110-113
    Solution Explorer, 109
    top-down, 107
  designing just enough, 104
  documenting, 119
  emergent, 105
  existing, 107
  Explorer, 114
  maintainability, 106-107
  structures, controlling, 113-117
    code mapping, 114
    existing codebases, 117
    intended dependencies, defining, 114
    layer validation, 115
  transparency, 105-106
  UML diagrams, 118
    activity, 118
    artifacts, sharing, 120
    component/class/sequence, 119

extending, 122-124
use case, 118
work item links, creating, 122
artifacts, sharing, 120
Austin, Robert, 86
automating
  builds, 181
    agents, maintaining, 185
    definitions, maintaining, 184
    BVTs, 182-183
    configuring, 181
    daily builds, 182
    deployment to test labs, 192, 196
    reports, 183-184
  code analysis, 152
  definition of done, 179
  scenario tests, 224-227
  task boards, 37
  tests, 223-224, 260

B

back to basics, 15
back-alley tours, 210
backlog
  iteration, 253-254
  product. *See* product backlog
  sprint, 27-28
ball of mud, 113
baseless merges, 167
behaviors
  distorting, 88
  unexpected, isolating, 154-155
Beizer, Boris, 219
Blank, Steve, 267
bottom-up cycles, 31
branching, 164
  benefits, 165
  by release, 165
  changes, 167
  viewing, 167
  work isolation, 165
broken windows theory, 90-91
Brown, Tim, 58

brownfield projects
  defined, 107
  dependency graphs, creating, 107
    broad coverage, 107
    code indexing, 108
    Quick Cluster layout, 109
    sequence of interaction between, 110-113
    Solution Explorer, 109
    top-down, 107
  layer diagrams, 117
bugs
  charts, 94-95
  dashboard, 95
  deferral, 245
  handling, 29, 223
  Ping-Pong, 12-13
  Progress Chart, 94-95
  reactivations, 95
  reproducing, 218
    DDAs, 215
    evolving tests, 219-221
    immersive app testing on Windows 8, 221
    solving, 218
  trends chart, 95
Build/Measure/Learn, 267-269
builds
  agents, 185
  automated, 181
    agents, maintaining, 185
    BVTs, 182-183
    definitions, maintaining, 184
    reports, 183-184
    configuring, 181
    daily builds, 182
    waste reduction, 12
  check-in policies, 137
  daily, 33
    chart, 94
    failures, 202
    testing, 196
  dashboard, 98

definitions, 184
failures, 202
process templates, 184
Quality Indicators report, 171, 203
test lab deployment, automating, 192, 196
reports, 183-184
Status chart, 94
Success Over Time report, 202
verification tests, 149, 182-183
Burndown dashboard, 92-93
business goals (DevDiv), 243-244
company culture, 244-245
debt crisis, 246
waste, 245
business value
problems, 47
release planning, 51
BVTs (build verification tests), 149, 182-183

C

Capability Maturity Model Integration (CMMI), 22
celebrating successes, 261
Change by Design (Brown), 58
changesets, 133, 167
chaos theory, 273
chaotic management situations, 3
charts
7-Day Bug Trend Rates, 95
7-Day Issue Trend Rates, 93
Active Bugs by Assignment, 95
Active Bugs by Priority, 95
Bug Progress, 94-95
Bug Reactivations, 95
Build Status, 94
Code Churn, 95
Code Coverage, 95
Manual Test Activity, 97
Recent Builds, 98
Sprint Burndown, 93
Task Burndown, 93
Task Progress, 93

Test Case Readiness, 96
Test Failure Analysis, 98
Test Plan Progress, 93, 96
User Story Progress, 93
User Story Test Status, 97
check-ins
cycle, 31-32
error catching, 132-133
check-in policies, 135
gated check-ins, 136-137
policies, 32, 135
work items, 140
CI (continuous integration), 179-180
class diagrams, 119
clean codebase
catching errors at check-in, 132-133
check-in policies, 135
gated check-ins, 136-137
shelving code, 138-139
clean layering dependencies, 113
code mapping, 114
existing codebases, 117
intended dependencies, defining, 114
validation, 115
clones (code), finding, 151
cloud, 263
feedback, 270-271
test environments, 198
CloudShare, 198
CMMI (Capability Maturity Model Integration), 22
code
automated analysis, 152
brownfield projects, 107
Churn chart, 95
clean
catching errors at check-in, 132-137
shelving code, 138-139
clones, finding, 151
coverage
chart, 95
monitoring, 203
unit test gaps, pinpointing, 147-148

dependency graphs, creating, 107
  broad coverage, 107
  code indexing, 108
  Quick Cluster layout, 109
  sequence of interaction between, 110-113
  Solution Explorer, 109
  top-down, 107
indexing, 108
integrating frequently, 199
maintenance
  build verification tests, 149
  data, varying, 148
  redundant code, 151-152
  unit test gaps, pinpointing, 147-148
  without tests, 145
metrics, 153
redundant, 151-152
reviews, 140-141
sequence diagrams, 110-113
shelving, 138-139
UI tests (Web performance tests), 224-227
  creating, 225
  running, 226
  test data, varying, 227
Cohn, Mike, 53
company culture, 244-245
comparing quantities, 82
compilers, versioning, 163
completing PBIs, 199
complex management situations, 3-4
complicated management situations, 3
component diagrams, 119
configurations
  automated builds, 181
  testing
    critical cases, 189
    labs, 187-189
    test machines, 189, 192
continuous delivery, 177-178
continuous deployment test labs
  automating, 192, 196
  cloud, 198

continuous feedback
  after every sprint cycle, 268
  Build/Measure/Learn, 267-269
  cloud, 270-271
  cycle, 266-269
  developers, 269
  priorities/execution, 268
  production, 269-271
  tests, 269
continuous flow, 262
continuous integration (CI), 179-180
controlling structures, 113, 117
  code mapping, 114
  existing codebases, 117
  intended dependencies, defining, 114
  layer validation, 115
Conway's law, 244
crowd wisdom, 83
culture, 244-245
cumulative flow diagram, 200-201
customers
  clear goals, 52
  paint points, 52
  problems, 47
  release planning, 53
  sprint reviews, including, 263
  user stories, 53
  validation, 63-69
  vision statements, 52
customizing
  dashboards, 98-99
  processes to projects, 39
    documentation, 41
    geographic distribution, 40
    GRC, 41
    Process Template Editor, 39
    project switching, 41
cycles
  continuous feedback, 266-269
  daily. See daily cycles
  process, 24
    bottom-up, 31
    check-in, 31-32

done, defining, 36
personal development, 31
release, 24, 27
sprint, 27
test, 32-36
Scrum, 7
time
PBIs, 176-177
reducing, 199-203

D

daily builds, 33
chart, 94
failures, 202
testing, 196
daily cycles
antipatterns, 131-132
automated builds, 182
branching, 164
benefits, 165
by release, 165
merging changes, 167
tracking changes, 167
viewing, 167
work isolation, 165
clean codebase
catching errors at check-in, 132-133
check-in policies, 135
gated check-ins, 136-137
shelving code, 138-139
Eclipse/Windows shell, 169
existing code maintenance
build verification tests, 149
data, varying, 148
gaps, pinpointing, 147-148
redundant code, 151-152
without tests, 145
interruptions, minimizing, 139
checking in work, 140
code reviews, 140-141
My Work pane, 139
suspending work, 140

programming errors, catching, 143
automated code analysis, 152
code metrics, calculating, 153
TDD, 143-145
scrums, 34-36
side effects, 154
operational issues, isolating, 157
performance, tuning, 159-162
unexpected behaviors, isolating,
154-155
transparency, 170-171
versioning, 162-163
dashboards
Bugs, 95
Build, 98
Burndown, 92-93
customizing, 98-99
overview, 91
Quality, 93-95
Test, 96-98
data, querying, 100
database schema, versioning, 163
DDAs (diagnostic data adapters), 215
debt crisis, 246
deferring bugs, 245
defined process models, 3, 78-80
defining done, 177-178
post-2005 improvements, 248-249
validating
build automation, 181-185
continuous integration (CI), 179-180
delivering software continuously,
177-178
dependencies
clean layering, 113
code mapping, 114
existing codebases, 117
intended dependencies, defining, 114
validation, 115
graphs, creating, 107
broad coverage, 107
code indexing, 108

format, 124
Quick Cluster layout, 109
sequence of interactions between, 110-113
Solution Explorer, 109
top-down, 107
unwanted, viewing, 115
deployment
builds to test labs, 192-196
continuous, 192-198
test machines, 192
descriptive metrics, 89
designs
architecture, 104
levels of requirements, 73
load tests, 228
manageability, 71-72
performance, 70
products
desirability, viability, feasibility, 58-59
storyboards, 60-62
security/privacy, 70
user experience, 70
desirability, 59
DevDiv (Microsoft Developer Division), 242
business goals, 243-244
company culture, 244-245
debt crisis, 246
waste, 245
improvements after 2005, 247
defining done, 249
engineering principles, 256
flow of value, 256-258
iteration backlog, 253-254
MQ, 247
product planning, 250-252
results, 256
lessons learned
broken quality gates, 261
product backlog, planning, 259
product ownership, 259

quality fundamentals, ensuring early, 259
social contracts, renewing, 258
successes, celebrating, 261
teams effects on each other, 260
test automation, 260
scale of work, 242-243
Visual Studio 2012, 262-263
continuous flow, expanding, 262
customer feedback, 263
geographic coordination, 262
including customers in sprint reviews, 263
public cloud, 263
Developer Team (Scrum), 22
development
continuous feedback, 269
daily activities. *See* daily cycles
potentially shippable increment, 130
DGML (Directed Graph Markup Language), 124
diagnostic data adapters (DDAs), 215
diagrams
activity, 118
class, 119
component, 119
extending, 122-124
layer
code mapping, 114
existing codebases, 117
extensibility, 117
intended dependencies, defining, 114
technical debt, reducing, 117
validation, 115
sequence
dependencies, 110-113
UML, 119
storing, 118
UML, 118
activity, 118
artifacts, sharing, 120
component/class/sequence, 119

extending, 122-124
  use case, 118
  work item links, creating, 122
use case, 118
work item links, creating, 122
Directed Graph Markup Language
    (DGML), 124
dissatisfies, 54-58
distortion, preventing, 89-90
documentation
  architectures, 119
  fitting processes to projects, 41
  models, 117
domains (UML diagrams), 118
  activity, 118
  artifacts, sharing, 120
  component/class/sequence, 119
  extending, 122-124
  use case, 118
  work item links, sharing, 122
done
  broken windows theory, 90-91
  defining, 36, 177-178
    post-2005 improvements, 248-249
    validating, 179-185
  measuring, 32
  server enforcement, 136-137

E

Eclipse development tools, 169
edge of chaos, 3-4, 273
elevator pitch, 53
eliminating waste. *See* waste,
    eliminating
emergent architecture, 105
empirical process model, 5, 80
engineering principles, 256
equivalence classes, 227
errors
  catching at check-in, 132-133
    check-in policies, 135
    gated check-ins, 136-137
  operational, isolating, 157

performance, diagnosing, 159-162
programming, catching, 143
  automated code analysis, 152
  code metrics, calculating, 153
  TDD, 143-145
estimating PBIs, 82-84
  benefits, 82
  crowd wisdom, 83
  disadvantages, 84
  inspect and adapt, 83
  quantity comparisons, 82
  rapid cognition, 83
  story point estimates, 82
  velocity, measuring, 83-84
exciters, 54-58
existing architectures
  code, 107
  dependency graphs, creating, 107
    broad coverage, 107
    code indexing, 108
    Quick Cluster layout, 109
    sequence of interactions between,
        110-113
    Solution Explorer, 109
    top-down, 107
  structures, controlling, 113-117
    code mapping, 114
    existing codebases, 117
    intended dependencies, defining, 114
    layer validation, 115
  UML diagrams, 118
    activity, 118
    artifacts, sharing, 120
    component/class/sequence, 119
    extending, 122-124
    use case, 118
    work item links, creating, 122
exploratory testing, 210, 219-221
extensibility
  diagrams, 122-124
  layer diagrams, 117
extra processing, 10

F

failures. *See* bugs
fault models, 236
feasibility, 58
features
  crews, 249
  product planning, 252
  progress, 254
feedback
  after every sprint cycle, 268
  Build/Measure/Learn, 267
  cloud, 270-271
  continuous
    Build/Measure/Learn, 269
    cycle, 266-267
    cycle activities, 269
  customers, 52
    clear goals, 52
    pain points, 52
    user stories, 53
    validation, 63-69
    vision statements, 52
  cycle activities, 268
  developers, 269
  effective, 64
  Feedback Client for TFS, 65-66
  priorities/execution, 268
  production, 269-271
  querying, 67
  requests, creating, 64-69
  responses, 66
  test labs, 269
  testing from user perspective, 269
  unit tests, 269
files, versioning, 163
flow
  continuous, 262
  cumulative flow diagram, 200-201
  inefficiencies, detecting, 200
  measures, 271
  remaining work, tracking, 200-201
  storyboards, 60-62

value
  defined, 5
  post-2005 improvements, 256-258
  product backlog, 8-9
  testing, 209
  transparency/waste reduction,
    reinforcing, 6

G–H

gated check-ins, 136-137, 179-180
geographic distribution, 40
goals, customer feedback, 52
graphs (dependency), creating, 107
  broad coverage, 107
  code indexing, 108
  format, 124
  Quick Cluster layout, 109
  sequence of interactions between,
    110-113
  Solution Explorer, 109
  top-down, 107
GRC (governance, risk management,
  and compliance), 41
Great Recession, 273
greenfield projects, 107

handling bugs, 29, 223
HR practices (Microsoft), 244
Hyper-V Server, 188

I

immersive app testing (Windows 8), 221
improvements after 2005
  broken quality gates, 261
  defining done, 249
  DevDiv, 247
  engineering principles, 256
  flow of value, 256-258
  iteration backlog, 253-254
  MQ, 247
  product
    backlog, 259
    ownership, 259
    planning, 250-252

quality fundamentals, ensuring early, 259
results, 256
social contracts, renewing, 258
successes, celebrating, 261
teams effects on each other, 260
test automation, 260
indexing code, 108
individual performance, measuring, 86
inspect and adapt, 37, 83
inspecting working software, 105
installing test machines, 189
integration
  continuous (CI), 136-137, 179-180
  feature crews, 249
  frequent, 199
IntelliTrace, 155
interruptions, minimizing, 139
  checking in work items, 140
  code reviews, 140-141
  My Work pane, 139
  suspending work items, 140
iron triangle, 78
isolating
  feature crews, 249
  operational issues, 157
  unexpected behaviors, 154-155
  work, 165
iteration backlog improvements, 253-254

J–K–L

Kanban, 38
Kaner, Cem, 90
Kano analysis, 55-58

labs. *See* tests, labs
layer diagrams
  code mapping, 114
  existing codebases, 117
  extensibility, 117
  intended dependences, defining, 114
  technical debt, reducing, 117
  validation, 115

layering dependencies
  clean, 113
  code mapping, 114
  existing codebases, 117
  intended dependencies, defining, 114
  validation, 115
Lean origins, 1
lessons learned. *See* DevDiv, lessons learned
load testing, 228
  designing, 228
  output, 232
  performance problems, diagnosing, 233-234
Logan, Dave, 244

M

The Machine That Changed the World (Womack), 1
maintainability, 106-107
maintenance
  builds, 184-185
  existing code
    build verification tests, 149
    data varying, 148
    redundant code, 151-152
    unit test gaps, pinpointing, 147-148
    without tests, 145
management
  designs, 71-72
  self, 15
    Scrum, 7
    Toyota example, 14
    transparency, 11
  situations, 3-4
  sprint, 100
manual tests
  Activity chart, 97
  playing, 216
mastering Scrum, 80-81
  contrasting techniques, 84
  estimation (Planning Poker), 82-84
  team sizes, 81
McConnell, Steve, 79

measuring
  done, 32
  individual performance, 86
  success, 104
  velocity, 83-84
merging branches, 167
methodologies (Scrum)
  cycles, 7
  potentially shippable increments, 8
  product backlog, 8-9
  self-managing teams, 7
metrics
  broken windows theory, 90-91
  descriptive, 89
  distortion, preventing, 89-90
  prescriptive, 87-88
  programming errors, catching, 153
Microsoft
  Developer Division. *See* DevDiv
  HR practices, 244
  Outlook, 100
  public cloud, 263
  Test Manager. *See* MTM
milestone quality (MQ), 247
minimizing
  interruptions, 139
    checking in work items, 140
    code reviews, 140-141
    My Work pane, 139
    suspending work items, 140
  overhead, 39
models
  documenting, 117
  process
    defined, 3, 78-80
    empirical, 5, 80
  projects
    artifacts, sharing, 120
    UML diagrams, 118-119, 122-124
    work item links, creating, 122
monitoring, 203
motion, 10

MQ (milestone quality), 247
MSF for Agile Software Development
    process template, 22
MSF for CMMI Process Improvement
    process template, 22
MTM (Microsoft Test Manager), 33, 211
  bugs, reproducing, 218
    DDAs (diagnostic data adapters), 215
    exploratory testing, 219-221
    immersive app testing on
        Windows 8, 221
    solving, 218
  build comparisons, 33
  manual tests, playing, 216
  Recommended Tests list, 213-214
  test cases
    inferring, 212
    organizing/tracking, 213
    plans, 213
    running, 216
    shared steps, 214
    test steps, 214
muda, 9-10
Multi-Tier Analysis, 159-160
mura, 9-10
muri, 9-10
My Work pane
  checking in work items, 140
  code reviews, 140-141
  personal task backlog, organizing, 139
  suspending work items, 140

N–O

negative tests, 210

OData (Open Data Protocol), 100
operational issues, isolating, 157
organizing test cases, 213
overburden, 10
overhead, minimizing, 39
overproduction, 10
ownership. *See* product ownership

P

pain points, 52
PBIs. *See* product backlog, items
peanut buttering, 47, 250
performance
    application problems, diagnosing,
        233-234
    backlog, ensuring, 259
    individuals, measuring, 86
    QoS, 70
    tuning, 159-162
    Wizard, 159-160
perishable requirements, 48-50
permissions, 24
personal task backlog, organizing, 139
pesticide paradox, 219
The Pet Shoppe (Python sketch), 47
planning
    products, 250
        backlog, 259
        experiences, 252
        features, 252
        scenarios, 251-252
        taxonomy, 250
        value propositions, 251
    release, 51
        business value, 51
        customer value, 52-53
        scale, 54
    tests, 213
Planning Poker, 27, 82-84
    benefits, 82
    crowd wisdom, 83
    disadvantages, 84
    inspect and adapt, 83
    quantity comparisons, 82
    rapid cognition, 83
    story point estimates, 82
    velocity, measuring, 83-84
plug-ins, 143
policies
    build check-in, 137
    check-in, 32, 135

Poppendieck, Mary and Tom, 10
post-2005 improvements
    DevDiv, 247
    done, defining, 248-249
    engineering principles, 256
    flow of value, 256-258
    iteration backlog, 253-254
    lessons learned
        broken quality gates, 261
        product backlog, planning, 259
        product ownership, 259
        quality fundamentals, ensuring
            early, 259
        social contracts, renewing, 258
        successes, celebrating, 261
        teams effects on each other, 260
        test automation, 260
    MQ, 247
    product planning, 250-252
    results, 256
potentially shippable increments, 8, 130
prescriptive metrics, 87-88
privacy (QoS), 70
Process Template Editor, 39
processes
    Agile, 2
    customizing to projects, 39
        documentation, 41
        geographic distribution, 40
        GRC, 41
        Process Template Editor, 39
        project switching, 41
    cycles, 24
        bottom-up, 31
        check-in, 31-32
        done, defining, 36
        personal development, 31
        release, 24, 27
        sprint, 27
        test, 32-36
    enactment, 20
    models
        defined, 3, 78-80
        empirical, 5, 80

team structures
  permissions, 24
  Scrum, 22
  TFS, 23
  templates, 21-22
product backlog, 8-9
  business value, 51
  creating, 51
  customer feedback, 52
  exciters, satisfiers, dissatisfiers, 54-58
  items
    acceptance tests, 27
    bugs, handling, 29
    completing, 199
    cycle time, 176-177
    diagram links, 122
    estimating. *See* estimating PBIs, 82-84
    minimum quality, 178
    progress chart, 93
    release cycle, 25
    testing, 213-214
  planning, 259
  QoS, 69
    ensuring, 259
    manageability, 71-72
    performance, 70
    security and privacy, 70
    user experience, 70
  release cycle definition, 25
  requirements, 73
  scale, 54
  sprint backlog, compared, 28
  user stories, 53
  velocity, 84
  work breakdown, 73
Product Owner (Scrum), 22
product ownership
  defined, 46
  explicit agreement, 259
  problems, 47-48
  QoS, 69-72

release planning, 51
  business value, 51
  customer validation, 63-69
  customer value, 52-53
  design, 58-59
  exciters, satisifiers, dissatisfiers, 54-58
  scale, 54
  storyboards, 60-62
requirements
  levels, 73
  perishable, 48-50
  Scrum, 50
  work breakdown, 73
production
  feedback, 269-271
  realistic test environments, 234-235
products
  backlog. *See* product backlog
  design
    desirability, viability, feasibility, 58-59
    storyboards, 60-62
  desirability, 59
  feasibility, 58
  ownership. *See* product ownership
  performance/reliability, 259
  planning, 250-252
  viability, 58
programming errors, catching, 143
  automated code analysis, 152
  code metrics, calculating, 153
  TDD, 143-145
programs, support, 163
progress, viewing, 254
projects
  brownfield. *See* brownfield projects
  Creation Wizard, 21
  greenfield, 107
  switching, 41
public cloud (Microsoft), 263
Python, Monty, 47

Q

QoS
  backlog
    ensuring, 259
    minimum, 178
  done, defining, 177-178
  potentially shippable increment, 130
  requirements, 69
    manageability, 71-72
    performance, 70
    security and privacy, 70
    user experience, 70
  understanding during sprints, 106
Quality dashboard, 93-95
quality gates, 248, 261
quantity comparisons, 82
query-based suites, 213
querying data, 100
Quick Cluster layout (dependency
    graphs), 109

R

rapid cognition, 83
Rapid Development (McConnell), 79
reactivations (bugs), 95
readiness, 96
Recent Builds chart, 98
Recommended Tests list (MTM),
    213-214
Red-Green-Refactor, 143
reducing
  cycle time
    build failures, 202
    code coverage/tests, monitoring, 203
    flow inefficiencies, detecting, 200
    integrating frequently, 199
    PBIs, completing, 199
    remaining work, tracking, 200-201
  waste
    Bug Ping-Pong, 12-13
    build automations, 12
    defined, 5

    flow of value/transparency,
        reinforcing, 6
    Taiichi Ohno's Taxonomy of Waste,
        9-11
    testing, 210
redundant code, 151-152
release planning, 24, 27, 51
  business value, 51
  customer validation, 63-69
  customer value, 52-53
  design, 58-59
  exciters, satisfiers, dissatisfiers, 54-58
  scale, 54
  storyboards, 60-62
  user stories, 53
released versions (solutions),
    tracking, 165
reliability, 259
remaining work, tracking, 200-201
Remove Customer Dissatisifiers, 252
renewing social contracts, 258
reports
  Build, 183-184
  Build Quality Indicators, 171, 203
  Build Success Over Time, 202
  production realistic test
      environments, 234
reproducing bugs, 218
  DDAs, 215
  evolving tests, 219-221
  immersive app testing on
      Windows 8, 221
  solving, 218
requirements
  perishable, 48-50
  product backlog, 73
  QoS, 69-72
results, 256
reviews
  code, 140-141
  sprints, 263
Ries, Eric, 267

risks
  testing, 236-238
    capturing risks as work items, 237
    fault models, 236
    security testing, 238
  work items, 237

S

satisfiers, 54-58
scale
  user stories, 54
  work, 242-243
scenarios
  product planning, 251-252
  tests, automating, 224-227
Schmea Compare, 163
Schwaber, Ken, 3
scope creep problems, 48
Scrum
  cycles, 7, 24-27
  daily, 34-36
  inspect and adapt, 37
  mastery, 22, 80-81
    contrasting techniques, 84
    estimation (Planning Poker), 82-84
    team sizes, 81
  overview, 80
  potentially shippable increments,
    8, 130
  process template, 21
  product backlog, 8-9
  product ownership, 50
  self-managing teams, 7, 11
  task boards, 37-38
  taxonomy of waste, 9-11
  team structures, 22
SCVMM test environments
    (System Center Virtual Machine
    Manager), 188
security
  QoS, 70
  testing, 238

self-managing teams, 15
  Scrum, 7
  Toyota example, 14
  transparency, 11
sequence diagrams
  dependencies, 110-113
  UML, 119
servers, done enforcement, 136-137
sharing
  artifacts, 120
  work item steps, 214
shelving code, 138-139
side effects, 154
  operational issues, isolating, 157
  performance, tuning, 159-162
  unexpected behaviors, isolating,
    154-155
simple management situations, 3
social contracts, renewing, 258
software, working, 105
Sogeti Test Management Approach
    (TMap) process template, 22
Solution Explorer, 109
Source Code Explorer, 167
Source Control Explorer, 163
sprint, 27
  backlog, 27-28
  bugs
    charts, 94
    handling, 29
    trends, 95
  burndown charts, 93
  code coverage/churn, 95
  crowd wisdom, 83
  daily builds chart, 94
  dashboards
    Bugs, 95
    Build, 98
    Burndown, 92-93
    overview, 91
    Quality, 93-95
    Test, 96-98

impediments, 93
inspect and adapt, 37, 83
managing with Microsoft Outlook, 100
metrics
  broken windows theory, 90-91
  descriptive, 89
  distortion, preventing, 89-90
  prescriptive, 87-88
overview, 80
Planning Poker, 27, 82-84
QoS, understanding, 106
quantity comparison, 82
rapid cognition, 83
reviews, 263
task boards, 37-38
team sizes, 81
test cases
  progress, tracking, 93
  readiness, 96
timeboxing, 31
velocity, 83-84
Stacey Matrix, 3-4
Stacey, Ralph D., 3
standard process templates, 21
standard test environments, 188
staying in the groove, 139
  checking in work items, 140
  code reviews, 140-141
  My Work pane, 139
  suspending work items, 140
storing diagrams, 118
story points
  estimating, 82
  measuring, 83-84
story units, 82
storyboards, 60-62
Strategic Management and Organisational Dynamics (Stacey), 3
structures, control, 113-117
  code mapping, 114
  existing codebases, 117

intended dependencies, defining, 114
  layer validation, 115
successes
  celebrating, 261
  measuring, 104
support programs, versioning, 163
suspending work items, 140
Swedish Vasa, 48
System Center Operations Manager, 157
System Center Virtual Machine Manager (SCVMM), 188

T

tacit knowledge, 41
Taiichi Ohno's Taxonomy of Waste, 9-11
task boards, 37-38
Task Burndown chart, 93
Task Progress chart, 93
taxonomy of waste (Taiichi Ohno), 9-11
TDD (test-driven development), 143-145
Team Companion, 100
teams
  behaviors, distorting, 88
  distortion, preventing, 89-90
  effects on each other, 260
  geographic distribution, 40
  meetings, 34-37
  permissions, 24
  project switching, 41
  self-managing, 15
    Scrum, 7
    Toyota, 14
    transparency, 11
  sizes, 81
  structures, 22-23
  task boards, 37-38
  velocity, measuring, 83-84
technical debt, 11-12
  defined, 11
  layer diagrams, 117

templates
 build process, 184
 process, 21
  custom, 22
  customizing, 39-41
  MSF for Agile software
       Development, 22
  MSF for CMMI Process
       Improvement, 22
  Project Creation Wizard, 21
  Scrum, 21
  Sogeti Test Management Approach
       (TMap) process template, 22
tests
 acceptance, 27
 automating, 223-224
 automation, 260
 bugs, reproducing, 218
  DDAs, 215
  evolving tests, 219-221
  immersive app testing on
       Windows 8, 221
  solving, 218
 cases
  inferring, 212
  organizing/tracking, 213
  readiness, 96
  shared steps, 214
  sprint, 93
  steps, 214
 choosing, 213-214
 configuration, 189, 192
  critical cases, 189
  deploying test machines, 192
  installing test machines, 189
 cycles, 32-36
 daily builds, 196
 dashboard, 96-98
 driven development (TDD), 143-145
 exploratory, 210, 219-221
 Failure Analysis chart, 98
 flow of value, 209
 handling bugs, 223

integrating frequently, 199
labs
  build deployment, automating,
       192, 196
  cloud, 198
  continuous feedback, 269
  Management feature, 188
  multiple, 196
  physical and virtual machines,
       189, 192
  production-realistic, 234-235
  SCVMM, 188
  setting up, 187-189
  standard, 188
  support, 186
  tests, running, 196
load, 228
  designing, 228
  output, 232
  performance problems, diagnosing,
       233-234
Management Approach (TMap)
       process template, 22
manual
  Activity chart, 97
  playing, 216
monitoring, 203
MTM. See MTM
negative, 210
Plan Progress chart, 93, 96
plans, 213
production-realistic environments,
       234-235
risks, 236-238
running, 216
scenario, automating, 224-227
security, 238
settings, 216
test-run failures chart, 98
transparency, 211
unit. See unit testing
waste reduction, 210
Web performance, 225-227

timeboxing sprint planning, 31
TMap (Test Management Approach)
    process template, 22
top-down dependency graphs, 107
tours, 210
Toyota self-management example, 14
tracking
  branch changes, 167
  test cases, 213
transparency
  architecture, 105-106
  defined, 5
  development activities, 170-171
  flow of value/waste reduction,
      reinforcing, 6
  Scrum, 8
  self-managing teams, 11
  testing, 211
transportation, 10
Tribal Leadership (Logan et al.), 244
tuning performance, 159-162

U

UML, 117-118
  activity, 118
  artifacts, sharing, 120
  component/class sequence, 119
  extending, 122-124
  Model Explorer, 120
  use case, 118
  work item links, creating, 122
unexpected behaviors, isolating, 154-155
unit testing, 143
  automated code analysis, 152
  build verification tests, 149
  code metrics, calculating, 153
  continuous feedback, 269
  data, varying, 148
  existing code without tests, 145
  gaps, pinpointing, 147-148
  redundant code, 151-152
  TDD, 143-145
unreasonableness, 10

unwanted dependencies, 115
use case diagrams, 118
user experience (designs), 70
user stories, 53-54
  Progress chart, 93
  Test Status chart, 97
*User Stories: For Agile Software
    Development*, 53

V

validating
  customers, 63-69
  definition of done
    build, automating, 181-185
    continuous integration (CI), 179-180
  dependency layers, 115
value
  business
    problems, 47
    release planning, 51
  customer, 52-53
    clear goals, 52
    pain points, 52
    problems, 47
    release planning, 53
    user stories, 53
    vision statements, 52
  defining, 15
  flow
    defined, 5
    measures, 271
    post-2005 improvements, 256-258
    product backlog, 8-9
    testing, 209
    transparency/waste reduction,
        reinforcing, 6
  propositions, 251
Vasa, 48
velocity, 83-84
versioning, 162
  branching, 164
    benefits, 165
    by release, 165

merging changes, 167
tracking changes, 167
viewing, 167
work isolation, 165
compilers, 163
database schema, 163
files, 163
support programs, 163
viability, 58
viewing
branches, 167
features progress, 254
unwanted dependencies, 115
virtual machines. *See* VMs
vision statements, 52
Visual Studio 2012, 262-263
Visualization and Modeling SDK, 122-124
VMs (virtual machines), test labs, 186
build deployment, automating, 192, 196
cloud, 198
multiple, 196
physical and virtual machines, 189, 192
SCVMM, 188
setting up, 187-189
standard, 188
support, 186
tests, running, 196
VS Developer Center website, 22

W–Z

waiting, 10
waste
DevDiv, 245
eliminating
build failures, 202
code coverage/tests, monitoring, 203
done PBIs, 199
flow inefficiencies, detecting, 200
integrating frequently, 199
remaining work, tracking, 200-201

no repro (bugs), 218
DDAs, 215
evolving tests, 219-221
immersive app testing on Windows 8, 221
solving, 218
project switching, 41
reduction
Bug Ping-Pong, 12-13
build automations, 12
defined, 5
flow of value/transparency, reinforcing, 6
Taiichi Ohno's Taxonomy of Waste, 9-11
testing, 210
Web performance tests, 227
creating, 225
running, 226
test data, varying, 227
websites
CloudShare, 198
unit testing plug-ins, 143
VS Developer Center, 22
Windows
immersive app testing, 221
shell, 169
wizards
Performance, 159-160
Project Creation, 21
Womack, Jim, 1
work
breakdown, 73
isolation, 165
items
checking in, 140
links, creating, 122
risks, 237
shared steps, 214
suspending, 140
working software, inspecting, 105

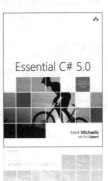

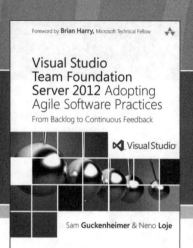

FREE
Online Edition

Your purchase of *Visual Studio Team Foundation Server 2012: Adopting Agile Software Practices* includes access to a free online edition for 45 days through the **Safari Books Online** subscription service. Nearly every Addison-Wesley Professional book is available online through **Safari Books Online**, along with over thousands of books and videos from publishers such as Cisco Press, Exam Cram, IBM Press, O'Reilly Media, Prentice Hall, Que, Sams, and VMware Press.

Safari Books Online is a digital library providing searchable, on-demand access to thousands of technology, digital media, and professional development books and videos from leading publishers. With one monthly or yearly subscription price, you get unlimited access to learning tools and information on topics including mobile app and software development, tips and tricks on using your favorite gadgets, networking, project management, graphic design, and much more.

Activate your FREE Online Edition at
informit.com/safarifree

STEP 1: Enter the coupon code: IOFNLCB.

STEP 2: New Safari users, complete the brief registration form. Safari subscribers, just log in.

If you have difficulty registering on Safari or accessing the online edition, please e-mail customer-service@safaribooksonline.com